KING CHARLES I

KING CHARLES I

KING CHARLES I

EVAN JOHN

*" Long experience has taught me how much easier
it is for princes to do evil than good."*
PETER PAUL RUBENS

ARTHUR BARKER LTD.
21 GARRICK STREET, COVENT GARDEN

PRINTED IN GREAT BRITAIN BY
MORRISON AND GIBB LTD., LONDON AND EDINBURGH

their government have been somewhat ignored by historians until quite recent years, and are perhaps overestimated to-day ; but they constitute a very serious indictment. Game Laws and the cruel mishandling of the Enclosure Acts were a sign that Parliament had become the organ of the rich. Property was almost an object of worship, its responsibilities forgotten, its privileges savagely vindicated. The Church, aristocratically controlled, tainted with flunkeyism, grew too " genteel " to recognize a saviour in John Wesley, and lost for itself—as now for all Christianity —the allegiance of the poor. The disastrous twist given to our industrial system at its birth set the seal on a long and tragic process, the slow depression in the wages and status of the working man. These things were distinguishing marks of the period which followed King Charles's defeat. The reader will have to judge for himself whether the seeds of them were visible in this reign, whether he attempted to prevent them growing, whether his victory might not have crushed them down.

The rule of the parliamentary oligarchy ended in 1832, when the Reform Act opened a way for representative democracy. It was hoped that a final solution had been found for the permanent problem of politics, and that government would retain something of the efficiency and the reasoned plan that a single mind can give it, while working at the dictation of the people's will and inviting their co-operation. In our time that hope has died. Our policy has the flabbiness of a great number of people trying to be charitable to each other's aspirations, cowardices, and vested interests ; it is administered by men whose outlook is either unintelligible or repulsive to the common man ; the people's will remains indiscoverable, or is discovered only to be deflected and manipulated for party ends. Some of us think that we must return to a form of rule that gives more scope to the monarchical principle, less to newspaper proprietors and parliamentary tacticians. We have all begun to doubt the magic of representative systems. We are certainly in a better position than our grandfathers for passing an impartial judgment on the institution of Monarchy.

It is a commonplace to say that Charles I relied too much on the magic of that institution, too little on its skilful and conscientious management. It is essential to discover how this came about, to examine the mental atmosphere in which such a mistake was natural, to understand what was meant by the Divine Right of Kings. Charles and his partisans did not regard Monarchy as a perfect instrument of government, but as the best possible in an evil and transitory world ; they believed that, as such, it had the sanction of another and more blessed One. The belief is a difficult one to recapture to-day, but to dismiss it out of hand is childish ignorance. Men died for that forgotten faith ; it is neither wise nor generous to stand and sneer upon their graves.

It is more profitable to trace the steps whereby the ideal was destroyed by a contrary philosophy. To do so it is necessary to go far afield, only returning from time to time to the centre of so much loyalty, a human creature whose story is the story of his kingdoms. Charles was in command when the crisis came ; his personal character was the axis upon which everything turned. He was not destroyed by some monstrous abstraction called the Evolution of England ; he fell because at definite moments he and his servants made definite errors, some moral, some mere miscalculations. It would be absurd to pretend that, at three centuries' distance, we can point an unerring finger at the particular mistakes which ruined him. Perhaps a forgotten word, a mere glance or expression of face, may have been more disastrous than all the Orders and Proclamations that survive. But it is worth while putting the story into new words if by so doing one can induce a single reader to join in the unending but not unprofitable pursuit of a quarry that can never quite be captured.

CONTENTS

CHAPTER ONE

YOUNGER SON

1600–12

THE story begins at Dunfermline, on a November night of the year 1600. King James VI of Scotland had come to see his newborn son. Jock Murray had brought him the news, riding down to the ferry and along the dozen miles to Edinburgh. The King gave him fifteen Scots pounds, and hurried away to Dunfermline. There, in a bedroom of the palace founded by Macbeth's supplanter Malcolm, the Danish woman whom James had married lay recovering from her third childbirth. Her son and daughter lived; this last child was expected to die in infancy, as did so many of his race. They would have to hurry on the christening or risk an unhallowed death in the palace. The Queen was accustomed to misfortune; it was an unhappy life she led with an unmanly husband and a crew of callous and insolent nobles. Even now they were trying to make her pretend friendship for a man she hated, Erskine, Earl of Mar. While she had been in labour, the Edinburgh hangman was solemnly mutilating, by Parliament's order, the dead body of her reputed lover, Ruthven. Her husband was fresh from the spectacle. To them came one of her women with an eerie tale. The child's nurse had been wakened with its screaming; starting up to find out what frightened it, she had seen a little old man, not of this world, bending over the cradle. As she stared he vanished, leaving behind him a long black cloak. If the child was to live, it was a bad omen for his future: if not, there was all the more need for a hurried christening. It was soon done, how and by whom is

still unknown ; possibly—for such is the irony of things—
by a Dissenting minister. And the child's name was
Charles.

His ancestry gave him a right to such romantic be-
ginnings, though to trace it back is to encounter Mary
Queen of Scots in the unromantic rôle of a grandmother.
As a matter of fact, she had been a close prisoner in England
since her son James was two, and dead thirteen years
before her grandson Charles—the next monarch after her
to die on an English scaffold—was born in Dunfermline
Palace. Yet it is worth while mentioning her name, for
something of her world survived. James, more successful
as King of Scots than he was to be in England, had done
something to humble the nobles who had bullied, betrayed,
and hounded her over the Border to her death. But their
attitude to the Crown was unaltered ; in some of them,
it was about as public spirited as that of American gang-
leaders towards the Federal Government. The Reformation,
an idealistic movement which many of them used—much
as gangsters used Prohibition—for the most sordid purposes, had in the end undermined their power. It was
already a smaller thing to be born head of a clan, to boast
an ancestor who had fought under Wallace—or betrayed
him to King Edward. New power was going to men of
humbler birth, notable for maintaining the gospel of
Calvin. A short walk from Dunfermline Palace stood
the ruins of what had been the Abbey Choir—until
John Knox's congregation put one of his sermons against
idolatry into practice.

Three years after the birth of Charles, his father left
Scotland. He had inherited a throne in England already
menaced by forces not altogether dissimilar from those he
had encountered among the Scots. English Calvinism was
strong and would one day be militant. England was not
governed so much by the nobles as by that uniquely
English product—gentlemen. On the whole they were
greatly superior to the Scottish lords in intelligence,

patriotism,[1] and sense of duty. Many of them, for motives good or evil, had been in secret correspondence with Scotland while Queen Elizabeth still sat upon the throne. They had promised their support to King James when the moment came for him to claim the succession.

It came in the March of 1603. One Saturday at midnight a tired English gentleman of the name of Carey rode up to Holyrood Palace ; as the Sabbath broke he was telling James that the old Queen had passed away at Richmond on Thursday night ; he had been in the saddle ever since. He had come to greet his King.

He was rewarded rather ambiguously ; when the little Prince Charles, still backward and a weakling, should be brought to England, Lady Carey was to have the care of him. Meanwhile, James set out at once, taking with him his eldest son, Henry Frederick, now Prince of Wales. The boy was nine years old, and he had been christened after his two grandfathers, Henry, Lord Darnley, and King Frederick of Denmark. If he resembled either, it was the Dane. He was energetic, good-natured, very fond of the open air. He grew up in England eager to carry on all that was adventurous in the Elizabethan tradition ; he quarrelled with the Cecils, representatives of the cautious and underhand side of Elizabeth's policy. He had no use for his father's ideas of foreign policy, pacifism and friendship with Spain. He championed the old firebrand, Walter Ralegh, whom James kept prisoner in the Tower. " Why," asked Prince Henry, " does my father keep such a bird in the cage ? " He idolized Henry of Navarre, now King of France, and longed to join him in a war against the Hapsburgs of Spain and Austria. Meanwhile he trained himself in every outdoor exercise. He loved horses, though he preferred plain hacking to his father's ceremonious hunting

[1] I use this word in a sense apparently becoming obsolete—love of one's country and of the type of life there lived : not contempt for foreigners ; certainly not militarism. Love of one's mother does not imply a dislike of other women, nor a desire for their organized massacre.

picnics. He played much tennis and golf—" a Scottish game very like Mall," wrote the puzzled French ambassador; he planted trees in Spring Gardens, near the Palace of St. James's, that had been allotted him. He was constantly riding off to Deptford to talk to Phineas Pett, the ship-builder, and inspect the fleet which King James kept in idleness. If he neglected his books, the English people loved him all the better for it. He grew so popular that his father grumbled that young Henry wanted to bury him alive.

Meanwhile little Charles had been brought to England, a year later than his father and brother : a more complete contrast to both it would be difficult to imagine. He had surprised the doctors by surviving infancy at all, and he bade fair to grow up dumb and a cripple. It is said that he could not speak properly till he was five, nor walk till he was seven ; he must have been still crawling when, in his fifth year, he was created Duke of York with lavish ceremony. Lady Carey fought against King James's project for operating on his tongue and putting his legs into iron boots. She insisted on letting time and nature work their cure. She may have been right ; certainly the hereditary rickets which had crippled his ankles passed off and left him with an excellent constitution. But a permanent impediment in speech (allied to the stammer of a naturally hasty and nervous mind) left him a poor speaker all his life and exercised no small influence upon his later fortunes.

Physically backward, Charles grew up very fond of his books. His tutor was a certain Thomas Murray, later the Provost of Eton, whose daughter Anne was to play Florence Nightingale to the wounded Cavaliers of the Civil War. The education Murray had to instil into his pupil was the usual one for a prince of that time, though to-day it would not disgrace a man whose sole business was learning. Charles learnt mathematics, and music in practice and theory ; he became something of an expert in theology ; he spoke French, Italian, and a little Spanish ; he was a

fair scholar in Greek and Latin. His first letter shows him
in the throes of the classics :

> SWEET, SWEET FATHER,
>   i learn to decline substantives and adjectives.
> Give me your blessing.
>   i thank you for my best man.
>   Your loving son,
>   YORK.

It can hardly have been from Murray that Charles
learnt the taste for art which distinguishes him from all
our kings. He shared it with Prince Henry, whose collection
he inherited, to be the nucleus of his own. Perhaps both
boys learnt it from Inigo Jones, an expert in all the arts
who had travelled Europe, served the Danish King, and
was now, in middle age, surveyor to Prince Henry, architect
of Whitehall Banqueting House, scene painter and costume
designer for the Court masques. Their librettist, Ben
Jonson, detested and quarrelled with him through twenty
years of enforced collaboration. Perhaps it was Inigo who
started Prince Charles on the career which was to give him
the reputation of " the best critick in Europe," and drew
Rubens and Vandyke to his Court.

It required greater efforts to make him proficient in
more athletic accomplishments, but he made them. In
the end he rode well, shot excellently, and held his own at
jousting, perhaps the most exacting physical test that man
has ever devised. Certainly he excelled his father in
horsemanship ; a courtier wrote that one could hardly say
the King rode, but only that his horse carried him. In an
age before sentimentality had spoilt the relations between
men and animals, horses and dogs played a large part in a
boy's upbringing. Charles always loved dogs, preferring
greyhounds to spaniels ; for greyhounds, he said, did not
flatter. In that preference of stiff nobility to fawning,
merry homeliness, lies the whole difference between him

2

and his son, Charles II—perhaps the difference between the two epochs in which they lived.

But success in outdoor pursuits came late, and at first Charles could only admire his brother's feats. He was very fond of him : it was perhaps from Henry that he caught a most uncharacteristic sympathy for Puritanism which worried good Mr. Murray in early years. It seems to have been a typical instance of the studious and the athletic schoolboy, sweetened by their affection for each other and for their sister Elizabeth. " I will give anything I have to you," wrote Charles to Henry, " both my horses and my books, and my pieces—or my crossbows,[1] or anything you would have." Henry returned the affection, not without raillery. Seeing his brother's devotion to books, he promised to make him Archbishop of Canterbury : the robe would hide his rickety legs. It was only a joke, and Charles was a little hurt. Yet, if fate had been kinder and the thing possible, England's temporal and spiritual life might have been well guided by Henry IX and Prince-Archbishop Charles.

Their mother, Anne of Denmark, is rather a shadowy figure. She differed from her whole family in a leaning to Roman Catholicism, and, it was suspected, died a convert. James allowed her no influence in politics. All we know of her indicates a " society woman," fond of frivolous display, eager to see her children make grand marriages, not above an occasional amour. Religion came to her in sudden and intense fits, not as a steady guide. We know nothing of her relations with Charles except that, when she lay dying, she pathetically urged him not to bother himself by staying beside her. " I am a pretty piece to watch beside," she said. Charles stayed. He was only eighteen at the time, and there is little trace of her influence on his later life.

---

[1] Crossbows were still in general use. Archbishop Abbot accidentally shot a gamekeeper with one, and the Earl of Berkshire chose the same unlikely instrument for committing suicide.

The odd man out in the family was undoubtedly King James. He had considerable ability and a very fine brain ; he was a good Christian and a sincere lover of peace ; he was kindly by nature, though selfish ; he had a very high conception of his royal office. But he was totally lacking in dignity, physical or moral. His appearance was slightly comic, he dressed badly, he slobbered. Even when sober, he had a maudlin way of addressing friends and servants. When he was drunk—which was frequently—anything might happen ; there is a picture of him, in a contemporary letter, riding out after dinner on a winter evening, and suddenly disappearing, head foremost, into a half-frozen stream, " so that nothing but his boots were seen." Divine-Right-of-Kings with its Boots in the Air, as Carlyle might have said. He was a great coward, so afraid of naked steel that he used to look the other way when he was using his sword to dub a knight. Sir Kenelm Digby complained that he would have had an eye put out, if a tactful bystander had not redirected the accolade. Charitable people traced this fault to the terrible night when his gallant mother, already carrying James in her womb, saw the many daggers hacking at Rizzio's body in the little supper-room of Holyrood ; the explanation is ingenious rather than convincing. If James was not personally vicious he was scandalously tolerant of vice, and allowed his Court to become a regular cesspool. His weakness for favourites of his own sex may have been innocent ; but it was politically disastrous, and it certainly contributed to his son's misfortunes. He was lazy at his work and neglected it for his pleasures. Great learning, shrewdness, and a real, if patchy, wisdom, gave him some right to his beloved title of " the English Solomon." For all that, he was a bad king.

It is not difficult to guess what his sons thought of him. To Henry, he was an unmanly pedant, careless of his own and his country's honour. Charles, refined to a fault (blushing like a girl, says the Venetian Envoy, at the sound of a coarse word), must have been disgusted at his father's vulgar talk, his drunkenness, his homosexual tendencies. One did not need to be sensitive to find the atmosphere of the Court a jarring one. Before Charles was old enough to take stock of it, there were the most disgraceful scenes. At a masque in honour of the Danish king's visit, the lady enacting the Queen of Sheba was quite drunk and, when the English Solomon tried to dance with her, he fell to the floor and was carried off to bed " covered with wine, cream, and jelly " ; meanwhile " Faith and Hope were sick in the Hall."

As Charles grew older in such surroundings, one gets an impression of his withdrawing into himself in suppressed indignation. He could do nothing to change matters, he was merely a younger son. His silence was misinterpreted as moroseness. A foreigner, obtaining a private interview, was surprised to find the Prince opening out in his congenial company, and revealing an active and interesting personality. It was a side of him hidden from King James's courtiers.

Things did not improve as time went on. If possible, scandals multiplied, some verging on farce. There was Lady Roos, who accused her husband of incestuous relations with his step-grandmother ; she produced a written confession of his, she produced a servant-girl Sarah, who had heard things from behind the window curtain of Lord Roos's Wimbledon house. James, combining Solomon with Sherlock Holmes, demonstrated that the confession was in a forged hand, and rode off to Wimbledon to prove successfully that the curtains in question were too short to hide an eavesdropper. Lady Roos was heavily fined, and Sarah whipped at the cart's tail.

The worst of all was the Essex divorce. Robert Carr, latest of a series of handsome youths to catch the King's eye, had fallen in love with the Countess of Essex. She was young and beautiful, Essex was rather a dolt, and they had been married when she was thirteen. Modern opinion

would regard it as a reasonable case for a divorce, especially
as the Countess said she had kept her husband at a distance.
But the seventeenth century thought otherwise, and the
Puritan Archbishop Abbot refused to touch the case. It
required all the influence of Lady Essex's powerful family,
the Howards, to set her free. James signalized their success
by making Carr Earl of Somerset. Within two years
society was buzzing with the tale that she had put the
business through by the slow poisoning of Carr's secretary,
Overbury, who knew too much to be a convenient divorce-
court witness, and may have been attempting blackmail.
The King was sufficiently horrified to have the Somersets
arraigned and condemned for murder, though he could
not resist the temptation to grant them pardon. It was
whispered that Somerset extorted it from him by threatening to disclose secrets : certainly the royal mercy did not
extend to the lesser accomplices, who had already been
hanged. The slow-witted Earl of Essex may have thanked
God he was not tied for life to a murderess, but he can
hardly have felt gratitude to the Court for the manner of
his release. He went abroad to the wars. One day he would
use his military experience to lead armies against King
James's son.

All this is an anticipation. It is necessary to go back
a little to two public events : Charles was too young to
understand them at the time, but they exercised a decisive
influence over his later life.

He was only three, he had not left Scotland, when
James called the Hampton Court Conference, to discuss a
petition from the Puritan clergy. Secure in the knowledge
that Puritanism would one day be a decisive force in
England, historians have agreed in condemning King
James's attitude. He thought of the Puritans as an unimportant sect, much persecuted by Elizabeth, likely to
die out rather than increase. They were not, like the
Roman Catholics, encouraged by foreign princes ; they
had not yet found so much support among the rich and

powerful as they were later to secure. We know that there were some country districts where people had hardly heard of them. But they were already numerous among the merchants and townspeople of the ports and among University dons. Some country squires were beginning to adopt their point of view. And the delegates who presented the " Millenary Petition " at Hampton Court represented a considerable section of the clergy. Their requests were humble and elementary, but in them lay the seeds of much strife. If we are to understand the history of the next fifty years, we must stop and inquire who the Puritans were and what it was they wanted.

The word " Puritan " was a vague one, but it was used to cover a number of seventeenth-century Englishmen whose aim was to " purify " the already Protestant Church of everything that was still reminiscent of Rome. But Puritanism has come to mean a state of mind, a philosophy, which, though it did inspire most of these men, is not peculiar to England or to the seventeenth century. It was strong among the early Mohammedans : it is traceable in mediæval monasteries (one even wonders whether their suppression did not release into the lay world a spirit which crystallized into the Puritanism of the next generation) ; it is at work to-day in several religious movements, especially those of American origin. A tendency towards it seems to be part of the stuff of human nature : social and political circumstances may at any time make that tendency a governing factor in a nation's life.

It is not primarily ascetic : the desire to impose irksome restrictions on others is an incidental vice, not of its essence. It was the bitter opponent of that great Roman Church which has always found a place for asceticism, always made high demands on some of its servants, and taught the spiritual value of suffering. The kernel of Puritanism (and the root of its hatred for Rome) is a hatred for symbols and intermediaries. The material world appears pure evil, only God and the human soul are good. No material

symbol can bring man nearer to God. Music and surplices
and stained-glass windows are not helps to worship ; they
are not even innocent adornments ; they are evil obstacles,
preventing communion between man and God. The
anointed priest is also an obstacle, not an intermediary ;
too often he is the dishonest lackey, detaining the soul in
an antechamber until he has exacted his customary *douceur*.
Where the priest governs and the religious symbols multiply,
the Puritan finds the atmosphere unbearable and he longs
to break away, to listen to his preacher and worship God
between bare walls or under the unadorned sky.

For there was one curious gap in the Puritan reasoning
and instinct. The preacher and " lecturer " became as
powerful and often as tyrannical as the priest. The Puritans
failed to perceive that words are merely symbols, and sometimes more misleading symbols than a surplice. The great
thinker Hobbes exposed the fallacy when he said, " Words
are wise men's counters,—they do but reckon by them ;
but they are the money of fools." But throughout Hobbes's
lifetime his countrymen and their Scottish neighbours were
submitting more and more to the despotism of mere words
and of that literal interpretation of Scripture which covered
so much self-seeking and even bloodshed.

Extreme Puritanism may be regarded less as an error
than as a stage of arrested development. Most men's
religious experience includes a phase in which all matter
seems unreal and evil ; few can learn, without this pre-
liminary, to use our very beautiful world for a good purpose.
Many of the Puritans, for one reason or another, seem to
have stopped in this phase and made it a permanent rule
of life. It made them bitterly hostile to the more worldly
of the Cavaliers who had never passed through such a
stage ; it set a blank wall of misunderstanding between
them and the born saints like Laud, who, with all his faults,
had no need to pass through it.

It is easy to see how minds of Puritan temper quarrelled
with every form of Art. Art is merely the skilful use of

ceremonies, the artist an intermediary between man and
Ideal Beauty. The curious inconsistency we have already
noticed permitted the art of words, a Puritan literature and
even a Puritan poet ; but there is no painter or musician to
set beside Milton. So long as *Samson Agonistes* remained a
string of words it could be published ; its stage presenta-
tion would have been illegal under the Commonwealth.
For the denunciation of Art was particularly strong against
that temple of symbolism, the theatre. It extended, to
our irreparable loss, over all that corresponded to drama
in the life of the poor—dancing, miming, and the village
maypole.

Such a temper of mind is doubly dangerous when it
has endured political subjection to an opposite type. It
accuses its rulers of treachery to God ; their care for art
and refinement appears effeminacy : their power of treating serious subjects with a light touch is denounced as
blasphemous. When they had thrown off the yoke, the
Puritans showed how deeply they were tainted with the
intolerance of their century. Not content with escaping
into the rarefied atmosphere they desired, they must haul
their neighbours out, to shiver in the unfamiliar, unsatisfying air. They must make the churches bare and disorderly
to the point of aggressive ugliness, suppress the theatre,
cut down the maypole. Many of them could not rest until
they had attempted to perpetuate their work by forcing
the Presbyterian system upon the country. If England
revolted, it was England they would change rather than
their own logic. And meanwhile many of them were
defeating a not ignoble purpose by showing that Puritanism
was compatible with a great love of money and a remarkable thirst for blood.

This side of Puritanism, however repulsive some of its
products, is intelligible enough ; as a protest against
religious deceit and mummery it is wholly admirable ;
and there is even something heroic about the extremer
forms, with their magnificent disregard for half the known

facts about human nature. What is harder to understand is the enthusiastic Determinism which links Cromwell's warriors with Mahomet's — the dreadful doctrine that God created a few men for eternal joy, the majority for eternal torment. It can be, and is to-day, restated in a form slightly more acceptable, but to most of us it seems that the denial of Free Will is the denial of Christianity. We prefer the modern scientific Determinism, which has had the courage to jettison the idea of God. But we must never forget that, to many seventeenth-century Englishmen, Predestination was a password and a war-cry. How it affected outward conduct is harder to see : an enemy might say that its origin was not in life, but in a perverted logic based on misinterpreted Scripture, and that no man could *live* such a theory for five consecutive minutes. This is a superficial view ; undoubtedly the certainty of being one of God's elect did produce, along with a pharisaic self-righteousness, an extraordinary driving-power, used for good as well as evil purposes.

It was against such ideas, imports, largely, from Geneva and the cities of Holland, that baby Charles was one day to champion an older, a more English, and surely a saner tradition. His opponents labelled his views " Arminian," after a contemporary Dutchman, Arminius, who fought Calvinism in its stronghold ; but he was none the less in line with his predecessor Elizabeth, with the cheerful Christianity of Chaucer, with all that had earned for pre-Puritan England the since meaningless title of " Merrie." Matter is not evil, sacraments and symbols are not evil (except where Rome, proclaiming Transubstantiation, confounds symbol and reality). Ceremony is necessary for man's intercourse with God, as with other men : its over-elaboration in Roman practice does not destroy the necessity. The only way that the Puritans could find to pull Charles from the English throne was by the slander, groundless, and in some cases deliberate, that he was at heart a Papist.

No one could bring such an accusation against King James. He was something of a Calvinist himself; his Divine Right of Kings was forged as a weapon to fight the Pope's claim to universal sovereignty. When the Puritan clergy and their bishops met at Hampton Court, he was in his element as arbiter of the theological debate. But point after point he decided with the Bishops. He upheld the sign of the cross in baptism, the white surplice against the black Geneva gown. He refused to let saints' days be eliminated from the calendar in order to concentrate on what we have learnt to call the English Sunday. He insisted that parsons who were paid to read the Book of Common Prayer should sign a declaration that they believed in it. Finally, suspecting that some points in the Petition were aimed against the government of the Church by bishops, he suddenly remembered the Presbyterian elders who had denounced his mother and made his own boyhood a misery. " No bishop, no king ! " he cried in a temper, and swore that he would make his clergy conform or would harry them out of the land.

The harrying was a mild affair, even compared with Elizabethan methods. But three hundred clergymen, refusing to sign the declaration that nothing in the Prayer Book was contrary to God's word, and to obey all its rubrics, gave up their benefices. Some emigrated to America, some became unofficial " lecturers," supported by a rich patron or a corporation. Rather ominously Parliament, disclaiming the name Puritan (still a word of abuse), expressed its dissatisfaction with the results of Hampton Court.

One positive, and excellent, result the Puritans had obtained. They had suggested that it was time that a Protestant nation hammered Tyndale's and other translations of Scripture into a national Bible. And work began on what was to be the Authorized Version.

A second event was soon to change the religious situation, very much for the worse. Little Charles, still under Lady

Carey's guardianship, only just escaped from playing in it a small and passive rôle.

Amid the hurriedly scrawled papers that remain to tell us of the feverish activities of November 1605, there is one that stands quite apart. It records evidence given by a certain Agnes Fortun, a Scottish servant of the Careys. It is written, very beautifully, in a different script from the other papers, and with Scottish peculiarities of spelling. Evidently the inquirers have been quite unable to understand the girl's broad Scots, and have sent out for a Scotsman to interpret and record her story. It is simple and homely. A few days ago, the family had been out (the baby taken to see King James), and Agnes alone in the hall. Two men had called at the door, one a very tall gentleman whom she recognized as Mr. Percy ; he was a Roman Catholic gentleman she had seen with Lady Carey at Greenwich. When she told him that the little Duke was out, he started asking a string of suspicious questions. Might he go up and see the rooms ? Why had such-and-such a passage been boarded up ? Was the little Duke taken much into the Park ? How many men guarded him on his outings ? Agnes grew canny, asked him to wait and see her master, though he might have to wait " a bonny while," she admitted. At that Mr. Percy turned to go : he would come back another time to see Sir Robert Carey. But he had a last look up the staircase before he went.

The beautiful handwriting stops ; Agnes and her Scottish interpreter are dismissed ; the hurried scrawl recommences. There are matters to be investigated even more important than an attempt to kidnap Baby Charles. Mr. Percy was one of many Papist accomplices, and they must be found and arrested before they disappear into their hiding-holes or fly the country. One of them is already in prison and under torture—Mr. Guy Fawkes, captured in the act of trying to blow up King, Lords, and Commons with a cellarful of gunpowder.

It is impossible to appreciate the effect of this revelation without understanding the state of the public mind towards Popery. There were many Papists in England, some said a third of the population : the concurrence of testimony makes a thirtieth the more likely figure. Their religion was proscribed and persecuted by law. Against them was directed a constant campaign of hatred ; how far it was sincere and religious in its motives will always be a matter of dispute ; it was certainly unscrupulous, and often supported by deliberate lying. Nothing that the Papists did, or refrained from doing, could mitigate the rancour of the attack. Their loyalty when the Armada sailed up the Channel was conveniently forgotten. As the century proceeded, and the Papists grew weaker and more patient under persecution, the campaign seems to have intensified, until it culminated in the criminal lunacies of Charles II's reign. It was bitterest of all in Scotland, where the fear of Roman Catholic reaction was most unjustified.

In spite of many not altogether disinterested agitators, the campaign was showing signs of dying down for lack of ammunition. Fox's *Book of Martyrs*, for all its wild exaggeration, could not keep alive for ever the memory of Mary's persecution. Then came the news that a small body of extreme Catholics had plotted to murder every person of importance in the country by blowing up the Houses of Parliament. Probably there were hardly a dozen that knew the design in all its ghastly completeness. The archpriest denounced the plot as " a detestable and damnable practice, odious in the sight of God " ; and one cannot help suspecting that, in the few concerned, it was not only religious perversion that worked, but also that homicidal mania which nowadays wrecks a trainload of innocent people or detonates bombs in a crowded street. But public opinion always hates details and distinctions, especially when they are accurate and thwart its taste for melodramatic generalization. After November 5, 1605, there were many Englishmen to dub "murderer" any one who had a good word for Papists, and see treachery to God and country in any neglect of an opportunity to harry them.

Law had provided such opportunities. By the Penal Laws of Elizabeth's reign, Papists had been excluded from official posts, prohibited from travelling five miles without a licence, directed to pay fines amounting to an enormous proportion of their incomes—in some instances two-thirds ; to hear Mass was technically High Treason ; a detected priest could be done to death, after a mutilation too horrible to put into print. Needless to say, the Penal Laws were never carried out with any thoroughness ; in a few districts, where Catholicism was strong, the enforcement was very infrequent. But to be a Catholic was to be excluded from public life (unless one was also a Peer), and liable to ruinous fines ; to be a priest was to live in hiding for fear of a terrible death. And the most constant factor in the next forty years of history was the demand of Parliament after Parliament for the rigorous enforcement of the Penal Laws.

Almost as constant were the efforts of James and Charles to evade the demand. No doubt their motive was to retain the loyalty of the large number of their subjects who were still Catholic ; no doubt they wished to placate Catholic princes abroad, at times to fulfil definite foreign treaties. But it is impossible to doubt that their effort was also inspired by tolerant and humane motives. Both these kings were in need of money, sometimes in desperate need ; the Penal Law fines went straight into their pockets ; Parliament held the purse-strings and Parliament could be most easily coaxed into unloosing them by a stringent persecution of the unpopular Papists. Neither King had any leaning towards Rome : one had only escaped from a Papist plot to murder him by a lucky chance. When we also consider how contemporary Europe (France excepted) was treating heretical minorities, it becomes apparent that to accuse the first two Stewarts of intolerance is neither a wise nor a tolerant thing to do.

What little we know of Prince Henry makes it likely that he would have been an extreme and perhaps a persecuting Protestant. A mere chance was about to snatch from him the hope of kingship, and bestow it on his younger brother.

CHAPTER TWO

THE CROWN IN SIGHT

1612–23

IT is a curious fact in our history that, of all the men and women who have sat upon the English throne, few have had more than a small proportion of English blood. Since the Conquest, we have had two French dynasties, a Welsh, a Scottish, and a German, all marrying into foreign more than into English families—with one Dutchman thrown in as a make-weight. Oddly enough, the least English in descent have often had the faculty, if not of seeming English in character, at least of becoming thoroughly popular with the average Englishman. Dr. Johnson was never more typical of his countrymen than in his admiration for Charles II, whose four grandparents were a Scot, a Dane, a Frenchman, and an Italian. In her own (most different) way, Queen Victoria, descended from four Germans of practically pure blood, became the beloved symbol of English domesticity.

It is a different story with Charles I. He was of foreign birth ; and Scots were more foreign and more unpopular than they are to-day. He did not differ radically from the Englishmen of his time in character or outlook : he would, for instance, fit quite naturally into one of Shakespeare's plays : but he did not understand (and was not understood by) a certain type of man which was rising to great wealth and influence in contemporary England. Over the ruins of the mediæval aristocracy, the Tudor rule had favoured the appearance of a new governing class. It was more interested in trade and industry : it was stupid about art, though not unappreciative : it was impatient of intellectual

subtleties, almost, one might say, impatient of principles :
it admired practical success and easy-going geniality. It
was fond of a joke, but it disliked irony. When it had
shuffled off the alien influence of the Renaissance and
repudiated Puritanism, its temporary and unnatural ally,
it was to give us, late in our history, the national legend of
John Bull, whom neither Chaucer nor Shakespeare would
have recognized as the typical Englishman. It has had
great influence to-day in forming the ideals of the respectable
Punch-reading classes.

Charles was not naturally interested in commerce, he
was a real expert in Art. He was ready to die for an abstract
principle. He had an analytical mind, and a weakness for
splitting hairs : this, combined with a certain dishonest
strain in his mind (hidden perhaps from himself), gave him
a fatal reputation for untrustworthiness. He was not
genial : no one in his senses could have referred to this
refined, melancholy creature as " bluff King Charlie." He
had very little humour, though he could be bitingly ironical.
He was not easy-going, but suffered from an enlarged sense
of duty. Finally, he was not successful. Long before the
final disasters, there was a feeling that his enterprises
could not be trusted to prosper. If this was partly due to
ill-fortune and the pressure of circumstance, it is human
nature—and particularly English nature—to admire good
luck and the ability to master circumstance. It is hardly
surprising that Charles the First could not become the
idol of squire and parson until he was safely in his grave,
and what masqueraded as his Cause enjoyed a posthumous
victory at the Restoration ; and even then there was
something remote and chilling about their idol.

It was into such hands that Fate put the English
Crown at one of the great crises of its unhappy history.
To round off the jest, Fate cleared the way to the throne
by sweeping off an elder brother already bidding fair to
be the *beau-ideal* of the typical English gentleman ; and
it chose for its means an over-strenuous game of tennis.

So low had King James's reputation fallen in 1612 that he was accused of poisoning his eldest son. Modern medical research has established that Prince Henry was already suffering from typhoid fever when he characteristically insisted on repairing to the tennis court and catching a fatal chill. Doubtful of his malady and fearing infection, the doctors denied his last request—to see his sister. He died forgetful of the Crown he would never wear, and calling out for Elizabeth.

A few months later, she and her surviving brother had also parted company. Henry died in the November of 1612 ; next February, Elizabeth was married in Whitehall Chapel, watched a special performance of *The Tempest* in honour of her wedding, and sailed from Rochester to an unkind destiny in foreign lands. The bridegroom—to the joy of Protestant hearts—was a Calvinist, Frederick Palatine : he was a south German princeling whose dominions formed an outwork of Protestantism against the Austrian Hapsburgs. They were soon to be overrun in the Thirty Years' War, and of all that dreadful business we shall hardly hear the last in Charles's lifetime.

Charles, though not formally invested as Prince of Wales for several years, held a seat in the House of Lords in virtue of the Dukedom of York. He became known as a peacemaker among the Peers, as his father strove to be among nations. Disputes in Parliament had a way of being adjourned elsewhere for the unparliamentary decision of drawn swords. Charles is credited with the prevention of several duels by timely reconciliation.

In one quarrel, starting not in Parliament but on the tennis court, he was himself a principal. It ended in reconciliation and lifelong friendship ; for the other principal was George Villiers, recently the younger son of a small Leicestershire squire, haunting race-meetings in out-at-elbows garments, but soon to be King's Cupbearer, Viscount, Earl, and Marquis of Buckingham, Lord High Admiral, the envy and bully of the Court.

3

This brilliant and disastrous personality, launched on his career by 1618, was to fall within ten years to the assassin's knife. He owed his initial success, as did most of King James's friends, to personal charm. It was of a different order from Somerset's, on whose ruins he rose. Buckingham's worst enemies have testified to his extraordinary fascination : it still breathes faintly in his letters. There was much good in him. He was an affectionate if unfaithful husband ; his wife, Kate, adored him and easily forgave the infidelities he humbly confessed to her, when a worser man might have concealed—or boasted about them. There remained to the end something candid and unspoiled about this spoilt darling of the Court. He did not love money as much as most of his contemporaries. He did many generous things and few mean ones.

He was a leader of fashion, and used his influence in foolish extravagances, some reminiscent of a later age : he introduced the sedan-chair into England, and was censured for degrading to the level of draught animals the human beings who bore him in exotic pomp. But he was not a mere fribble. Clarendon, exactly the kind of slow plodder to detest a fribble, had a genuine admiration for him. Attempts have been made to deny Buckingham any ability except in trivial matters. They have failed.

He was the product of a vile system which pushed courtiers into responsible positions ; he knew himself a mere courtier, he was (it seems strange) modest about his political ability, and he did his best. He refused the governorship of Ireland, because he could not look after the business ; he refused to let it be done by a committee while he took the title and the credit. When he became Lord Admiral, he appointed a board of real experts and helped them, as we shall see, to rescue the Navy from an appalling condition of decay. Goaded into assuming military command,[1] he showed himself a very brave soldier, and, for all his inexperience, a not incompetent one. One

[1] See pp. 113 and 124.

seasoned veteran who fought under him said that time
might have made him the equal of the greatest captains.
Sir Henry Wotton, a sober critic, attributed his later
reputation to this—" His enterprises succeeded not according to the impossible expectations of the people." It was
not entirely his own fault if he dazzled men into expecting
the impossible.

Nevertheless, he was one of the most disastrous servants
the English Crown has ever had. His foreign policy was
incompetent. It impressed Europe with its Byronic
gestures; it made England a force to be reckoned with
again; but its fruits were negative. Secondly, he could
never shake off the atmosphere in which he had risen. He
saw everything with a courtier's eye, in terms of personal
friendship and personal enmity. Holding few offices himself (besides the merely ceremonial ones) he exerted his
influence to displace Somerset's friends, relatives, and
dependants, and substitute his own. Like the two kings
he served, he lacked the power to choose good subordinates,
and the level of ability was no higher for his interference.
If he was not venal himself, his nominees were grossly so.
Though he generally treated Parliament with respect, he
quarrelled with half the nobility of England—already
hating him as an upstart—and with more than half the
foreign ministers with whom he came in contact. English
policy, the happiness of a people, were at the mercy of his
touchiness, his occasional insolence, his irresponsible manner.
Such was " Steenie," King James's darling, the greatest,
perhaps the only friend of King Charles. He was not
unworthy of friendship, but his long continuance in para-
mount position at the King's Council was a national
disaster.

One of Buckingham's first acts was to champion Ralegh,
left championless by Prince Henry's death. He had been
in prison for thirteen years. Imprisonment was not the
soulless torment it has become to-day : a prisoner was
allowed his own possessions about him, his friends and

family. It was not intended as punishment so much as restraint from mischief : Ralegh was spending his days in chemical experiments, in writing a history of the world, in political pamphlets curiously accurate in their foreshadowing of coming conflicts.[1] But restraint was just what he most chafed at.

The business began with Ralegh bribing two of Buckingham's brothers. James released him, listened to his mad scheme for fetching gold from Spanish America without fighting the Spaniards, and promptly began to discuss them with Gondomar, the Spanish ambassador. Ralegh found the greatest difficulty in raising followers. He has captured the affection of posterity, and we have forgotten his avarice and cruelty, remembering only his courage and his grand dreams of Empire. But he was thoroughly unpopular with his contemporaries, and now he had outlived the best of them : he could not understand the new age which loved money as much as his own, but would not risk life or even comfort to get it. Worst of all, he could not find sailors. Drake and Hawkins were dead, only the dregs of the seaports would follow Ralegh to the Spanish Main. He reached South America ; his advance-parties, marching inland, were forced into the battle with Spanish garrisons which he had promised to avoid. They fell back bearing no gold, but only the dead body of Ralegh's son. Empty-handed, he returned to Plymouth, expecting neither Buckingham's favour nor mercy from the King. Within a few months of his homecoming he died, very bravely, by the axe. He had spent some of his last hours in composing two almost perfect lyrics. With him died the Elizabethan age.

James had yielded to Gondomar's demand for his blood, and sacrificed him to the cause of European peace. Peace still prevailed. The two religious camps into which the Continent had fallen watched each other in silence ; even the Pope seemed to have accepted the Reformation as inevitable. If war still threatened between Spain and her

[1] *Harleian Miscellany*, v. 194.

Dutch rebels, France was at peace with herself and with others. Italy enjoyed a much-needed tranquillity. The danger was to come from a new quarter.

Trouble was stirring right in the heart of Europe. It was six years since Frederick Palatine had married Charles's sister and taken her to his pleasant domains on the Rhine and Upper Danube. Now he was suddenly offered a chance of doubling them and striking a blow for Protestantism at the same time. His neighbours the Bohemians (Czecho-Slovakians, as the march of modern science has taught us to call them) had always been a thorn in the Pope's side. Now their ruling classes, infected with Protestant doctrine, had used their ancient constitution to plead that the Crown was elective, depose their Catholic king, and offer the kingship to Frederick. But their king was not merely king of Bohemia ; he was also Holy Roman Emperor, with vague rights that extended from Milan to the Baltic : he ruled vast hereditary domains from his capital of Vienna : he was a Hapsburg, cousin to the Spanish king. To accept the Bohemian offer was to provoke a European war. Frederick accepted ; within a year, the embattled forces of Catholicism had obliterated his army at the battle of the White Hill, swamped Bohemia, and surged into the Rhenish Palatinate. The Thirty Years' War had begun.

In England, Protestant feeling and loyalty to the Royal Family were united as they had not been for years. Parliament cried for war in support of King James's son-in-law : it voted an inadequate sum of money for the purpose. A voluntary loan was raised in supplement. Prince Charles, who had shut himself up in his room for two days when the news arrived from the White Hill, subscribed £50,000 [1] from his own pocket. Buckingham joined in the clamour and subscribed £5000. Only the King was immune from the

---

[1] All the figures have been multiplied until they roughly represent the values of 1933. To arrive at a satisfactory index figure is a complicated and controversial business. I have adopted the cautious and conservative figure of 5.

enthusiasm. He had condemned Frederick's folly ; the Bohemian rebels were too like English Puritans and Parliamentarians for his taste. He knew something of the vast forces that his son-in-law had challenged : he alone at the Palace had shown no surprise at the news of the White Hill. He was not going to challenge Spain and Austria in order to restore an intruder to a throne from which the lawful owner had lawfully expelled him. A small force might go to defend or recover the Palatinate—not Bohemia. Even so, James preferred diplomacy to war.

Meanwhile Parliament was wreaking its indignation on a private individual. An old man called Floyd, a debtor in the Fleet Prison, had let slip some injudicious words. He had referred to Frederick's defeat with satisfaction ; he had called him and Elizabeth, Goodman and Goody Palsgrave. It was a nickname that the Queen had invented to show her annoyance at her daughter finding no grander match than a petty German prince. But Floyd was not the Queen, and he added to his crimes the heinous one of being a Roman Catholic. The warden of the Fleet reported him to the House of Commons. The evidence was contradictory, the prisoner denied all guilt, and was not allowed to see the witnesses who testified against him. The Commons vied with each other in inventing disgusting ways of torturing the old man, Sir George Goring outbidding others with a proposal for cutting off his nose, ears, and tongue, whipping him, making him swallow his Popish beads, and finally hanging him. Sir Edward Sandys brought the House to its senses, and persuaded it to confine its sentence to the pillory and a fine of £5000. One member still objected, and suggested that Floyd (already in prison for debt) should be whipped if he could not pay the fine. The House did not accept the suggestion, for it did not recognize a leader of opinion in the ingenious proposer. He was the new member for Calne, in Somerset, and his name was John Pym.

The Lords did worse. At the King's request, they

reprimanded the Commons for their extraordinary assumption of judicial power ; for the Lower House had no jurisdiction at all, except where their own members were concerned. But the Peers were undoubtedly a Court of Law : they multiplied Floyd's fine by five ; they also condemned him to whipping, branding, and life imprisonment. One Peer—Prince Charles—fought the barbarity : he managed to get the whipping cancelled : a year later, he had Floyd released from the Tower.

He was to show humanity again in the case of Francis Bacon, accused of corruption. The case was not a bad one, judged by the low standards of the age, but Bacon was unpopular and he had been a focus for much shady finance. The method chosen was impeachment, the revival of a mediæval custom whereby Parliaments attacked ministers of the Crown. The Lords sat as judge and jury, the Commons acted as prosecuting counsel. Prince Charles saved Bacon from unnecessary humiliation at the trial, and succeeded in getting his sentence reduced. He was rewarded with one of those letters of almost crawling flattery which the philosopher addressed to benefactors in high place.

Bacon was a dependant of Buckingham, and Buckingham voted for his acquittal : he was in a minority of one. The impeachment was part of a general attack on courtly corruption, in which it had been hoped to implicate the favourite. He was known to have had a hand in the granting of monopolies. This device of government was defended on the ground that it fostered new industries : it amounted to a prohibition of all competitors in some particular trade ; it had been used to reward courtiers, to the detriment of commerce, and to raise income—for even courtiers paid the Government heavily for their monopoly.[1] Buckingham, two of whose brothers held profitable monopolies, saw his chance for a grand gesture : if his father had

[1] Modern practice is odder. While I write, the Government is establishing a very important monopoly, and paying the monopolist large sums from public funds for exercising it.

begotten two sons to be grievances to the Commonwealth, he said, there was a third to help in punishing them. With a Bill to limit monopolies and the sentence on Bacon, Parliament professed itself satisfied. Buckingham had won a little popularity in a somewhat unheroic manner. He was about to play for a second round of applause, equally undeserved, equally ephemeral, and terribly damaging to the monarchy.

For a long time there had been talk of marrying Charles to a Spanish Infanta. The King was beginning to wonder whether an agreement, so cemented, might not include a clause whereby Spain should help Frederick Palatine to recover his Palatinate. King Philip IV, on his side, hoped to induce England to repeal the Penal Laws against its own Roman Catholics; he also hoped that, in order to win his bride, Charles would become a convert to Rome. Spain had little power to restore the Palatinate, now engulfed in European forces beyond the control of any single government; if James had attempted to grant tolerance to the Papists, Parliament would make government an impossibility; and Charles was so obstinate a Protestant that one misguided foreigner called him a Puritan. One way and another, the Spanish match was being discussed in an atmosphere of optimism rather than reality.

That it was being discussed at all was rousing the Commons to protest. They disclaimed the power to control foreign politics, but they demanded the privilege of discussing them, and giving advice; they recorded their demand in the Parliamentary Journal. James was quite uncompromising. Where a deliberative assembly has sovereignty, the extreme inconvenience of its debating foreign politics must be faced. Where no such sovereignty is claimed, the debate may do incalculable harm; the speakers will be in ignorance of the essential facts, they will raise hopes and fears abroad with mischievous consequences; they will be misled, with or without money passing, by the resident envoys of foreign powers ; they may end by wrecking a delicate negotiation and precipitating a war. James sent for the Parliamentary Journal and tore out the offending page. But he had miscalculated the strength of the war party, and he had reckoned without Buckingham.

Our envoy at Madrid was the Earl of Bristol, an admirable man, who had advised against the whole business of the Spanish match, and then been told to proceed with it. Founded on unrealities, the negotiations were costing Bristol infinite trouble, and they did not seem to progress an inch. How far the Spanish were sincere is still a matter of dispute : probably their chief minister Olivares wanted to see the match concluded ; probably there were powerful factions thinking otherwise. Buckingham, who never underestimated his power to charm, intrigue, and persuade, thought he could do better than the patient Bristol. After a talk with Gondomar, he went off to James and told him that so long as things went through the usual channels, nothing would ever be done : he suggested a plan that was simple, bold, and (in any hands but Buckingham's) quite sensible. Buckingham proposed to take Prince Charles to Madrid himself, insist on the Spaniards making up their minds, and eclipse Bristol by standing best man at the wedding.

We have here our first glimpse of Charles in his personal relations. Unfortunately it only shows us a silent young man, already won over to the schemes of his brilliant friend, watching Buckingham cajole and bully consent out of the reluctant old King. Charles's secretary, Cottington, was present, and spoke against the venture. James defended him from Buckingham's furious tongue : " No, no, Steenie," he said ; " he answered me directly the question I asked him, and very honestly and wisely.": But Buckingham had his way. He carried off Charles to his country house to say good-bye to Kate, and talk over their plans. They were to take with them Dick Graeme from Westmoreland. At Dover they would pick up the unwilling

Cottington, and a gentleman in Buckingham's service called Endymion Porter, who, besides his beautiful name, had the advantage of a Spanish grandmother and an education in Spain. They must themselves use false beards and false names, though their imaginations provided nothing better than Tom and John Smith. The King was already regretting his consent, but they were too quick for him.

At Gravesend, the ferrymen took them for two young sparks going abroad to extinguish each other in a duel, and reported them, too late, to the authorities. At Canterbury the Mayor tried to arrest them as conspirators. But they reached Dover, crossed the Channel (both were sick and Buckingham the sicker), and had reached Boulogne by noon. That night they slept at Montreuil.

It was the first and last time that Charles set foot on the Continent, and it must have been the most exhilarating adventure. For a few short days he was a private gentleman, with a horse under him, a friend beside him, foreign lands to see, and a romantic bride to win. They were recognized at Paris, but no one gave them away. Buckingham had spent some of his penurious youth there and could do the honours of the city—already noted for romantic adventure and insanitary odours. Disguised in periwigs, they coaxed their way into the gallery when the French Court was rehearsing a masque. Here they saw, as Charles wrote home, " the Queen, little Monsieur, and Madame " at their dancing. The Queen was a Spaniard (called Anne of Austria to confuse one), and sister to the Infanta he was riding to woo. Her beauty, he said, spurred him on : judging by a later event, Buckingham may have been the more moved. Neither has a word for " little Madame," though her name was Henrietta Maria ; when she heard who had passed through Paris, she said, " He need not have gone to Spain for a bride."

But gone he had, and very happily. One of Bristol's messengers met them on the road and reported that he had never seen the Prince look merrier. He had just had a triumph. Dick Graeme had offered to steal them a goat for supper, and Charles had told him not to try his Border tricks on French peasants. He satisfied both honesty and sportsmanship by paying the goatherd and, while his friends began a clumsy chase, pistolling the goat running from his running horse. When they crossed the Spanish frontier, he executed a little dance of joy. Cottington may have felt more anxious : at home stolid Englishmen were prophesying that their Prince would soon disappear into a Spanish prison and what Clarendon called " the bottomless abyss of Reason of State." But such suspicions were unjust to the ancient and honourable nation to whom Charles was now entrusting himself.

Madrid was enthusiastic in its welcome. King Philip provided magnificent quarters for them and for the Englishmen who came posting after them. The Lenten fast disappeared in balls and festivities. The great dramatist, Lope de Vega, wrote a song for Charles, and Velasquez drew his portrait. The Infanta proved a real beauty, not the dark-skinned Delilah that good Protestants feared (and were later to get from France), but a fair-haired, pink-and-white girl, more Flemish than Mediterranean. Charles promptly fell in love, and hung round the streets for a glimpse of her coach. One morning he got Buckingham to give him a leg over her garden wall : she fled screaming from this violator of decorum, and he was confronted by an old dragon of a Marquis who produced the key of the garden door and insisted on immediate decampment. The indiscretion was forgiven ; Charles was young and a lover, and it was spring-time in Madrid.

Beneath the surface, things were less idyllic. The Spaniards were gravely disappointed to find that Charles had not come in order to proclaim his conversion to Popery, that he dutifully sat and listened to their grave friars without the least hint of agreeing with them. There is something in the outward trappings of Catholicism very tawdry and repellent to a mind unused to them. If Charles concealed his discomfort, his attendants were less considerate, Buckingham definitely insolent.   The Infanta was kept well guarded behind the bars of an iron etiquette ; Charles complained he had less chance to see her than had Archie, the Court Fool, who had followed him from London.   Negotiations went ill ; the Spaniards' demands were rising.   They refused to use force against a Hapsburg Emperor to restore Frederick ; it was only natural, but, without such force, Frederick might whistle for his Palatinate.   Olivares had got on well with Bristol, he was beginning to detest Buckingham.   Spanish decorum was outraged by the free-and-easy way in which the favourite treated his Prince ; Spaniards accused him of making love to their wives, and insulting their religion.   More and more Englishmen arrived and behaved worse and worse.   It is odd to hear that they attributed their ill-success with the Spanish women to the parching effect of too much sun and the purifying effect of too much Roman Catholicism. Charles wrote to his father about the constant stream of courtiers, and his " Dear Old Dad," as James styled himself, promised to stem the tide.

It was too late.   One of the new arrivals, Sir Edmund Verney (one day to die grasping the standard at Edgehill) obstructed a priest who had come to do his duty by a dying English convert, and struck him in the face.   King Philip could stand no more : he demanded that Charles should dismiss every Protestant in his suite.   It was time for Charles to go home.   Rightly or wrongly, all his friends assured him that the Spaniards had never been sincere about the match.   But he told Philip he was only going home to persuade his father into tolerating the English Catholics.   He rode to Corunna, Buckingham throwing a parting insult to Olivares.   Once on an English ship, Charles began to find the Spanish match an evil dream ; England was preparing such a welcome for him as should make it an impossibility.   From Portsmouth to London, from London to Royston, church-bells pealed, bonfires crackled, windows blazed with candles, and free banquets were spread in the street for all but Papists to make merry. Even the Cambridge undergraduates got an extra course for their dinner. The great, the patriotic, the Protestant Duke had rescued England's heir from the land of Popery and wickedness : soon they would be sending armies and fleets to revenge the Armada. At Royston their " Dear Old Dad " stood at the top of a stairway to embrace and blubber over the two prodigals. His life-work for Europe's peace was ruined, but his poor tired heart was warmed by such joy and relief as he had seldom known.

CHAPTER THREE

Protestant Crusade

1623-25

KING JAMES was to know little more joy on this earth. He was barely king. Buckingham's pride had been wounded. Charles was suffering from a violent revulsion : he had tried to do as his father bid, and it had put him in a false position : he had fallen in love, and the affair had turned sour. Behind them, all that was articulate in England was clamouring for war, and the merchants were rubbing their hands at the prospects of Spanish plunder. James had been honestly striving for peace, and had thought to find a guarantee for it in Spanish friendship. England only knew that peace with Spain meant peaceful penetration of English life by an alien influence, Gondomar insulting over Ralegh, our colonies discouraged, our fleet held idle. The long delays over the marriage treaty seemed to prove that Spain had never been sincere ; Bristol was a dupe or a traitor who had sat still while Spaniards tried to tamper with the Prince's religion. The only remedy was war. A Parliament was called, and Buckingham was its hero. The frantic efforts of the Spanish envoys to accuse him of treason only increased his popularity. A new Bill was devised for harrying the Papists at home, a petition was sent up for war with Spain. King James was beaten.

Parliament's idea of a war with Spain was the Elizabethan one—an attack on Spanish America, raids on the Spanish ports. Thanks to Buckingham, there were means to carry it out.

Elizabeth, strange to say, had done little for the royal

navy. It certainly could not have defeated the Armada
but for the merchantmen who volunteered, or were ordered
by government, to rally round it as a nucleus in time of
peril. James had spent more money than she, but unfortunately he had kept in power the man who had nominally
commanded against the Armada—Lord Howard of Effing-
ham. He was now Earl of Nottingham, and to say that he
had been resting on his laurels is to understate the case.
His treasurer, his controller, and surveyor grew rich with
presents from contractors and dockyard officials. These
in turn were mere sharks : they complained that they had
to buy their jobs at such a figure that they could only
recoup themselves by rifling government stores. They
received large sums of money for the building of ships,
and they did not even pretend to build them. If ships were
sold or sunk, their names remained for years on the pay
and provision list while somebody pocketed the difference.
The sailor's pay of 50s. a month was in arrears, the contractors received twice as much as Elizabeth had allowed
for their food, and the food was not appreciably better.
Mutiny was checked by barbarous punishments. At the
head of this mass of corruption stood, or rather slept,
Nottingham. If he was unable to cure it, he had his
reason. He had attained the venerable but inactive age
of eighty-two.

Those of us who do not believe in mankind's moral
progress must at least admit a great progress in efficiency.
By modern standards, most armies and navies, since the
fall of Rome, seem to have been systematically starved,
neglected, and robbed of their pay. But there was a danger-
limit beyond which our ancestors could not reasonably go.
Nottingham was politely superannuated, with a handsome
present in his pocket, and Buckingham stepped into his
place. When the Treasurer Mansell resisted further
inquiry, he and his colleagues, Messrs. Bingley and Shipley,
were less ceremoniously cashiered. Buckingham had not
the right experience for the work, and appointed a Board.

Its most active member was a Mr. Lionel Cranfield, a City merchant, risen from 'prenticeship, who had obligingly married a relation of Buckingham's. He had already done excellent work on the Customs. Buckingham had the sailors' pay raised by half, and then insisted on every possible economy. Four years' work reduced the expenditure from £265,000 to £150,000, while the number of serviceable ships rose from 23 to 35.

Such an achievement would alone make Buckingham's admiralty notable. The test of war did not entirely belie it. When we came to fight France and Spain combined, Buckingham (it is sometimes forgotten) was able to land and protect an army on a small island a mile from the French coast, a hundred and fifty from Spain, and nearly four hundred from our nearest base.

But for the moment it was only Spain we had to tackle, and Buckingham was finding unexpected opposition at home. It arose on the King's Council : there sat several sober lords who disliked him and knew what war meant ; there sat Mr. Lionel Cranfield, now Earl of Middlesex, who did not want to see " the toil of his long years blown away in gunpowder." [1] While Buckingham had been in Madrid, Cranfield had been at work. His earldom of Middlesex was wheedled out of James when James was sending out a dukedom to the Marquis of Buckingham. Middlesex had even dreamt of supplanting his patron, had brought up a handsome young relative from the country, treated his face with seventeenth-century beauty preparations, and introduced him to the old King. He had worked on James's pacifism, and been hand-in-glove with the Spanish ambassador. He was suspected of putting spokes into the wheel of the Virginia Company because Spain disliked English colonies in America. Buckingham's return, the outbreak of the war-fever, put him into a terribly dangerous position. But he stuck manfully to his guns. He argued that England could not afford a war. He told Prince

[1] Wade, *John Pym.*

Charles to his face that honour compelled him to marry the Spanish Infanta. There was a germ of truth in that, but it is hardly the kind of thing a City merchant could say to a Prince.

Buckingham's remedy was a parliamentary impeachment, and he easily found agents. Middlesex had a host of enemies in Parliament : one cannot save a Treasury £100,000 a year without disturbing a good many secret incomes. And Middlesex, for all his reforms, had managed to acquire a respectable fortune himself. But it was a sorry business, with Middlesex, harassed and perplexed, standing for hours together to answer the Commons' accusations, and Prince Charles dropping in an acid word here and there. Charles may have regretted it one day, certainly he was glad to consult Middlesex privately in later years. Middlesex might have solved his worst problems, even saved his Crown : now he was being condemned and disqualified from office for ever. In London men were wondering what the Commons thought they were doing, but the Commons had the bit between their teeth and Middlesex had no friends but the shrewd old fool who sat impotent on the throne. " You are making a rod for your own back," said James to Buckingham ; and he told Charles that he would soon have his bellyful of impeachments. But he could do nothing to prevent the fulfilment of these uncannily accurate prophecies.

Bristol came home from Madrid, and Buckingham was afraid that his account of happenings there might be a little too truthful for convenience. He dared not let him approach the King too closely, and procured an order confining him to his estates in Dorset. It was nothing that Bristol had refused a Spanish title and a pension : it was enough that Olivares had offered them. Bristol's welcome was a poor one for an honest man whose worst fault was patience and trustfulness. But nothing was good now that came from Spain.

Meanwhile there was a war to wage. If we had a fleet,

4

we had no army. A few men had been recruited for the recovery of the Palatinate, and had done quite good work. Some larger effort was needed, and a military commander. Few men in England had any military experience, Buckingham himself had none. When King Louis, Spain's natural enemy, sent us Count Mansfeld, a German freebooter with a bad record, he was welcomed at Court and applauded in the streets ; 12,000 raw recruits were gathered to make an army for him. Meanwhile England began to look for allies.

A first glance at Europe was not particularly reassuring. Of the Protestant powers, Holland was the likeliest : she was preoccupied by war with the Spaniards at home, but her fleet would be a useful adjunct to our own. Denmark and Sweden were at odds with one another, but offers were made to both. The King of Sweden was by way of being a great man—Gustavus Adolphus. At twenty-five he was already an old hand at the game of war : he was right in demanding a very great deal of money before he would intervene in Germany. Christian of Denmark was Charles's uncle, and his terms were far lower. They were accepted, money was sent as an earnest, and Christian prepared to march for the Palatinate. Gustavus had to wait for a richer paymaster.

There remained one great force which might or might not be set in motion against the Hapsburgs, and that force was France. The attempt to secure French alliance was of crucial importance in Charles's life. It failed. It revealed him as a diplomatist easily outwitted. It involved him in a piece of dishonesty which greatly complicated his problems at home. It provided him (we are studying not only politics, but the story of a human life) with a wife and a domestic happiness rare in the history of kings.

If there has been one factor more constant than others in the shifting chaos of European politics for the last three centuries, it has been the foreign policy of France. While all governments are tenacious of advantages, just or questionable, France has been the most clear-sighted in securing them, the least hampered by illusion. She has been even more successful than is warranted by her military superiority. She has admitted religion and idealism to an extremely limited place in her policy, and erred on the side of suspicion (the national vice) rather than over-confidence in the good faith of others. She has ridiculed, often with great justice, their idealistic pretensions. Meanwhile, when not actively aggressive, she has been wrapping the heart of her country in layers of territory which only Frenchmen believe to be French, and, outside them, in further layers of foreign allies. It is a remarkable fact that the only period in which France appealed to an international ideal— Liberty, Equality, and Fraternity—ended with French armies marching from Egypt to Moscow, and French annexation stretched from the Elbe to the Adriatic coast.

It was the fate of Charles, as a young and inexperienced man, to encounter this great force, still unexpended to-day, and then just finding its enduring channels under the lead of one of the decisive personalities in European history. Charles and Buckingham began negotiations with the crowd of nonentities who held office under the young Louis XIII, in a vacuum created by Henry of Navarre's death. They ended by encountering Cardinal Richelieu.

This very great man was not only the principal exponent of France's traditional policy : he changed the shape of European politics to suit the pattern of his own iron mind. Himself a priest, he thrust religion into the subordinate place it has since held : an official of the Roman Church, he engineered Protestant alliances to defeat the forces which, but for him, would have undone the work of the Reformation. He turned the religious conflict of the Thirty Years' War into an undisguised struggle between France and the Hapsburgs of Austria and Spain.

It might be imagined that England, bent on a Protestant crusade against the Hapsburgs, would have made an admirable instrument in Richelieu's hands, as Sweden became in later years. But France was not yet ready, and Richelieu was not firmly enough in the saddle. Charles refused to be a mere instrument, and was always riling the French by his insistence on being the senior partner in the alliance. Finally, England was a rival, and to judge by past history, a very dangerous one. When Gustavus of Sweden grew too successful, Richelieu remarked, " It is time to stop the progress of this Goth " : for further progress was not to the interests of France. For the same reasons, it was better to encourage England to expend her strength in making a breach for France to enter later. England's strength proved negligible, but Charles never forgave the French. He saw in Richelieu not only a treacherous ally, but an active enemy, always intriguing for his ruin. In after years, when he was asked whom he most blamed for the Civil War, he did not point to Pym or Hampden or Argyle, but to Louis XIII. And the old gossip, Mme de Motteville, calls Richelieu, quite simply, " l'auteur de la Révolution Anglaise."

How much truth there was in the accusation we cannot tell. Charles only knew himself in conflict with a force he could not understand and believed to be evil. He had no pretensions to being a great man ; he lacked that dangerous but invaluable faculty of seeing a situation stripped of every moral factor, as a conflict of naked strengths. To Charles, the moral aspect was all that mattered : he was always at a disadvantage in dealing with men whose moral system differed from his own. He felt himself tricked, and tricked for an unworthy purpose. And two nations, whose interests were very similar, found themselves drifting apart, until the projected alliance was threatening to become a war. It is time to examine the steps whereby this came about.

The idea of alliance was of many years' standing. France had tried to dissuade James from the Spanish match and marry Prince Charles to a French princess. A monk was sent to watch the English negotiations in Madrid and was delighted to watch them break down. He immediately came to England to renew the French proposals. Discussions were opened between Buckingham and Marie de Medicis, the Queen Mother of France and the patroness of the rising Richelieu. They were held up by her insistence that any marriage treaty must include a pledge to stop the persecution of the English Catholics. For Prince Charles, in the revulsion of his return from Madrid, had told the House of Lords that he would never bargain again with a foreign power on the subject of the Penal Laws, and James had made a more formal promise to the Commons of the same tenour. The French envoys were told to return : they must find a husband for Henrietta in some less Protestant country.

They had a last resort. Before leaving, they went to Buckingham, and Buckingham told them to stay. There was still hope. The French minister, La Vieuville, scouted the difficulty : the stipulation about the English Catholics was a mere formality, intended to throw dust in the Pope's eyes and induce him to give a dispensation for Princess Henrietta to marry a Protestant : King Louis had no serious interest in the fate of English Catholics ; James could write a private letter, and need not act upon it. James began to listen again. But La Vieuville had gone too far, and King Louis dismissed him. Richelieu stepped into power. Louis had shown that he meant business, and Richelieu, still needing the Queen Mother's backing, was under a double necessity to press the original demand in all seriousness.

James had abandoned his safe and honourable position, and was open to all manner of temptation. Buckingham knew how to tempt. Louis gave every sign of being an invaluable ally. He would not pledge himself in writing, but he promised to embroil himself with Spain by allowing Mansfeld to pass through France with his army of English recruits. As to the Palatinate, he urged his good brother of England to " confide in my affection, which I will show

by my deeds and acting rather than words and promises."
His good brother was tempted to confide. Meanwhile,
Buckingham won over Prince Charles and began to badger
the King. A pledge to Parliament was nothing : Parliament wanted war with Spain, and it could only be carried
on with French assistance ; Parliament had no business
in foreign affairs ; the Penal Laws were a barbarous ana-
chronism. King James gave way.

It was the last December of his life, and he happened to
be in the vicinity of Cambridge. He met the French
envoys in the " Combination Room " of St. John's College.
They presented him with a treaty in which England
promised to stop persecuting her Roman Catholics for
their religion. James, crippled with gout, signed with a
wooden stamp. Charles signed a second document, binding
him to agreement whenever he succeeded his father. The
honour of the English Crown was sold for a foreign alliance
and the prospect of a grand marriage.

In after years Charles said the agreement was a mere
matter of form, intended only for the Pope's satisfaction.
It is impossible to accept the excuse, after the business
of La Vieuville's dismissal. It would have been better to
plead youth, the influence of Buckingham, " Reason of
State." There is a thing which we connect with Nietzsche's
name, as our ancestors connected it with Macchiavelli's—
the curious doctrine that governors are in some way
superior to the morality which is the only spiritual justification for the continuance of government. It is as common
among politicians as among kings : it is present among
commercial directors wherever " Business is business " is
made to mean that dishonesty on a large scale is not
dishonesty. It is universal, inevitable, and generally
disastrous. If Charles was travelling towards a scaffold,
it was, perhaps, no inconsiderable step that he took in the
low-ceilinged room of a Cambridge College.

Sealed in dishonour, the bargain brought no profit.
Louis broke it in spirit almost as soon as it was signed.

While James issued a secret order to suspend proceedings against the Papists, Louis was refusing to admit Mansfeld into France, refusing to commit any act of war against Spain. We can learn from de Brienne's memoirs what one honourable Frenchman thought of his king's diplomacy. Louis was obdurate : he would send a few horse to Germany, a little money to Holland. He suggested that Mansfeld should sail straight to Holland and help the Dutch beat the Spaniards from Namur : Namur threatened the French frontier more than the Palatinate. The great coalition against the Hapsburgs, in which Buckingham had been encouraged to believe, was falling to pieces. And our envoy in Paris was soon writing that France would do nothing, that negotiations were on foot for a treaty between France and Spain. Prince Charles was comparatively young, but he was learning a lesson in diplomacy.

If France refused to be embroiled with Spain, we were already on the edge of war. Some allies we must have. Parliament had always distrusted alliance with Roman Catholic Powers, always urged friendship with Holland. Negotiations were already under weigh, and in order that they might run more smoothly, England was prepared to swallow one of the most barbarous insults ever offered to her.

Round the edge of the world, some twenty Englishmen had established a small dépôt in the East Indies, close to the great Dutch fortress of Amboyna. They were protected by a treaty in which Holland promised to refer all disputes to an international tribunal. But Amboyna, possibly under instructions from Amsterdam, was determined to be rid of its rivals.

One evening a Japanese soldier in Dutch pay was talking to a sentinel on the ramparts. He asked a question about the fortifications. He suddenly found himself hurried away to a dungeon and subjected to the most fiendish tortures (the Dutch were acknowledged experts) until he confessed that there was a plot to surprise the fortress, concocted between the Japanese mercenaries and the English traders. These, too, were seized and tortured. At Amsterdam they will still show you an English Bible on whose margins one poor wretch has scribbled what was being done to them from day to day. Confessions were extracted, the Englishmen put to death.

There may have been a substratum of truth in the story of a conspiracy. England was hardly likely to believe it; England, when news of the whole ghastly business arrived, believed that the Dutch inquisitors had put the whole tale into the mouths of their victims. It is hard to believe that there is any other period of our history when we should have accepted such an outrage without war. There was some indignation, and James protested with sincere but impotent wrath. Some people even blamed our East India Company for publishing the news at such an awkward moment. Within a month we had signed a treaty of alliance with the Dutch.

Meanwhile Mansfeld had sailed for Holland with his 12,000 recruits. Mansfeld had seen war in Germany: his method of feeding troops had been to lead them into enemy country and allow them free licence to plunder. In the territory of an ally he could not be bothered to think out a new system. The Dutch wished to use his army for delivering Breda, besieged by the Spaniards. James insisted that it must march for the Palatinate. Before the dispute was settled, the 12,000 had been reduced by cold, sickness, and starvation to 3000 effective men. The greater part of the rest had perished, hundreds of miles from the real enemy.

As the news of the disaster spread across England, King James lay dying. Charles was with him, Buckingham so assiduous in attendance that the doctors accused him of trying to poison his master. But it was disappointment and failure that were hastening James to the grave. On March 27, 1625, he passed away.

Like many men whom the world accounts failures, he

had perhaps attained his inmost ambition. He had been lazy, cowardly, and weak ; he had forfeited dignity ; without growing evil, he had scandalously tolerated its growth in others. But he had increased his one talent, and died a wise man. Unfortunately, his wisdom was not of that kingly sort which can impose itself on outward circumstance, and it was a sad muddle he was bequeathing to his son.

CHAPTER FOUR

ACCESSION

1625

A WEEK after his father's death Charles left St. James's, where he had lived as Prince of Wales, to walk on foot, and without formality, past Spring Gardens to Whitehall. He was King. Those who saw him pass spoke with approval of his dignified bearing and handsome, serious face : they were glad the new reign had begun. One wonders if any of the same spectators were there to see it end, twenty-four years later, with the same man treading the same path on a bitter January morning, guarded by soldiers, to his death. Certainly if any one had prophesied such an ending, they would have scouted the notion as fantastical. There were no clouds in the sky ; the monarchy seemed imperishable. Nothing but good was known of the young King. He was reserved, shy, something of an enigma. But they hoped to know him better soon, to love and respect him as his father had never been respected.

One thing was made clear with comforting promptitude. If James's Court had been a scandal, his son's was going to be a model to Europe. Drunkenness and vulgarity gave way to sobriety and good taste. One of the King's first acts was to dismiss Christopher Villiers, Buckingham's brother, as a drunkard. Sexual immorality had to hide itself. Charles attacked it in the least odious way—by example. He was to live for twenty-four years in the full glare of a frequently hostile publicity and remain untouched by any scandal worthy of a minute's acceptance. He was not cold by nature, he was deeply attached to friends, and to his wife and children ; he had the same difficulties as every other man since civilization began, except that (as

46

his son was to show) a King's temptations are greater.
That he fought them with complete success was one of his
greatest assets, as man and as king. His Court and policy
were not influenced by a succession of mistresses : he
enjoyed the respect even of his political opponents. His
times (like all times) were immoral, and sin was not condemned with any exaggerated emphasis : but men still
admired self-control, and were not yet touched by that
indiscriminate worship of broad-mindedness which ends in
admiring men and women for the remarkably easy feat
of leading an impure life. There is no gain without loss,
and, without adopting the sneer that makes chastity and
stupidity synonymous, we may perhaps trace to Charles's
unbending virtue a certain stiffness and lack of sympathy.
We have the best of all authorities for knowing that, on
their own ground, " the children of this world are wiser
than the children of light." But while Charles adopted the
only attitude consistent with his view of human dignity, it
cannot be said that he neglected any innocent custom that
could broaden and refine life. He was fond of music and
the theatre. Archie, the Court Fool, kept his place. Games
and hunting-parties, regattas, masques, and dances remained
part of the yearly round. The enemies of merriment were
also the enemies of the King.

At the same time, the Court must be Christian, and
Protestant. An Irish Earl who presumed on his Catholicism,
to absent himself from prayers and even to disturb them by
loud talk in the next room, was told to come in to service
or leave Whitehall. Cottington was dismissed from his
secretaryship : he had recently experienced the first of
several conversions and become a Papist in Madrid. He
appealed to Buckingham, who told him candidly that he
regarded him as an enemy and would not lift a finger in
his behalf. Cottington had the naïveté to ask for the
return of some rich tapestries which he had sent Buckingham in order to curry favour ; Buckingham had the generosity to reimburse him for his unsuccessful extravagance.

If Buckingham's brother had been dismissed, Buckingham was as powerful as ever. There was an unbreakable bond of friendship between him and the King. And the King had decided, rightly or wrongly, to continue the policy which had brought him to the throne on a wave of popularity. So far as England was articulate, England was applauding Buckingham ; England was shouting for war with Spain. To oppose the demand would be the act of an arbitrary despot, a deliberate thwarting of Parliament's expressed petition. And in this matter Parliament seemed to represent the nation, weary of James's peace policy and the corroding influence of Spanish friendship. Not without misgivings, Charles committed himself to the rising tide. It was to be his misfortune to be more consistent and more thorough than his subjects, and to be left high and dry.

There was no doubt who was going to direct the war. Buckingham seemed popular, except among jealous Peers ; his abilities were still untried, but he was energetic and whole-hearted. He had wavered before, as personal considerations dictated. Now he had thrown himself into the policy of war, and he had the personal backing of King Charles, who was not going to waver at all. His first duty was to go to France, to fetch home Henrietta, and see if he could not induce King Louis to abandon his dishonourable neutrality. The first part of his mission was easier than the second. On June 1 he saw Henrietta married by proxy outside the great west door of Notre-Dame. But considering that he was charged to escort a young bride to her husband, he exercised his charm in a rather questionable direction.

Louis XIII's appearance in history is that of a vague shadow at Richelieu's back. He was a rather cold-blooded creature, married to a beautiful Spanish wife. Buckingham, failing to get anything whatever from Louis, failing completely to draw him into war with Spain, made indiscreet love to Anne of Austria. He let the whole Court see on what his eyes were fixed, and Anne did nothing to rebuke him. He wooed her at dusk in a private garden, until he frightened her into calling to her attendants for help. When duty compelled him to start home with Henrietta, Anne accompanied the party to Amiens. Parted from her there, Buckingham had hardly gone twenty miles when he made an excuse to double back. He arrived in Amiens again in the morning and found Anne in bed. He threw himself on his knees and covered the bedclothes with kisses. The bystanders were scandalized to hear their mistress tell him to depart, " without overmuch anger." After such a scene it is not surprising that Louis refused in future to accept any English embassy that contained the Duke of Buckingham. Buckingham, it is said, replied that the next time he came to France, it would be at the head of an army.

As the ships approached England, Charles rode down to Dover to welcome the girl of whom he had only had a brief and uninterested view more than two years ago. But a naïve note from Henrietta begged him to return : she had had a tossing, she was not looking her best, would Charles give her time to recover herself on dry land ? Charles rode back to Canterbury, while Henrietta disembarked. Next day saw him in Dover again, by ten in the morning. Henrietta was still at breakfast—we do not know if it was the beef and beer of England or whatever *petit déjeuner* the French favoured when coffee was still unknown. She left it, and ran downstairs to the room where a husband awaited her.

Monarchy makes strange demands upon human creatures. Here were two young people in whom life ran strong, two bundles of illogical preferences, now under the obligation to surrender the one unreasonable fancy to which reason rightly bows. Knowing each other only through courtly liars, they had already exchanged a pledge from which nothing could release them as long as life remained ; and on the success of their union hung the happiness of a million humbler souls, to preserve or gamble away.

All went well. As soon as she saw her husband, Henrietta fell on her knees—she was only sixteen—and tried to kiss his hands. Charles raised her gently and kissed her on the lips. " Sire," she said, and one wonders how often she had rehearsed it, " I am come to this country to be used and commanded by your Majesty." Then formality broke down. Charles was looking at her shoes, and, remembering some one had made the ungallant suggestion that she was not tall enough for him, she guessed what prompted his glance. " No, Sire," she said, " I wear no false heels. This *is* my height ! "

They went off laughing to a picnic on Barham Downs, but as soon as they were alone, Henrietta was telling Charles that she was young and ignorant, and would he please tell her when she did wrong, not leave it to a third person. Charles reassured her and hoped she would do the like by him. It looked as if the miracle was going to happen with unexpected swiftness, and themselves be already on the threshold of a happiness they had hardly dreamt. They had forgotten that Henrietta was French, Charles English, and that he had a friend who was also his evil genius.

The marriage treaty had given Henrietta the right to bring with her a large French retinue, including a bishop and many priests of the Church which Charles disliked and many of his subjects abhorred. France had chosen them for zeal rather than discretion, and, with them, as ladies-in-waiting to the young Queen, came some Frenchwomen who represented the worser qualities of their great and attractive nation ; one at least already enjoyed an evil reputation among her own people. They had begun to grumble as soon as they arrived. The house appointed for their mistress at Dover was dreadfully old-fashioned, the bed a scandal : the first meeting—so successful in putting Henrietta immediately at ease—was held to be disgracefully, insultingly informal. Charles did not know what trouble was brewing, but he had made up his mind that the

Queen of England must not be exclusively surrounded by Frenchwomen : two English ladies must ride in her coach to London. He tactlessly chose Buckingham's mother and sister, and Henrietta, already hating Buckingham, was furious. At Canterbury she overcame her anger. Charles supped with her, carved her some venison and pheasant with his own hand, and was delighted to see her take no notice when a priest reminded her that it was a fast day. When she retired for the night, even her ladies admitted that the cathedral city had provided a bed *moins infâme* than the Dover horror. It was arranged that they should enter London by barge, a not unusual method made more prudent by the Plague, which had begun to rage in the streets. The entry was not a success. Of course the French ladies thought that the thunder of cannon, pealing bells, and blazing bonfires were a poor and bar-barous substitute for the refinement and *galanterie* that Paris would have provided for a Royal welcome. Of course—since it was June—London contributed a heavy downpour of rain. The climax to a wretched day was reached with the discovery that Henrietta was expected to sleep in an Elizabethan bed, so old-fashioned that even the English could not remember when it had been really *à la mode.*

No one foresaw how serious these frivolous quarrellings would become before they were cured once and for all. At one moment it almost looked as if Henrietta might become the perfect wife at once, even a popular figure in London. One good Puritan was so charmed by her beauty that after seeing her at a public dinner, he went home to pray for her conversion from her idolatrous religion. But her position was a very trying one. She was a mere girl ; for all her attempts at humility, she was as high-spirited as became a daughter of Henry of Navarre : she had been badly brought up in a Court corrupted by his immorality, sinking, after his death, into mere levity and extravagance. Now she was surrounded by mischief-making women, egging her on to assert herself. Mme de Motteville blames them for " preventing her knowing her husband's good intentions, and the love he bore her." At her back were priests whose religion compelled them to speak of him as a heretic, his subjects as bloodthirsty persecutors of the truth. Worse still, she knew his heart was in partial bondage to a man she hated. In after years she declared that Buckingham not only fomented deliberate trouble, but brazenly told her he was doing so. If " these are the forgeries of jealousy," she had good reason to be jealous. But there were observers that threw the blame upon her. " The King loves her absolutely, and she," wrote an Italian, with some exaggeration, " has from the first day shown an aversion from his person and from all the English nation." Even Frenchmen complained that she treated everything English with uncompromising rudeness.

But Charles could afford to wait until time or circumstances cured his domestic troubles. Meanwhile there was a war to conduct, and he was summoning Parliament to supply him with the means.

The name of Parliament raises graver issues than lovers' tiffs. We have come to regard the quarrel between King and Parliament as the only important matter in Charles's reign. If this is an exaggerated view, yet it is undoubted that this quarrel grew until it had absorbed and focused upon itself every other conflict in England, and that its outcome has profoundly affected the history of the human race. In the next chapter we must interrupt the narrative in order to discuss the nature of Parliament, its origins, the causes and the rights of its struggle with King Charles. These things have been discussed again and again from the very reasonable point of view of the Parliamentarians, and *ad nauseam* from the irritating point of view of comfortable Victorian gentlemen enjoying the benefits and shielded from the evils of Victorian constitutionalism. We will try to re-examine the matter as it may have appeared to a seventeenth-century king, and as it appears in the light of certain neglected facts in our history, before and after the defeat of Monarchy.

In the first year of the reign, few indeed can have foreseen the proportions of the coming struggle. There had been friction under King James; the main causes of trouble were beginning to appear. The House of Commons had control of a large proportion of the Royal revenue: this had emboldened them to protest, with varying success, against Elizabethan restrictions on their power. The Queen had forbidden them to discuss foreign politics, and they had acquiesced. She had denied that they had any jurisdiction over the government of the Church: that was a matter for her, for the bishops, and for Convocation—the elected parliament of the clergy. Again they had acquiesced, less willingly. She had imprisoned their members for words spoken in the House, words she described as seditious. They had protested, but ineffectually. When the new king came from Scotland, they told him that their acquiescence was no precedent for the future. New causes of dispute arose: the Commons wished for fresh and more stringent laws against the Catholics, fought for a Bill that might lay the foundations of Sabbatarianism, began to discuss both Church and foreign politics. The result was a very considerable friction, though no one foresaw that a great conflict was in preparation. There may have been courtiers who hoped to see such friction crushed by acts of despotism: there may have been parliamentarians scheming to fan the flame until the throne grew uncomfortably warm. But when a member called down God's curse on all who sought to break the marriage solemnized in Parliament between King and People, the whole House cried, Amen. Only when James was dying and Buckingham at their head did Parliament suddenly find its will prevailing against a king, its foreign policy adopted, its power to impeach a King's minister recognized.

To that outburst, so dangerous to monarchy, Charles had given his countenance. Now that he was king, he

5

hoped to reap a harvest of popularity. He was eager to call a Parliament quickly, and even asked whether his father's last Parliament could be summoned to reassemble at once. He was told that custom demanded fresh elections on the death of a king. It was three months before they were finished, and the hundred Peers and the five hundred Commoners came to find lodgings in a plague-stricken city. In the week of Parliament's meeting, 165 Londoners died, among them the dramatist Fletcher: debates proceeded to the sound of passing-bells in the street outside.

June 18 was appointed for the opening day. The King sat on his throne, splendidly robed, the Peers sat round him; before them stood the bareheaded Commons. There were many famous men in the Hall, many to grow famous with the years. There sat Essex, the wronged husband, the future general of Roundheads; Mandeville, who had condemned Ralegh and arraigned the Somerset poisoners, one day to be Earl of Manchester and Essex's colleague in the field; Lord Saye, who would send them troops but manage to avoid fighting himself, and turn up smiling to greet Charles II at the Restoration; Ben Jonson's young patron, who would soon be Duke of New-castle, spend five million in the Royalist cause, see his Whitecoats cut to pieces at Marston Moor, and yet live to patronize Dryden. Among the Commons stood Stanley, one day to be the "Martyr Earl" of Derby; Wentworth, for whom waited a swifter and more cruel fate; Eliot, already nearing the end of his short and tragic life; Hampden, to die in agony in the little house at Thame; Pym, who would be King Pym of London, and yet live to hear a London mob come howling for his blood. If any man foresaw what was coming, it may have been Pym, though even his bold and powerful brain, focused with such astonishing clearness on the next step, can hardly have seen the ultimate goal. From most the whole future was mercifully hidden. They could hardly have guessed that the legacy of doubtful law, the pressure of class interest, the riddle of religious strife would grow into a single conflict, envenomed by mishandling and wilfulness, faction and greed, until it split England and broke the puzzled hearts of many an honest man.   Nor could King Charles know, as he rose to speak, that the passing-bell outside marked something other than the havoc of the Plague.   It tolled the death-knell of the house of Stewart.

CHAPTER FIVE

Origins

1066–1832

"Circumstances, which some gentlemen pass for nothing, give, in reality, to every political principle its distinguishing colour and discriminating effect."—BURKE.

THERE is not, and perhaps there has never been, such a thing as an absolute monarchy. Absolutism is a relative term. Even the Oriental despot must work through viziers and pashas and satraps. He may appoint what servants he will, he may flog and torture them for disobedience, he may dismiss and put them to death. But they are men, they have wills of their own ; as they obey his word, they dilute it, perhaps unconsciously, with their own personalities. If he is constantly crossing their wishes or violating their conscience, they can sometimes defeat him by putting him, or rather his office, into commission. They revere his person, they strip him of power and rule his kingdom themselves. Thus Turkey has been governed by a clique of eunuchs, and Japan, for a thousand years, worshipped its Emperor but obeyed the regents put up by a feudal aristocracy. If the monarch is too wary or too active to be so treated, there is still another course open to his servants : they can murder him. And they frequently do. The only despots secure from this danger are those whom religion has surrounded with a divine legend. Peru affords a good example ; it is not exactly Oriental, though it can be reached by going long enough in an easterly direction. There the Incas imposed the minutest despotism on their servants and all their subjects, ordering their food, lodging, and occupation, and even invading the last sanctuary of human liberty, by prescribing to them their choice of wives. For to the Peruvians, the Incas were direct descendants of the gods.

Now there was nothing Oriental about Charles or his opponents. They were Englishmen and Christians. But it is interesting to see (since human nature is one) what different forms things may take under a different sky. In Christendom, men have rights, men are equal before God. Murder, and especially the murder of kings, is not embarked upon without a considerable twinge of conscience. The plan of putting kingship into commission, loading it with honour and stripping it of power, strikes us as odd. It had been successful in Venice, where a ring of merchant families had put the Duke into their pocket. It needed a century to perfect the experiment in England : the English gentry were probably unconscious of imitating Italians, though Charles actually cried out that he would not be made a Doge of, and died to prevent it. Finally, though he claimed a divine authority for his office, he could not follow Oriental examples and claim personal divinity. He was a Christian, and a Christian king has as much and as little divinity as the meanest labourer in his fields.

Another thing that tells against the king in Europe is that his servants have not considered themselves as deriving their authority purely from him. They derive it from heredity, from immemorial custom, from the possession of land and wealth. At times they went so far as to claim that he derived his kingship from them, to vote themselves or their cousins king, and, outvoted, to devastate the country with civil war. The practical inconveniences of this system soon destroyed it in every country except Poland. If there are traces of election in our own Coronation Service, they are only traces.

Still, even in England, the nobles retained great independence. Their duties to the central government were strictly limited by custom, their local power almost despotic. When what we call Political Evolution (our ancestors called it God) prompted the King to make a nation out of the patchwork of their private estates, they still did a deal of local governing, though it was now in his name ; and they insisted on their right to advise him about carrying on the central government. To give such advice—and frequently to enforce it—they became a formal assembly with its own methods of procedure, and, since its main concern was talk, it was called Parliament.

Then a most interesting thing happens. An eccentric aristocrat of foreign extraction raises rebellion and supports himself by introducing an idea already in full working order abroad ; de Montfort is defeated, but the next king adopts his idea. Tired of the advice somewhat monotonously provided by the larger landowners, Edward I calls a new assembly, to represent the smaller landowners and the town merchants—two from each county, two from each borough ; the advice he asks from them is how best to raise more money. It is agreed that he will abide by what they say on the subject : in financial matters, " advice " becomes " consent." He is still not conferring a privilege so much as demanding a service : and it is often a great nuisance. No one likes to interrupt business in order to follow the King to London, or Gloucester, or even York. The town councils vote the job on to the most unpopular, or send the black sheep of the community ; even then they pay them. But the advantages of a Parliament are beginning to appear. Not only does the King raise his taxes according to their advice : he listens to their grievances and redresses them. They are embodied in local petitions, which he may grant or refuse : *Soit droit comme il est desiré* is his formula for accepting a petition. Otherwise, *le Roi s'avisera*, the King will think about it. When greater grievances demand a wholesale change in English law, he seals acceptance with *le Roi le veult*.

It is one of the burdens of a king's life that he cannot do anything without creating a precedent. Convenience

and then justice demand that he shall not disappoint
hopes and defeat calculations by a sudden change of front,
except under the pressure of emergency. Subjects may
even plead a king's former acts against him. Custom
becomes law. Custom binds the King to go on calling to
Parliament the same nobles and bishops, two members
from each county, two from the same towns—though
those towns may be decaying and ceasing to be towns at
all. Custom also gives the Lower House the right of
deciding on all financial matters. They grow more important. The King, the largest landowner in the country, had
once paid for central government from his rents and dues,
had, in mediæval phrase, "lived of his own." The Commons
had helped him by granting to each new king, for life, the
right to levy customs at the ports. If he wanted still more,
he must come to them each time for a grant. Falling
values, wastage of Crown lands, a huge rise in prices, play
into their hands. A king cannot wage war, hardly carry on
a peaceful government without their help. It has never
been refused, it has hardly ever been granted on conditions.
But it is often grudged. The only thing a king can do
without his Commons' consent is to take a compulsory
" loan," and forget to pay it back, or to drop the pretence
and call it a " benevolence." And if he does this too
often there will be trouble.

All this is a definite limitation of royal power, and every
king accepts it, willingly or reluctantly. It leaves untouched
his power of acting as he pleases, without even advice, in
those spheres of government in which it has not been
customary to consult Parliament—foreign affairs, war and
peace, Ireland, and the details of Church government. It
also leaves untouched his power to do anything at all, in
the teeth of custom, law and even bare justice, when
really serious danger threatens the community. This
absolute power in some spheres of government, this emergency dictatorship in all, were put together under the
single title of Prerogative. It is difficult to see how the

nation could have survived the centuries without it. It was frequently abused, but the bitterest Parliamentarian did not deny its necessity : Cromwell exercised a Prerogative, and a far wider one than Charles. The dispute concerned not its existence but its limits.

That it had limits Charles never denied. His contemporaries on the Continent laughed at him for not attempting to establish unlimited despotism. His detractors have accused him of working to that end, but the facts contradict their accusation. When enemies charged Strafford with suggesting absolutism, Charles declared that it was a lie ; he would have punished any minister who made such a suggestion ; he was " very well content with that authority which God has put into my hands " ; did his good subjects, he asked, conceive him a fool or a tyrant ? Charles had so often been accused, and sometimes justly, of saying one thing and doing another, that it will be better to let the reader judge of his sincerity in this crucial matter from the narrative of his reign. But if he recognized limits, he was adamant about defending them from encroachment : the full maintenance of his Prerogative was the duty for which he had been born upon this earth. Slackness in such a matter was treachery to his ancestors, to the happiness of his subjects, to the welfare of posterity. And when a duty had such sanctions, it was, to the seventeenth-century mind, a duty to God. Indeed, if God is anything but a distant and meaningless abstraction, if He lives in the hearts and adventures of men, as well as in the farthest star, then the Divine Right of Kings becomes something a little less laughable than our age would like to make it.

Rightly or wrongly, we have come to think of politics in terms of biology : man is a superior kind of animal, his mass movements are described in such phrases as social organism, racial evolution, herd instinct. The seventeenth century had never heard of Darwin, and it thought in terms of religion. Man was a spirit, a fallen angel, a son of

God. If he had brutish instincts they were implanted in
him by a spirit, though an evil one. If he had a body,
subject to material accidents, it was merely an expression
of his soul, a shadow of that heavenly counterpart which
clothed the soul in the regions beyond time, where the
dead and perhaps the unborn dwelt. But even among
such shadows God was active and all-pervading. If a
custom had endured for ages it had His approval : it
might grow obsolete in a changing world ; but the man who
presumed to alter it must bring overwhelming evidence
that his motive was pure—not the faction or tyranny which
the Devil sows in men's hearts. That is what Charles
meant by the Divine Right of Kings. That is what his
opponents meant by the sacred rights of Parliament. If
any one finds it impossible to understand the theory
(admittedly a bold one) that God created this world and is
still immanent in every blade of grass and every passing
thought in our minds, he will also find Charles, all his
principal followers, and nine-tenths of his enemies radically
unintelligible. He will save himself a great deal of unnecessary irritation by closing this book here and now,
and sending it back to the library.

If government is to survive at all, it must rest on some
axiom beyond dispute and almost beyond discussion.
Recently our axiom has been that universal suffrage pro-
duces an assembly roughly representative of the national
will. The fact that this proposition has ceased to be
axiomatic and is freely discussed shows that we are within
measurable distance of revolution. The seventeenth
century would have dismissed it as impractical—and
untrue ; our ancestors were apparently more alive than
we are to the effects of apathy, temporary excitements,
and the manœuvring of interested electioneers. Their
axiom lay in obedience to a set of laws whose chief sanction
was their antiquity, changed occasionally by a Parliament
representing the richer and more intelligent classes, administered by a single man, on whom the affection and

loyalty of the people could concentrate. This man must be raised to a position where fear and ambition and avarice have ceased to have any meaning. If his lot is not always happy, it is enviable (for men pursue power more greedily than they pursue happiness) ; he must therefore be guarded by a strict rule of heredity which will extinguish all hope of supplanting him in the mind of his most powerful and most unscrupulous subject. He must be beyond the reach of intimidation, responsible to no earthly power. So placed, he may be a bad interpreter of the national will, but he will be in some sort an impartial one, the best that can be discovered in this perplexing world. He will guard the national liberties from the tyranny of aristocratic cliques, of religious sects, of mere money. This system was not unchallenged, but it had seen us through many perils. It had rescued us from the Wars of the Roses and set us free from Papal tyranny. Its strength under a selfish homicide like Henry VIII and a persecuting Papist like his daughter had left fewer permanent scars than its weakness under Edward VI, a minor under aristocratic control. By and large, it had stood the test of time. It had God's sanction.

We have said that it was not unchallenged. It remains to see what was now challenging it, and whether England would be better for its defeat.

We must examine the organ through which its opponents worked ; for Parliament meant something very different from what it means to-day. We must discuss their theories, though we need not fall into the ingenuous habit of judging the Parliamentarians solely on what they said in the House —or rather on reports of their debatings left us by avowed sympathizers like d'Ewes and Rushworth.[1] And we know

---

[1] Rushworth, our fullest authority, became Cromwell's secretary. He records some of the Opposition speeches (particularly Pym's) in great detail. Contemporaries accused him of serious suppressions, of which one instance will suffice. Both he and d'Ewes speaks of the Royalist Finch defending the Prerogative in December 1640 with extraordinary ability, so as greatly to affect his adversaries. Neither reports his arguments.

enough of contemporary England to analyse the driving-force which lay behind their theories.

There were among them a few Republicans, drawing their inspiration from a somewhat romantic vision of classical Greece and Rome, and from the less romantic reality of contemporary Venice and Holland. These two were the only contemporary republics (except neglected Switzerland), for it was like England's contrariness to increase its crop of that rare phenomenon, the English republican, just when Europe was everywhere accepting despotism.

But far the greatest number of Charles's opponents were Monarchists : Cromwell so avowed himself within a year of cutting off the King's head. They thought that the original balance of King, Lords, and Commons could be preserved, or rather restored. Fundamentally, the whole quarrel was about the limits of the Prerogative ; appealing mainly to late mediæval precedents, they argued that the Tudors had recently stretched their Prerogative to quite unhealthy lengths. They had violated the privileges of Parliament and debarred it from discussing religion, foreign politics, or the choice of royal ministers. Such a policy could only be justified by the recurrent national emergencies of the Tudor age. It was now intolerable.

There were some very weak spots in this argument, upon which the King could seize. The Commons had never interfered in foreign policy or the details of Church government : the impeachment of royal ministers had been a rare and exceptional thing. But Charles, for reasons we shall soon see, could not rely on such criticisms ; his main contention was a more general one. He denied that the Tudor emergencies had ceased. He did not suggest that an earthquake or a foreign invasion was imminent, nor arrogate to himself powers suitable to such an occasion. He pleaded a different kind of emergency, and one which justified him in disregarding Parliament's views, particularly on religion and the choice of ministers, occasionally in imprisoning its members, finally in ruling for eleven years,

in defiance of custom, without calling a Parliament at all.
The emergency he pleaded was this, that the parliamentary
machinery had been captured by a faction, unscrupulous
in its methods, unpatriotic in its aims, whose triumph
would mean the destruction of English liberty, the imposi-
tion of a tyrannical and unpopular religion, the unbalancing
of the whole national life in the interests of the few.

It is sometimes assumed that such a plea is too absurd
to need examination, and that Charles was crying Wolf !
at his own shadow for interested motives.   Yet there are a
dozen arguments to support it : in Charles's speeches and
proclamations, in the writings of contemporary thinkers
(not all Royalists), and in certain ascertainable facts about
the history of the time.   They do not amount to proof ;
but they amount to a very strong presumption that
Charles's view was as well-founded as that of his opponents,
and that its triumph might have left us a better England
than the one we know.   For if his defeat was followed by
two centuries in which we were happier than our neighbours,
that happiness was very unequally distributed, filched
increasingly from the poor, denied, through long years of
racial and religious tyranny, to the dwellers on an adjacent
island.   And it was perhaps less than was warranted by
the advantages of our position, our natural wealth, and the
splendid qualities of our race.   Now that we are losing
some of those advantages, we may well look back and
wonder how it was that we did not make better use of
them.

Those centuries were dominated by the triumph of
Parliament over the Monarchy. They ended, in 1832,
with a recognition that Parliament, with its corruption
and its " pocket-boroughs," represented, not the nation,
but a narrow clique of wealthy men : and the result was
the great Reform Bill. It is difficult to trace the steps
whereby Parliament became such a body : it is arguable
that it was well on the way to becoming so when King
Charles ascended the throne in 1625.

The local rule, that a constituency should be represented by a resident, had been lately swept away. Seats were handed about in the oddest way. Pym sat for three different boroughs within four years, lending some colour to the suspicion that he owed them to Lord Bedford's patronage. But they were all in the same region, and his record is nothing to that of Mansell, Nottingham's corrupt Admiralty official, who sat for two Welsh counties, a Welsh borough, a town in Norfolk, and a town in Cornwall. It will appear later how easy it was to find a Devonshire seat for an unknown Irishman called Clotworthy—and for what purpose. It is not surprising that such things should go on in boroughs, where the electorate might be a few venal aldermen : in the middle of Elizabeth's reign a " verie simple man " had suddenly presented himself in the Commons and, asked how he got there, replied that he had presented £20 to the Mayor of Westbury and to " one Watts." Again, Liverpool was regarded in Charles's time as a safe seat for Lord Derby's candidate. It is harder to see how the county seats (with their 5000 or 10,000 electors)[1] were captured ; but Berkshire was regarded as being in Lord Pembroke's gift, and it was only natural that he should bestow it on his son.

It must be added that some of this " patronage " worked in favour of the King (though that hardly made Parliament more representative). It is also true that the Commons made efforts to check it in several cases : they had certainly sent the " verie simple man " to the rightabout, and even got him his money back. Their motive may have been to assert their independence as a representative body. Their efforts were not very successful.

How deep these practical abuses went, we can only guess : corruption does not willingly leave written records. What we can more easily examine is the official system of representation.

[1] No figures are available until the end of the century and the beginning of the next. Then 5500 voted in Oxfordshire, 9300 in Cheshire.

There was no question of democracy, in our sense of a
Parliament based on a wide and equal suffrage. The idea
did indeed crop up towards the end of Charles's life when
he was a defeated prisoner. Cromwell, among whose
troops it appeared, toyed with the notion and then crushed
it out of sight. It is one of his few actions that would
have had the unqualified approval of the Long Parliament.

The boroughs differed immensely : in some there were
a large number of electors ; some were controlled by a
small ring of merchants ; some were so small as to be
under the influence of a local landowner. Their distribu-
tion was odd. A system does not inspire confidence by
allotting as many seats to Cornwall as to Lancashire and
Yorkshire combined, despite a different balance in population. In the counties there had once been votes for all
who came to elections. A fifteenth-century enactment
had confined them to freeholders, and the freeholders were
now a diminishing class.

Many of the anomalies were due to the fact that the
whole face of society had changed since the system had
crystallized. And behind all minor changes there was
one which amounted to a revolution. Mediæval Parliaments had represented a great number of different classes
and interests. Apart from the Bishops, there were the
richer landowners in the House of Peers ; there were the
lesser landowners of the shires, socially distinct ; there were
merchants, cut off from both by the mediæval gentleman's
distaste for commerce ; finally, there were the lawyers,
drawn from the preceding classes, but with separate
interests expressed in a separate guild. What was happening in the seventeenth century was that all these classes
were rapidly becoming one. The intermingling of Peers
and Commoners was still incomplete : the delay gave
Charles a breathing-space ; but their final alliance was
his ruin. Wealth was bringing them together. In 1628 it
was said that the Lower House could have bought up the
Peers (the King excepted) three times over. They were

more than three times as numerous, so that this somewhat
vulgar boast meant that they were, man for man, not quite
so rich. But they were beginning to intermarry freely.
Hazlerig, the King's opponent in the Commons, was
brother-in-law to Lord Brooke, the Roundhead general.
Lord St. John became Earl of Bolingbroke and a Parliamentarian, while Mr. Oliver St. John pleaded in the courts
for Hampden and supported him with speeches in the
Commons. He was a connection of Oliver Cromwell, and
when Cromwell came to sit in the Long Parliament he
found seventeen of his relations there : co-option was to
increase the number to twenty-four, before his soldiers
" purged " this family party and finally took away its
bauble.

Lawyers and landowners were becoming quite in-
distinguishable : most squires entered one of the Inns of
Court in order to learn their duties as J.P.s ; they frequently
left younger brothers there for life. Successful lawyers
bought landed estates ; so did successful merchants. The
country gentry were investing surplus rents in commerce,
sitting on the governing bodies of City companies and sending their sons into commerce. Several Earls were principal
shareholders in the City ; one, a few years after Charles's
death, apprenticed his son to a London tradesman. The
process was to be checked for a time, even reversed in the
eighteenth century. Then the vast wealth of " nabobs "
and industrial *parvenus* tempted the landed gentry to
begin it again. It has ended in our own day (for good or
ill) by making social distinctions quite meaningless. A
fraudulent Company puts a baronet among its directors, a
Countess uses her title and her photograph to advertise
a face-cream.

But it is the political aspect which is here in question.
Parliament had ceased to be a microcosm of warring
interests, it was becoming the organ of a class whose distinguishing mark was riches. So far as it obeyed its selfish
interests, its aim would be to destroy the pressure of the

Crown above, to depress the status of the poor below. It becomes clear that there are national emergencies other than foreign invasion. It becomes possible to connect the tragedy of King Charles with a greater and more lasting tragedy.

In the Middle Ages, the poor, cruelly as they no doubt suffered from civil wars and the violence of the strong, had a certain security. Many possessed land, if only a few strips, and could not legally be dispossessed ; most owned their own houses : dues and services could not be raised above the immemorial " custom of the manor," and failure to pay did not mean eviction. The system collapsed, a thousand causes contributing to its ruin. If some of the poor ceased to be serfs, or even slaves, an alarming proportion became vagabonds, while the lands they had tilled were given over to the rich man's sheep. Most of them became wage-earners, working on land and with instruments that were their masters' property. A parliamentary statute, passed in the reign of a weak king, directed that their wages should be fixed by the J.P.s—all landowners themselves, all employing wage-earners. For a long time they fixed not a minimum wage, but a maximum, above which no man must ask. Only in one trade, the weavers', did the King's Council interfere to fix a minimum.

Meanwhile the landowners, in the teeth of continual edicts from the King, were " enclosing " the commons ; this process was tragically mismanaged, with the cruellest injustice to the poor. It was conducted by the larger ladnowners, with their hired lawyers, whose chances of future employment rested on the reputation they could win among landowning gentry. Some of the land came under more productive control, some was laid out in game preserves, and in ornamental parks whose beauty almost justifies the theft. The process was bitterly resisted by the Crown. Not till Charles had been twenty years in his grave did Parliament pass a General Enclosure Act, facilitating the passing of private bills. Not till the final

collapse of monarchy under George III did the thing
acquire its final swiftness and momentum. Meanwhile
competition was telling against the smaller freeholders.
They were bought out, they lost their parliamentary vote,
the King's revenue suffered, but the estates of the gentry
were nicely " rounded off." Yeomen became tenant
farmers, liable to rack-renting and eviction. The rich
were becoming masters of the land.

As J.P.s, the landlords decided all petty cases in their
district, and some which were not petty—to the poor. No
doubt there were many good Christians, glad to show
special consideration to a poor man's plea. But there
were others whose circle of ideas centred on the rent-roll,
the sanctity of game, the prestige of the gentry. There
were two possibilities of appeal from their decisions. There
were the ordinary law courts, administered by lawyers
who were also gentry ; becoming expert by long years of
unpaid toil, they naturally demanded high fees for pleading, and some of the judges expected handsome presents.
Here was no place for the poor. There were other courts,
under directer royal control, less expert, more arbitrary,
far less expensive. Arbitrary justice may sometimes be
the terrible thing that it is represented, and on one of
these courts, Star Chamber, enemies have succeeded in
fixing, at least for the educated, a terrible stigma. To
the poor and uneducated even the name of Star Chamber
may have had no sinister sound. Its fellows, High Commission, the Council for Wales, the Council for the North,
even were demonstrably guardians of the poor man's
rights. From them he could get a justice which was
cheap, swift, and tolerably impartial between rich and poor.
They were given the informative name of Prerogative
Courts. The other courts, more free from Royal control,
waged a long war against them (for they attracted many
suitors, and seriously diminished lawyers' fees) by issuing
" writs of prohibition," on one excuse or another, to
transfer their cases to Westminster. But the war re-

6

mained indecisive until the lawyers persuaded the House of Commons to take their side and the Long Parliament abolished the Prerogative Courts, nominally as instruments of tyranny. Dr. Reid, who has made a special study of the Council for the North, returns an uncompromising verdict upon this abolition. It greatly increased lawyers' fees, but it " established a system of justice which, at least in the North, amounted to an absolute denial of justice to the poor man. . . . To the wage-earners, and to the poor especially, the disappearance of the Council for the North was pure loss."

Justice was not the only matter in which the Crown was in constant friction with the gentry. They were responsible for the administration of the Poor Law. After the destruction of the Monarchy, the system became the national disgrace that we can read of in the records of the Speenhamland system or even the novels of Dickens. One historian of the Poor Law has said, " There are grounds for believing that never since the days of Charles I have we had so much provision of work for the able-bodied, or so complete a system for looking after the more needy classes," [1] It was enforced by the King's Council. It disappeared with the successful assault on Royal power.

Roads and bridges were under a similar control : in the next century they were so badly kept that the gentry invented the characteristic remedy of farming roads out to joint-stock companies, erecting turnpike gates, and recouping the shareholders out of tolls levied on all who rode or drove along what had once been the king's highway. Another duty of the squires was to enforce the militia regulations, see that every Englishman kept arms and was drilled in their practice, levy a rate to pay for his target practice. How well they did their work we shall soon see. Professor Firth has published an amusing letter from a local magnate protesting against the iniquitous sum at which he is assessed for gunpowder ; his excuse is

[1] E. M. Leonard, *Early History of English Poor Relief*, p. 132.

the perennial one—" the abundance of rates and taxes
wherewith we are continually charged." It may not have
been only the tradition of Agincourt which made the long-
bow popular with the English squire long after Europe
had begun to laugh at it.

But it is not the occasional inefficiencies of squire-
archy that mattered, it was its existence, its friction with
the Crown, and its omnipotence in local government. It
was now joining hands with the merchant plutocracies
in the towns, who fixed urban wages and prices, laid down
conditions of work, policed the streets, ruled markets,
and levied local tolls. Their power was based on mediæval
charters ; their constitution may once have been a democratic one ; but the ladder which led to positions of influence
was now a very difficult one for the poor apprentice to
climb, very easy for the rich man's son, for any that could
" bring money into the firm." And the vicious circle was
established by which wealth meant power in local politics,
and political power increased private wealth. Now the
ruling classes of the towns were joining hands with that
other class which dominated the countryside. Its omnipotence was checked locally by a few royal courts, a few
king's officers, by the constant interference of the Privy
Council. Such obstacles could only be swept away by the
capture of the central sovereignty, and to effect that
capture the gentry and merchants and lawyers had the
admirable weapon called Parliament. They would use it
for that purpose, while they claimed for it the right to
dictate the policy of England and of those two other nations
whose king was our King, whose fate hung upon the
happenings at Westminster. And their triumph would
enable them to pass laws which could regulate, not piecemeal
and here and there, but uniformly from Land's End to
Berwick, the conditions under which millions of the poor
and humble must live and work, marry and worship,
rejoice and mourn and die.

They had their way. For two centuries after Charles's

death, the power of the Crown would decline, the power
of the rich increase. While prices rose, the poor man's
wages fell lower and lower, the wealth of his betters piled
mountainously up. Their rule grew harsher as it grew
more absolute. Elegance and penury produced two
separate species, sundered by scorn and misery. The
physical presence of the poor (except of those trained and
adorned for domestic serfdom) grew distasteful to the
rich man, whose ancestors had eaten and made merry
with his dependants at the long board of the Elizabethan
manor. In the end he was helping the *parvenu* he
despised to build up the industrial nightmare of the
growing towns ; Parliamentary Acts, comfortable economic
fallacies, even religious teaching, guarded machinery and
starvation wages ; evicted villagers swelled the armies of
slum-dwellers on whose misery the machines could feed ;
and, while in France a peasant priest shared this world
and the next with his fellow-peasants, Miss Jane Austen's
young ladies made a genteel match with a curate worth
£1000 a year in Consols. It is impossible to doubt that all
these things would have been profoundly modified, many
of them prevented altogether, by the continued pressure of
a monarchy above the rich man's head.

Against so vast a background of human happiness
and human misery, the rights and wrongs of the storm
in the Westminster teacup begin to lose some of their
significance. We are even tempted to ask whether John
Hampden, Esquire, really did so much for England when
(otherwise untaxed for many years, able to bequeath,
among other legacies, a sum of £200,000) he withheld his
contribution of seven or eight pounds to the upkeep of
the Royal Navy. And perhaps Sir Thomas Wentworth of
Wentworth Woodhouse was a better patriot in later years
than when he went to a few months of light imprisonment
rather than pay £200 out of his £30,000 a year to finance
a war for which Parliament had petitioned.

If this is an unfair way of arranging undoubted facts,

yet it brings out one neglected point about Charles's opponents. They were nearly all rich men, some amazingly so. Translated into modern values (as they are here) the figures are most significant. A comparatively poor King was at odds with subjects abnormally rich. One of them, Eliot, probably ruined himself in the opposition : most of them grew even wealthier, certainly Saye, probably Pym, who started from humble circumstances. Among them Cromwell, inheriting £1000 to £2000 a year, and marrying money, was not counted a rich man. His colleagues in Parliament never quite forgave this obscure squire who lived to quarter his arms with the leopards of England and be buried in the Abbey at a cost of £300,000.[1]

There are two explanations of the gentry's abnormal wealth, apart from the natural working of their influence in local government. They had been, for generations, very lightly taxed. Many benefited from the decay of the mediæval system ; their ancestors had raised large rents from their lands and paid for it by helping the central government by service or money in time of war : now, in more peaceful times, they continued to enjoy their rent, and paid nothing to the Crown. Their only taxation may be (inaccurately but not misleadingly) lumped together as " subsidies "—a levy on property, very unjustly assessed, which Parliament granted to the Crown, at whatever percentage it thought fit.

Secondly, all through the Middle Ages, a great reserve of untouched wealth had been piling up. While barons died childless or forfeited their lands by rebellion, the undying monasteries grew richer and richer. A century before Charles, their vast wealth had been suddenly poured out. It might have been expected that Henry VIII would have employed it to make the Crown master of England, land-lord of countless acres. It might have been hoped that he would have used some of it to enrich a Protestant Church

---

[1] It is said, however, that there was little waste of public money. The undertaker's bill remained unpaid.

and continue the work which (with all their faults) the monks had done for education and beauty. To reckon so, is to forget the English gentry. They swallowed it all. Henry VIII died considerably poorer than his father. The manor-houses of the Tudor gentry outshone the royal palaces. Mary burnt poor men at the stake; the plunderers acquiesced, but they did not disgorge. When England grew Protestant again, their corridors might be visited by the grey ghosts of forgotten monks. But Lord and Squire could drown superstitious fears by a hearty damning of the Pope, by teaching their sons to fight him and all his works. They could certainly bequeath them a good income for the purpose.

Here a question rises insistently to the mind. If Charles was really fighting the rich in the interests of the poor, why did he not say so? Why did he flourish nothing but the Divine Right of Kings in the face of history? There are several answers, and each is interesting.

It is perhaps too much to expect historians of King Charles's reign to read his own speeches and proclamations. They are too busy in studying Pym's speeches—though for all Pym said, he may not have cared a brass farthing for the welfare of the poor. Charles makes several express stipulations for that welfare; but his main contention is that the Crown is the guardian of all society, the guarantee that each class shall pay its due of justice or service to the other. Charles was himself a gentleman: he was brought up in an atmosphere where government by the rich was the only possibility, and any appeal against it the grossest demagogy. He had been born to a different duty—that of ensuring that that government was just. While he had the power, he and his servants never neglected it.

Secondly, what Charles could not say, his followers said for him. The attempt to write the history of the Great Rebellion in economic and social terms was made at the time: it has been obscured since by the legend of a struggle between a king and a rising tide of democracy.

Harrington, a follower of King Charles, wrote *Oceana* to demonstrate the power of the rich : he recommended a law limiting all estates to £15,000 a year. *Oceana* was censured (and censored) by the Puritans as too democratic. Far more striking is a letter addressed to Charles as early as 1626 and published among his papers. The anonymous author gives a list of the classes attacking Buckingham in Parliament, and, through Buckingham, the royal power. Side by side with Puritans, malcontents excluded from office, and the Papists (even a Royalist cannot leave Papists alone), there appear four significant classes : the merchants of London, " Lawyers in General," Republicans learning their ideas from " commerce with the Low countreys," and finally " Covetous Landlords, Inclosers, Depopulators, and Justices of the Peace who have got an habit of omniregency and an hope to extend the same against the King in Parliament, as they do on his Subjects in the Country." [1] Such a contemporary document does something to justify King Charles's contention that, even in defending Buckingham, he was fighting something slightly different from a band of patriotic brothers with the interests of the nation at heart.

The attack was reinforced by the spread of Puritan ideas. The gentry were one day to repudiate and even persecute Puritanism : meanwhile it was an excellent stick with which to beat the King. Not till his power to interfere in local government had already been destroyed by the Long Parliament did some of them begin to rally round him, largely on the religious issue, and even draw swords against their former allies. Temporarily defeated, they triumphed at the Restoration : they restored the Church, but they were careful not to restore the power of the Crown. [2] But the subsequent history of England lends some colour to the notion that what perished, what Charles

---

[1] The letter was published in *Bibliotheca Regia*, 1658.

[2] Mr. Chesterton has put the matter wittily but penetratingly. " Charles II was never in the old sense a King ; he was Leader of the Opposition to his own ministers."—*Short History of England*, p. 179.

had been somewhat unskilfully defending from the start, was not without value in the national life.

If there was so much good in the Cause, why did it so signally fail ? The destinies of England were in the hands of the gentry. One hesitates to agree that their motives were so sordid or their apathy so complete that they allowed the kingship to go down before a narrow religious faction and be replaced by a Parliamentary rule whose effect (if not its purpose) was the government of England by the power of money. The word " gentleman " is ceasing to have any meaning now, except in tailors' catalogues. But it reminds us of many lovable things—some pleasantly eccentric, some very admirable, a few heroic. It has about it an atmosphere of patriotic endeavour and just dealing, an evening glow which all the mists of modern envy cannot obscure. One would be sorry to conclude that its power was founded on the factiousness or treachery which ruined Charles.

Indeed, it was not only factiousness and treachery. There were many good men, and a few far-sighted who were ranged against him. How this came about only the full story can show. It was partly the intricacies of an ancient constitution which divided and confused every issue. It was partly the good in Puritanism, the evil in its enemies. It was partly the follies of the King's ministers. It was partly the character of the King.

A ruthless, self-centred tyrant might have saved the situation ; an adroit and unscrupulous tactician would have stood an even better chance. The Crown had descended to no such man, it had descended to a refined, conscientious and kindhearted gentleman with a taste for theology and a passion for Art. He had already allowed Buckingham to rush him off his feet into a disastrous mistake, how disastrous we are now in a position to appreciate. He had encouraged Parliament to force its will upon a reluctant king. He had opened the gates to a tide that would engulf him. He was King himself now, and Buckingham was his minister, and soon Parliament would not be on their side.

It was, perhaps, the mistake of youth, inexperience, failure to grasp the real issues. Its effects would not last for ever. There was something more permanent, something ineradicable in his own nature. That nature has been so obscured by alternate calumny and foolish praise that it is hard to come by the truth. But there was in this man, raised by chance to defend an ancient institution at the crisis of its history, a dark strain which gave colour to the calumny and almost justified some of the crimes his enemies committed in destroying him. There was a real love of justice and fair dealing, combined, in the oddest and most culpable way, with one or two acts of real duplicity, a constant preference for delay and prevarication rather than the straight, bold answer, a deliberate dallying among crooked ways. This side of Charles has been greatly over-emphasized, his nobler as well as his gentler qualities unjustly neglected. It is even possible to argue that he loved nothing so well as honesty and straightforwardness ; that he was forced reluctantly into other methods by the dishonourable manœuvres of his adversaries ; that he had his back to the wall, a kingdom to defend, and no other weapon to defend it. Such a case can be made out by charitable reinterpretation of the facts, by refusing to blame Charles for all his servants' acts, by the rebutting of undoubted slander. It never quite convinces. One cannot quite shake off the feeling that a different kind of man, possibly less well-intentioned, less scrupulous for the letter of the law, would have given smaller hold to the slanders, controlled his servants better, appealed to clearer issues, and commanded a wider loyalty. He might have gone down fighting, but he would have left a greater name and stamped his personality more heroically upon our annals. The great poet Browning finds no better word for King Charles than the line in which a friend speaks of him to the betrayed Strafford : " Be merciful to this most wretched man." It is a poor epitaph for a king.

CHAPTER SIX

FALSE START

1625

KING CHARLES had risen from his seat : he was addressing his first Parliament in plague-stricken London.

The curse of his childhood was still upon him, and he halted and stammered ; being, as he said, "unfit for much speaking," he would leave all details to his Lord Keeper. He himself spoke mainly about the war. He excused his father's hesitation in declaring it, partly due to the lack of means for maintaining it. He had entered upon it himself by the advice and entreaty of the Commons ; he had acted freely and willingly, but he was a young man, and perhaps he had been rash : they must not do themselves and him the dishonour of withholding their help now that he was committed. He did not doubt their love and loyalty, or their eagerness for war with Spain ; only he must impress on them the need for haste. War brooked no delay ; nor did he want their lives endangered by too long a stay in plague-stricken London.

Before he finished, he mentioned one more thing ; it seemed small at the time, but it would one day destroy him. Lying tongues were at work ; men had begun to say that he was less staunch a Protestant than his father. The Commons must not listen to such tales : he had sat at Gamaliel's feet ; he had learnt his lesson.

When Charles sat down, he had made a good impression. He had been pleasantly brief and direct, and had not, like "Gamaliel," vexed his Lords and Commons with a lecture on political theory and the Divinity of

Kings. The Lord Keeper was also brief, perhaps unwisely so. He was the worldly Bishop Williams, who had
opposed the policy of war and was not to keep his office
much longer. Now he was merely the mouthpiece of the
Government, and he gave a catalogue of its various com-
mitments : the Palatinate, the fleet, assistance to Dutch
and Danish allies, the securing of Ireland from a Spanish
attack ; for all these things money was needed and needed
quickly. My Lord Bishop talked, and King Charles sat
watching his Commons. It is not likely that he anticipated
difficulties or serious friction. He believed that there
were trouble-makers among them, " seditious fellows," as
he had called them, four years ago, in a letter to Buckingham ; now, he imagined, their mouths would be stopped
by this declaration of war for which they had clamoured.
The worst he might anticipate was new trouble about the
laws against English Catholics, by promising King Louis to
protect them : he had broken a pledge to his Parliament. Something would have to be done ; what, he was
still uncertain. Meanwhile the only fruit of his treaty
was a wife, likely to prove a bad bargain, with whom he
was already quarrelling. The bishop's speech ended, the
Commons departed to debate in St. Stephen's Chapel, and
Charles went back to an unquiet home.

Two days later, Sir Thomas Crew came to him to
announce that the Commons had chosen himself as their
Speaker, and to ask for His Majesty's approval. He
conveyed their thankfulness that Charles had already
shown himself a good and Parliamentary monarch, pointed
out that the exemplary king, Hezekiah, had also been
twenty-five at his accession, was optimistic about recovering the Palatinate and abusive about " those locusts, the
Jesuits." Finally, he asked that Parliament should enjoy
its customary privileges during the session—freedom from
arrest for debt or misdemeanour, freedom of debate (Mr.
Speaker was sure that no member would overstep " the
limits of duty and modesty "), and a charitable con-

struction to be put on all their words, rather than the
open ear for malicious interpretation. Charles was pleased
to consent. All was well; if, behind the reference to
Jesuits, lay a hint about enforcing the Penal Laws, that
was only to be expected from every House of Commons.

The next news to reach Whitehall was less reassuring.
Charles might be full of good feeling towards the Commons,
but he did not know how to co-operate with them. He
was—and was always to be—badly represented in the
House. While he worked at the Palace, no minister or
secretary of state was explaining to them the exact details
of the Government's needs. They might have resented a
demand for a definite sum of money, they may possibly
have appreciated the policy of leaving everything, rather
vaguely, to their love and loyalty; but it proved a
disastrous mistake. Left without a lead, they began to
wander. Several members even answered the King's
request for haste by a proposal to adjourn until the Plague
abated: some suggested that no subsidies should be
granted until they had inquired how the last grants made
to King James had been spent. The House rejected both
proposals; it even refused to present any grievances—
there could be no grievances with a new king on the throne.
But a word from Pym introduced the favourite topic of
religion. Sir John Eliot, more of a pagan philosopher
than a Puritan, combined in one speech praise of the
Ancients for their attitude to religious unity and an appeal
for the enforcement of the Penal Laws. The Ancients'
anxiety for religious unity began and ended with persecuting the early Christians, and it is a little difficult to
fathom Eliot's meaning, unless he approved of Nero and
his lions. But a petition was drawn up begging for
stricter measures against the Papists and asking for the
reform of undoubted abuses in the English Church;
among the rest was a plea for the readmission of Puritan
clergy. Then at last the King heard that Parliament
had begun to debate the question of money for the

war. It was not long before he heard the result of their deliberation.

The Commons had once promised King James that if his diplomacy failed they would help him in a war to recover the Palatinate "to the utmost of our lives and fortunes." The proposer of the resolution had declared that "the drawing back in so good a cause should not be charged on their slackness." James, faced with war, had appointed a committee of experts, a War Council, which suggested four and a half million as a minimum annual sum. It was well within England's power : Cromwell (having "removed the bauble" and rid himself of Parliamentary control) was to extract far more ; Scotland, with vastly inferior resources, was voting Charles £2,000,000. The English Parliament decided to grant him about half a million. If they had wished his reign to begin in spectacular failure, they could hardly have done otherwise.

It is extremely unlikely that the Commons had any such wish. There may have been a party already working to weaken the Crown. If so, it was an obvious move to hustle the King into war and then leave him without funds to wage it, though the King would not be far wrong in describing such a manœuvre as Treason. It is more likely that the majority were mainly influenced by a not unnatural desire to spare their own pockets and those of the taxpayer. When the adjournment to avoid Plague was suggested, one member had pointed out that it would save them the necessity of granting money. The House had rejected this disgraceful argument, but it was not feeling generous. Charles had relied on their loyalty and enthusiasm. One cannot altogether blame him if the result was a bitter disillusion with the very idea of Parliaments.

The main trouble was that the Commons wanted a war, but not too much of it. They contemplated no alliance except with their friends the Dutch. They had the vaguest ideas about recovering the Palatinate. Their idea of war was circumscribed to the destruction of Spanish influence in England and the plundering of Spanish ports, treasure-ships, and colonies. This policy had appealed to Elizabeth's parsimonious soul : it might help to cripple a trade-rival and open up new markets ; if the booty was sufficient, it might be made to pay for itself. Sir John Eliot hoped it would do more, and pay off the debts of James's peaceful years. He suggested that if it failed to do so, funds could be raised for the Protestant Crusade by fining the English Catholics ; but the House rejected this cruel and tyrannous suggestion. Yet when Middlesex had talked sense about the cost of war, the Commons had adopted Buckingham's suggestion of impeaching him. Now they were learning how far-reaching and expensive were Buckingham's plans and they began to hedge.

Undoubtedly Charles should have known their temper better. An assembly in which such things could be said and done, such complete ignorance of the European situation prevail, needed coaxing and exhorting into a wiser and more honourable mood. He had done nothing ; he had left them to themselves ; and the result was a vote of money that would only cover a tiny fraction of his needs.

Charles never blamed the Commons for their action ; he had no desire to fix a quarrel on them. Even now there was a chance that the vote was merely an earnest of future generosity. He sent his thanks for the grant, answered the minor petitions of the Commons, and talked of closing the sessions soon and releasing them from the dangers of plague-stricken London. Many did not wait for the formal closure, but departed forthwith for their homes. It is just possible that Charles had hoped for this, and hoped that it would be his opponents who would go. It was in vain : throughout his reign, important decisions would be taken in a depleted House ; but it was always the Opposition that ruled, the Court members who were too apathetic to attend. It was so now ; and the members who remained behind proceeded to the congenial subject of religion. They also began to discuss the vital matter of the Customs.

For two hundred years it had been the rule for Parliament to grant to each successive king a Tonnage and Poundage Bill which empowered him to collect the Customs during his lifetime. Now disputes arose ; one member argued that the merchants only paid customs in return for the protection of the King's navy, and that they were at present suffering from continual loss by piracy ; another raised the question of changes in the rates and methods of collection, a much juster grievance. It was probably without disloyal or obstructionist motive that the House voted a Bill, not for the King's lifetime, but for one year only—until all disputable points had been discussed. But the foundation had been laid for one of the major quarrels of the reign.

Meanwhile Charles had decided that the Commons must be coaxed into a second vote of money, before he dismissed it—or saw it dribble home without his dismissal. He consulted Buckingham, and it was resolved that some one must be found to rise in the House, state the needs of the Government, and make a definite proposal. Late one night Buckingham called together his supporters at York House, between the Strand and the river, and there the business was arranged. But one man, Sir Humphrey May, left the meeting much perturbed. A night's sleep did not quiet his anxiety, and, meeting Sir John Eliot early next morning as they walked to Westminster, he communicated his worries, and begged Eliot to go and speak to Buckingham himself. Eliot hesitated, unwilling to be late for Parliament, and May (it is an interesting sidelight on procedure) promised to hold up business until he got back. Eliot turned off down the Strand and knocked at the door of York House.

It is time to speak in more detail of Sir John Eliot. He came from Cornwall ; his ancestors, of Devonshire origin, had bought up the priory and monastic estates of St. Germans and rechristened it, after the manner of *parvenus*, Port Eliot. But the family was no longer *parvenu* when John was born : his father's early death left him a wealthy

squire in his teens ; at twenty-four he was elected by the
neighbouring borough of St. Germans to sit in King James's
Parliament. He was not typically Puritan ; he was a
classical scholar, and, if he hated the Roman Church, it
was in the spirit of Marcus Aurelius rather than of Bunyan.
But he was typical of the West Country in his hatred of
Spain, and he shared (and often led) the enthusiasm of the
House for enforcing the Penal Laws against the Catholics.
He had been a dependant of Buckingham and become, by
his favour, Vice-Admiral for Devon ; he discharged his
duties honestly and with unusual energy. At some personal
risk he carried through a stratagem for capturing a dirty
scoundrel who had set up business as a local pirate ;
but his victim had a pull in the law courts, Buckingham
was away in Madrid, and Eliot suddenly found the pirate
free and himself in gaol. Within a month of Buckingham's
return, probably through his influence, he was released,
sat in Parliament, advocated war, and took part in the
dubious impeachment of Middlesex. It does not help us
much to talk about " the fiery Cornishman " or even " the
excitable Celt," but there was certainly a strain of nervous,
almost hysterical exaggeration in his speeches ; one
Parliamentarian, quoting Tacitus, said that he " brought
himself into danger without benefiting the liberties of
others." At Charles's accession he was still in Buckingham's
circle and wrote to him in the fulsome phrases which the
seventeenth century addressed to a patron. Why he had
not been called to York House at nighttime we do not
know : there may have been a rift already ; but it was as
Buckingham's friend that he was accosted by May in the
morning, and as such that he knocked on Buckingham's
door.

The Duke was still in bed ; poor Kate Buckingham
was bundled out to dress in another room, and Eliot admitted to a bedside conference. We have only Eliot's
account of what passed between the two men. He represents himself as urging that to propose a further vote

of money would be dishonourable to the King. His Majesty's thanks and acceptance for the first vote implied that it had been sufficient : to ask more was to impeach the King's word. This silly argument was followed by a sensible one—that a vote taken in a depleted House was an unworthy manœuvre. Then he tried to work upon Buckingham's personal interest with arguments " some more fit for use than for memory or report " : Buckingham, as favourite, would lose much reputation for allowing further taxation to be suggested. Finally, Eliot was sure that the House would never pass the vote : Buckingham would have harmed his own reputation and the King's to no purpose. Buckingham had an answer for everything. The King's acceptance of a meagre grant was no bar to his asking more : his honour was not concerned in such matter, but in the sailing of his fleet, held back by want of money. If the members had chosen to go home, that was their business. But if the remnant refused to help their King it was better to ask them, if " merely to be denied." In other words, it was better to throw the odium on the Commons, to let the world know that it was they who were refusing funds, not King Charles who was abandoning his cause. It is a little difficult to understand why Eliot professed such indignation at this last argument, why, as he himself reports, it first turned him against Buckingham : he called it " the secret," a clue which revealed to him, little by little, the other villainies of his former patron. To Eliot, with his almost superstitious reverence for the House of Commons, it was villainy to appeal from it (as the Court was to do again and again) to a wider public opinion. The House could do no wrong, or, if it did, Buckingham had no business to show it up to the world. Eliot left the bedroom already half-way to becoming the Duke's enemy.

In one matter Eliot's prophecy was justified before the morning was out. He had not long reached the House—Buckingham, perhaps, was still at his belated toilet—when

7

the proposal for further Supply was made and lost. In a
sparse assembly, an Admiralty official rose to explain
that the navy was landlocked at Plymouth for want of
money ; that Mansfeld and the Danish king could not
advance on the Palatinate without English gold ; that
the King and Duke had already run deep into personal
debt to meet the expenses of the war. Something must
be done, if possible by Parliament's help, if not by " some
new way." If the members felt themselves too few to
vote money, would they make some declaration that at a
second session they would relieve His Majesty's wants ?
The members refused to bind the House for the future :
they may have been nettled at the hint that some unparliamentary method of raising money was under consideration ; they were certainly not going to grant a
further supply. The proposal was still-born.

Charles kept his temper. He even gave a gracious
reception to the petition on religion. But one matter of
religion had now cropped up, on which it was impossible
for Charles and the Commons to agree.

A certain Essex clergyman, Montague by name, had
employed his leisure by writing a book against Popery.
So far, so good ; Montague was in the fashion. But his
arguments were on unorthodox lines ; they lacked thoroughness and the accustomed venom. He had asserted that
Rome was not indisputably the Scriptural Antichrist, nor
the Pope *ex officio* a man of sin ; while denying that the
Church could compel men to confession, he suggested that
the perplexed soul might unburden itself to a clergyman ; he rejected Transubstantiation, but believed Christ
to be mystically present in the Communion elements ; he
even argued that paintings and images in Church, though
they must not be made objects of veneration, might be
as useful as a sermon for teaching religion to the simple.
He adopted, in fact, the ordinary attitude of the ordinary
Anglican to-day.

The book had been out a year. Two other clergymen

had reported Montague to the Commons; the Commons had reported him to his Archbishop, Abbot, the moderate and honest Puritan. Abbot, evidently disliking the whole business, had advised Montague to revise his book and make quite sure that he meant exactly what he had said. Montague was perfectly sure : he went to King James, and the royal theologian, himself a Calvinist, had given him every encouragement. Montague wrote a new book, called *Appeal to Cæsar*, claiming complete orthodoxy, had it duly licensed, and published it. The angry Commons now applied to Abbot again, but Abbot would do nothing until the matter came before him in a more official way : he probably had no desire to see the Commons interfering with his Church. They took the matter into their own hands. They suspended judgment about Montague's doctrine. But they declared that *Appeal to Cæsar* was a disturbance to Church and State and a dishonour to King James (he had read and approved it) ; and that to publish it while the Commons had the first book under discussion, to attack the two clergymen who had reported to the House, was a breach of Parliamentary privilege. Montague was summoned and, as we should say, " bound over."

The issue raised was a fairly clear one : it may seem trivial ; it was of quite deadly import. The Commons were claiming the right to regulate the Church ; they were showing that they intended to use that right against any opinions that did not tend to preserve and widen the breach with Rome. There were a few Puritans who expressed what every Christian must feel—a desire for the reunion of Christendom. As Protestants, they made it quite clear that such reunion must be on their terms and not the Pope's. But at the same time they were doing and saying everything they could to make reunion impossible on any terms. King James had given them no countenance. What would the young king do ?

Charles always deprecated religious controversies ; his

final policy was to forbid them altogether, as causing bad blood and hindering the Church from its more important work ; in four years' time he was even to suppress *Appeal to Cæsar* by royal proclamation. Meanwhile Montague was certainly being provocative, and insisting that his view was the only possible one for the Church of England. On the other hand, his opponents had flung down a challenge which Charles could not possibly disregard. As king, he could not accept the Commons' claim to interference : Tudor Parliaments had voted England Protestant and placed the English Church under Royal supremacy instead of Papal ; there, for Charles, the matter ended, and the King must remain supreme. As a Christian, he was as entirely in agreement with Montague as his father had been. He was an uncompromising Protestant, he abhorred the idea of Popery re-establishing itself. But he would run great risks and give his enemies a terrible vantage-ground rather than subscribe to the facile and bitter dogma— " the farther from Rome, the nearer to God." He could never admit that violent denunciation of the Pope was necessarily the mark of a good Christian. He had written to the Pope from Madrid, in words which might be used at any reunion conference to-day :

" I am and ever shall be of such moderation as to keep aloof, as far as possible, from every undertaking which may testify any hatred to the Roman Catholic religion ; nay, rather will I seize all opportunities, by a gentle and generous mode of conduct, to remove all sinister suspicions entirely ; so that, as we all confess one undivided Trinity, and one Christ crucified, we may be banded together unanimously in one Faith. That I may accomplish this, I will reckon as trifling all my labours and vigilance, and even the hazard of kingdoms, and life itself."

It is true that a young man may write anything in order to wheedle an old one into granting a dispensation for his marriage. This particular young man was to inherit a kingdom in which men gloried in increasing sinister suspicions, some for interested motives, some from mere

fanaticism ; his youthful pledge was never broken in deed
or word : he lost his kingdom and his life mainly because
it was so easy for his adversaries to persuade men that by
fighting against this obstinately Protestant king they were
really fighting Popery.

It was unfortunate that Montague's case should provoke
the vital conflict so early in the reign. Charles saw quite
clearly what was at stake : two interpretations of Christianity
had come into collision ; when some one said it was merely
a case of Parliamentary privilege, the King " smiled, but
made no further reply." He made Montague his own
chaplain and protected him from Parliamentary prosecution.
The Bishops, to whom the doctrinal points were submitted,
decided in Montague's favour, while they deprecated the
attempt to bind any one down to a definite opinion upon
" curious particulars disputed in schools." But they
suggested that some of the arguments used against Montague were so dangerous that they should be suppressed
by law.

Their decision was published at Oxford, whither Charles
had moved Parliament in hope of avoiding the Plague.
At Oxford a more violent quarrel came to a head, as, sooner
or later, it was bound to do. Charles had no one but
himself to blame for the impossible situation about the
Penal Laws. He had told the Lords, James, the Commons,
that there would be no more negotiations on the subject
with foreign powers. The Commons were now clamouring
to know why those Laws were not more rigorously enforced.[1]
The act of bad faith at Cambridge was coming home to
roost.

Parliament had hardly reassembled at Oxford when
a member laid before the House a document that had
come into his possession ; it was a pardon, signed by the
King, remitting the death sentence on a Jesuit priest.
Eliot affected to believe it could not be genuine, or at least

[1] The answer to their question was not hard to come by, for the terms
of the marriage treaty had been published in the *Mercure François*.

not signed in full knowledge ; the King could not have been so wicked. A minister promised that the main aim of the Penal Laws would be maintained : the Government would make quite sure that the Papists were made powerless to do harm. It was not enough. There was war : what was the use of fighting Spain if Papists at home were not harried ? There was not the slightest evidence of espionage, but members grew particularly suspicious of Papists living near the seacoast. They demanded nothing less than the full execution of the law.

Charles was entangled in the meshes of his own double-dealing, and he must decide which of his obligations he would throw over. There could be little doubt. Continued opposition in the Commons meant that the conduct of the war, government itself, might become impossible. He had some reason for saying that the French had tricked him into the treaty, though, by refusing to put anything in writing, Louis had avoided any actual breach of contract. Buckingham explained to the disgusted French envoys that everything would be done to treat the Catholics lightly, but that the Penal Laws could not be suspended at present. Then he went off to Parliament, assembled in Christchurch Hall, with a final offer. He made a long defence of his foreign policy, contrasting the sad plight of Protestantism a few years ago with the present hopeful situation. The enemies of Spain were united : Mansfeld had an army in Holland, now reinforced ; King Christian of Denmark was preparing to march for the Palatinate ; the English fleet lay at Plymouth, waiting to sail. Nothing was lacking but the money which England was pledged to supply. Buckingham had heard grumblings about the extent of his schemes ; he assured the Commons they had been adopted by the advice of the War Council and the King's Privy Council. Finally, if the Commons were still doubtful, let them name the enemy against whom they wanted the main endeavour to be made. Buckingham's last appeal for co-operation was backed by a message from the King :

if Parliament would grant supplies for the war, it should reassemble in full during the autumn, and not dissolve until the domestic grievances had been thoroughly thrashed out.

It soon became clear that co-operation was impossible. The Commons proceeded to pick Buckingham's speech to pieces. Mansell, who had been a member of the War Council, told them that he himself had opposed one of Buckingham's plans and been overruled. Another member claimed that, when the last subsidy was granted to James, the mention of the Palatinate had been struck out expressly, as too costly a venture. Wentworth, who had always (to do him justice) opposed the war, argued that in any case the decision of one Parliament could not bind its successors : such a plea, officially adopted, would have made hay of the Commons' claim to be a responsible organ of government. Another member argued that Buckingham had entered into alliances without their consent, and they were not bound to support him : there was a little more reason in this, though one wonders what a modern Cabinet would say to it in time of war. But beneath all the arguments lay one ominous fact—the Commons were turning against Buckingham. They eagerly adopted two reports against his work as Lord Admiral. The Moorish pirates had carried out a successful raid on Cornwall ; privateers from Dunkirk were harrying the east coast trade. Secondly, there was a story, not without ground, and yet, as we shall see, most unfairly put, that Buckingham was lending ships to King Louis to be used against French Protestants, now in rebellion. England was at war, the Commons, who controlled her financial power, had lost confidence in the Government. They talked of inquiring into the expenditure of the last subsidies granted to King James. When a private member proposed a further grant, the House decided not to put the question.

That afternoon, Charles called his Council together and announced that he was about to dissolve Parliament.

The worldly-wise Bishop Williams thought it would make an ill beginning to the new reign ; Buckingham went on his knees to dissuade the King ; he was still confident that he could win back the Commons to his side.   Charles could see one thing only : Parliament was claiming sovereignty, claiming to direct the war, to control the royal ministers.   He sent for the gentleman of the Black Rod, whose summons preceded the dissolution of Parliaments.   The Commons, warned of their fate, began to draw up a protestation of loyalty.   Fears were expressed that the King might be about to punish members for words used in the House.   A man called Phelips had been among the boldest, and, remembering the old Macedonian who had appealed from Philip drunk to Philip sober, he cried that he would appeal from King Charles misinformed to King Charles rightly informed.   But already Black Rod was knocking at the door : he summoned the Commons to appear before King and Peers, as they had appeared two months ago, when Parliament first met at Westminster.   Now it was to hear the sentence of dissolution.

Charles punished no one for words spoken in the Commons ; he was soon to be busy summoning a new Parliament ; he still gave no sign that he suspected deliberate disloyalty.   But Phelips had hit one nail on the head when he spoke of Charles misinformed.   For Charles did not understand, and was never to understand, the nature of deliberative assemblies.

One of the virtues of the modern system of government is that a man cannot become Prime Minister without a thorough experience of the way in which assemblies can be led or coaxed.   The weakness of the old system was that a king could have no such experience, and chose ministers with quite unparliamentary qualifications.   It had worked tolerably well under Elizabeth, partly because the Commons had not learnt their power or did not care to use it, partly because she herself had considerable talent for flattering them, and yet manœuvring herself out of the necessity for granting their demands. Even so, there had been serious friction, and she had sent members to prison. Charles had no such adroitness as Elizabeth. He was naturally unversed in the science of Parliamentary tactics : it was being evolved during his reign, and it was to be used against him by his opponents. Meanwhile the House floundered for lack of any leadership, and it floundered along dangerous paths.

For the Tudor Age was dead, and the gentlemen of England assembled in the Commons were feeling their way towards making unprecedented claims. Already the Prerogative was threatened at a crucial spot—the choice of ministers. At no time could a king feel much sympathy for such a claim as was implied in the attack upon Buckingham. In time of war it appeared mere treason. It was all the worse because it proceeded from a House of Commons that knew little—and appeared to care less— about the state of Europe, and seemed principally concerned with evading any but the most meagre taxation.

It has been suggested that the Commons were objecting to Buckingham's schemes not because they were expensive and planned without their co-operation, but because they were inefficiently conducted. To assume this is to read history backwards ; Buckingham's spectacular failures were in the future, and they were in no small degree due to the withdrawal of Parliamentary support. There is no sign that he was held responsible for the disasters that had overtaken Mansfeld in the last reign. The most that can be said is that the Commons had begun to feel that such disasters were likely to recur under King Charles, that they were somehow scenting that Buckingham was the wrong man to lead the Protestant Crusade.

It was a little late in the day to give expression to such a feeling. Buckingham had already gathered a fleet and an army at Plymouth. It was about to make trial of Parliament's favourite plan for plundering the coasts and the fleets of Spain.

We are in the autumn of 1625. Considering past and future achievements, the date may be taken as the low-water of England's power to inflict serious damage on her neighbours. The navy was numerically strong, better equipped than it had recently been, and yet not well enough, utterly lacking in experience of war. Round it were gathered, on the Elizabethan plan, the commandeered merchantmen who had done so much to defeat the Armada : the chances of their defeating a Spanish fishing-fleet were now uncertain. They were lucky to be reinforced by a Dutch navy. They were to convey what passed for our army to the attack on a Spanish fortress.

There had never been a standing army in England, and for nearly a century the machinery for producing one in time of war had decayed with fearful rapidity. Henry VIII had been the last king to do anything effective for our military organization. He had renewed and enforced the ancient statutes which decreed that every able-bodied Englishman must keep arms and be frequently drilled in their use. The system had provided what was once called the *fyrd* and was soon to be called the *militia* : as a body, it was only available for home defence, but its members could be severally recruited as volunteers or called up by press-gangs and " Commissions of Array." The militia of London, generally called the " trained bands," mustered 15,000 magnificently accoutred men, supported by the guns of the Honourable Artillery Company, Henry's own creation. Henry took to France one of the largest expeditionary forces that ever left our shores before the year 1914 : yet what military strength he left behind him could shatter the chivalry of Scotland on Flodden Field. England was a power in Europe.

Since that day everything had fallen to pieces. The gentry allowed the militia to lose its weapons and shirk its drills : the London trained bands sunk to a tenth of their numbers. When the poor rose against the introduction of Protestantism, the Government used German and Italian mercenaries to crush them. Elizabeth dismissed even these, more from parsimony than patriotism. Her efforts (as Mary's before her) to reorganize the militia had little effect. Ancient custom once broken, lethargy and corruption prevented its restoration. Middlemen cheated the Government of its troops, taking pay and provisions for men who only existed on paper : they cheated the troops that did exist of their pay and provisions. At the crisis of the reign, when an Armada and a Spanish army were converging to destroy us, everything was in chaos. The only thought was to collect as many men as possible, trained or untrained, at the Tilbury rendezvous. Many came unarmed and refused to wear the only steel caps the Tower could provide. Some were told to go home again unless they had brought their dinners with them. The commander, Sir John Norris, had seen service in Holland : he remarked that he was the only soldier at Tilbury, and the only man who was frightened ; he had some notion of what seasoned Spaniards might do. It is not impossible that Norris was the originator of that ancient military joke—" Thank Heaven we have a Navy."

The threat passed, no one troubled to provide against its recurrence. It could hardly be expected that James would do much to remedy the decay, and he did nothing at all. If any of his subjects, Englishmen or Scots, were interested in the game of war, they had to go abroad to play it in Holland or Germany. The chances of invasion were exceedingly remote, and James had no ambition to send armies for the invasion of other countries. England had now repudiated King James's policy, and expected his son to make successful war without an army.

It was a sad muddle that Charles rode down to inspect at Plymouth, a month after the Oxford dissolution. The lack of money was responsible for the more obvious troubles. The soldiers were unpaid ; they could get no food from the Devonshire farmers on whom they were billeted ; they had begun to pilfer the countryside. Sickness and desertion were thinning their numbers, and the press-gang hardly repaired the wastage. It had been a mistake to recruit them so soon, for the officers were doing little to train them for battle. Sir Edward Cecil, who had seen fifteen years of Dutch wars, was their commander. Essex, also a soldier, though with less experience, was second in command. Under them Buckingham had placed his brother-in-law, Denbigh, as vice-admiral. Cecil was gloomy about the quality of the troops. When Charles arrived, he was busy chasing the pirates of whom Parliament complained, and failing to catch them. Charles reviewed the men on Roborough Downs, somewhat prematurely promised Cecil a peerage, and left Buckingham to see the expedition off.

Buckingham allowed a malicious sense of humour to get the better of him. The recorder of Plymouth was a certain lawyer called John Glanville, who had made himself prominent in the Oxford Parliament. Buckingham thinking it would be a good joke to send the lawyer to sea, appointed him secretary to the fleet. Glanville protested that his pocket could not stand the absence from Plymouth law courts and their fees; that his old mother was dependent on him for advice and support; that he was useless as a secretary, because no one, except one confidential servant, could read his handwriting. Buckingham was as inexorable as the press-gang: Glanville, he said, could surely take his accomplished servant with him. After a false start, due to unkind winds, the fleet sailed. It bore the lawyer away from his aged mother, to share its inglorious adventures, and to write an account of them, illegible perhaps in the original, now published in excellent print.

Far away to the south, among the pinewoods of San Lucar, the Marquis of Medina Sidonia took his ease in a castle overlooking the Atlantic. Late one night, they brought him news that a fleet was in sight, heading southward for Cadiz. Messengers galloped to warn Gibraltar and Malaga, to raise the levies of Andalusia. The peasants assembled, cursing Olivares for letting English devils loose on them again : rumour had it that there was an Essex among them, and no one could distinguish father from son. Other horsemen were spurring for Madrid, one to be promptly imprisoned for loitering on the way. Then Giron, governor of Cadiz, wrote that the English and Dutch had opened fire ; one of his forts was being fiercely bombarded. King Philip read the message, but refused to be alarmed. He had only one anxiety : it was November, the annual treasure-fleet was due home from the Indies ; at any moment it might come into sight of Cadiz harbour. Madrid began to speak of it as lost, and wonder how much church plate would have to be melted down that winter. But on the minor point King Philip was quickly justified and reassured. Giron wrote that he had a skirmish with the English, and that " there was no need to trouble about such men."

Cecil had effected the meeting with twenty Dutch ships. Instructions had purposely been left vague, but a council of war decided to attack Cadiz. Essex, in the van, disregarded orders by rushing ahead to chase some Spanish vessels into Cadiz roads. Cecil, with sense and generosity, decided to support him. His ships refused to follow ; they countered Essex's bold disobedience by a sullen and cowardly one of their own. The Spaniards reached an inner harbour and blocked its mouth with sunken hulks. Cecil asked the Dutch to spend that night cannonading Fort Puntal with five of their ships, and ordered twenty English to assist ; he chose the hired merchantmen, shallow in draught, which could ride close in to the target. Hidden by the darkness, they did nothing of the sort. Dawn came to find the Dutchmen still at it, tired and reeking with powder. The English had not fired a shot.

Cecil landed his men and captured the fort. He also landed food for them, but the officers on the beach said

they had no orders for its reception and sent it back to
the ships. The hungry men were led out of the captured
fort, and kept marching under the sun to find an elusive
enemy. Some had had no food for a day and a night
when they marched into one of the Marquis Medina's
estates, and discovered a wine-store, laid up for the fleet
of the Indies. In half an hour they were a mob of drunkards.
Meanwhile Spanish galleys had slipped through to provision
and reinforce the vital spot of Cadiz town. Refortified
since an elder Essex had captured it thirty years ago, it
was judged impregnable—certainly to such soldiers as the
men were turning out to be, "verie unserviceable and
unfitt for a designe." There was nothing to do but to
get them back on to the ships.

There was one hope left—to hang about in hope of
catching the treasure-ships. Their capture would make
amends for all. It would more than recompense the King
for Parliament's grudging of money. It would silence
grumblers at home, and cover the new reign in a blaze of
glory.

Cecil sailed out of Cadiz and strung his ships across the
Atlantic in the hope of netting the great prize for his
master. But the naval contractors had done their foul
work, and Buckingham's Commission had not effected a
sufficient cure. Old tackle and rotting spars hampered the
sailing ; bad beer and mouldy food spread sickness among
the men. The fleet could not keep the sea for more than a
month. One by one the ships made for home with their
burden of disease, and dropped wearily into Plymouth
harbour. They had accomplished exactly nothing.

In his studio at Brussels, Peter Paul Rubens broke off
from his task of covering vast canvases with rococo
warriors and overripe females, and sat down to write to a
friend in Italy. He had heard news from London. The
English grandees were in ecstasies at the disaster, "which
they impute to Buckingham's rashness."

Rash he had undoubtedly been. He had led England

into the war she demanded, and opened it with a venture
after her own heart. But it had not occurred to him that
Parliament might grudge money, or that a great nation
might have lost her prowess in arms. There had been no
system for making a trained fighter out of that military
nullity, the ordinary man. The royal navy was the better
for Buckingham's efforts, but not good enough. The hired
merchantmen had proved ineffectual cowards. Buckingham had engaged us in war with a first-class power, and it
almost looked as if we had ceased to be a fighting people.

But the proverbial ill-luck of the Stewarts had also
dogged King Charles's fleet. Two days after Cecil had
left Cadiz to form his cordon across the ocean, the treasure
fleet, warned to sail by devious routes, had crept in, and
dropped anchor in the harbour.

CHAPTER SEVEN

Evil Genius

1626

THINGS were going ill for the Protestant alliance and for King Charles its champion. There was a new threat in Germany. There was the news from Cadiz, the proof of England's weakness ; nor did it look as if Charles and his Parliament would agree on a remedy and succeed in curing it. Finally, there was France, now hardly pretending friendship ; it would soon be a question whether she could be kept from open enmity.

The news from Germany was not yet alarming. Christian of Denmark had received his first subsidies from England ; they were inadequate, but he was marshalling an army. Mansfeld had collected another, though his methods of feeding it on the country did not make him popular in Germany. But down in the South, the Emperor had found a new general. From among the rebel and Protestant nobility of Bohemia came a red-haired rogue and adventurer called Wallenstein, converted by the Jesuits, already an Imperialist. He was as unscrupulous and as callous as Mansfeld, and ten times more able. He had offered his services to the Emperor and was recruiting a huge army of adventurers ; there were many of King Charles's subjects among them, Irish and Scottish exiles ; some even were Protestants, for Wallenstein paid well and asked no questions. Unless Charles could send more money to his uncle, King Christian would be hard put to it to meet the cosmopolitan horde.

For the present, the situation at home was more disquieting. England had entered the lists in traditional

style by an attack on Cadiz, and our ancient prowess had
been sadly to seek. It might be thought that the only
thing was to make peace at once and keep it, at any sacrifice
of self-respect, until the nation had been hammered into
some kind of fitness for war. But peace was impossible ;
we could not so betray our allies ; such a surrender would
completely destroy the country's confidence in its king,
and make government an impossibility. Nor was it in the
least likely that England would consent to be hammered.
Parliament, stinting supplies for war, would certainly
refuse to pay for such a process in time of peace, and would
prohibit it in the name of English liberty. War only gave
the opportunity. Charles trusted Buckingham to make
better work of our next expedition : when it came, two
years later, it was indeed a great improvement. Buckingham's energy and enthusiasm almost compensated for his
inexperience, his mediocre talents, and the grinding lack
of funds.

The shortage of money was a complete bar to the
satisfying of our principal need, a trained professional army.
It was difficult to convince men of the necessity. The
pressure of actual danger forced Dutchmen to tax themselves properly for war purposes ; elsewhere on the Continent, armies were the product of growing despotisms.
England was an island, protected by an adequate fleet ; it
required a civil war to turn us into a military nation again.

That the fleet was no more than adequate was not
entirely due to lack of funds : some of the blame must
fall upon Buckingham and King Charles. After the Cadiz
fiasco, Cecil was indeed dismissed ; his attempts to throw
the blame on Essex earned him the cold shoulder at Court ;
he retired to find employment in the Dutch army again.
But there was a serious delay in ferreting out the real
culprits, the naval officials and contractors : they were of
Buckingham's following and they lay undisturbed in their
burrows until a year later, when fresh evidence of inefficiency and corruption made Charles appoint a Commission

8

of Inquiry. Even then no real cure was effected. If Charles was to lay some of the foundations of our naval greatness, it required the despotic efficiency of Cromwell, the patient work of James II to build anything permanent upon them. Luckily the naval decay, which had set in soon after the Armada, had destroyed Spanish power more swiftly than English, and we were safe from attack.

But it was not for her own security that England had put herself at the head of a Protestant alliance. Buckingham's schemes were as far-reaching as his resources were short. The one to which Charles had sacrificed most was bearing least fruit : the King had increased his difficulties enormously in order to marry a Frenchwoman and a Papist ; neither he nor his allies had gained any compensating advantage. And now the petty details of a woman's life were about to help in the upsetting of the European balance.

Henrietta still hated Buckingham : Buckingham was still enthroned in her husband's heart. She was surrounded by Frenchwomen clamorous in their grievances and their contempt for all things English, by priests whose religion, in defiance of the marriage treaty, was still proscribed in England. It was an impossible position for a young girl, and she cannot be blamed for proclaiming her discomfort in some rather silly directions.

When she was down in the country, at Titchfield, she refused to have a Protestant service read in any part of the house she was occupying. Charles could not allow such an outrage on public opinion and insisted on her giving way. But at the same time he was foolish enough to press upon her three members of the Buckingham family as ladies-in-waiting. Henrietta indulged in not unnatural reprisals. While the Protestant service was in progress, she marched her women into the room and helped them to drown the preacher with laughing and chatter. When the poor man retired to the garden to rest from his interrupted sermon, some one let off a shot-

gun in the hedge behind him. He pretended that there
was a plot to murder him, that the gun was aimed at him,
that the bench on which he had been sitting was pitted
with pellet marks. An ingenious Frenchman demonstrated that this was impossible : the marks covered the
whole bench ; the reverend gentleman was extremely fat ;
if he had been sitting on it, the pellets must have passed
through his body. Unable to show a single puncture, the
parson had to own to a lie. But international relations
were not improved.

Meanwhile the priests of Henrietta's household were
urging her to press on Charles her greatest and most
undoubted grievance. They themselves were exempted by
treaty from the Penal Laws ; but other priests were still
liable, whenever detected, to a horrible death. Charles,
hoping for the co-operation of Parliament, had pledged
himself, however reluctantly, to the barbarous system
which has filled the country houses of England with
" priests' holes," and cast a shadow for many centuries
over thousands of innocent English lives. He could do
nothing to satisfy Henrietta, much as he loved her, much
as he needed her love and encouragement. Already he
was struggling with a new trouble, likely to make things
worse ; for quarrels were arising between him and her
brother's government.

The coronation service in the January of 1626 emphasized the unhappy situation in the most public manner.
The ritual was without flaw, though long afterwards it
was said that it was a bad omen for the King to wear white,
the colour of sacrifice. But Charles's favourite bishop,
Dr. Laud, presided. After a moment's hesitation, probably
due to ignorance of the procedure, the people burst into
the most gratifying roars of " God save King Charles ! "
But beside his throne stood an empty chair, for the priests
had forbidden Henrietta to take part in Protestant ceremonies. It was a symbol of a still-born alliance between
two countries, of a divided and unhappy home.

Its happiness was not increased by Henrietta's next move. She drew up a list of stewards for the estates that Charles had given her under the marriage settlement, and put on it several names he was bound to dislike. She presented it to him when he was in bed and trying to get to sleep. He promised to consider it in the morning, but she badgered him into an immediate argument. It was particularly provocative of her to tell him that the list had been drawn up with her mother's approval; no man likes being kept awake at night to hear about his mother-in-law. The dispute ended with Henrietta in tears, crying out how miserable she was and refusing to listen to anything her husband said. He could do nothing with her; he told her to be quiet and turned over to sleep.

That she was miserable no one can doubt. Husband and wife were both going through one of the most trying times in their lives, and it looked as if the expected would happen: a French and Papist princess would remain for ever a foreigner in England and a stranger to her husband. Neither of them was cold by nature, easy-going, or self-sufficient: the not unhappy *modus vivendi* that Charles's parents had arranged in the same palace, long after real love had departed, would never suit this sensitive, highly strung young couple. Perhaps, to their permanent loss, they would drift apart, and even find consolation elsewhere.

It was clear that there must be some underlying cause behind the constant jangle of petty incidents. Henrietta was sure of it, and summed up three-quarters of the trouble in the one word "Buckingham." Charles was coming to a different conclusion; he threw the blame on to Henrietta's French attendants, partly because they kept her back from any attempt to accept her position as an Englishman's wife (she was very slow even to learn the language), partly because he believed them to be a set of deliberate mischief-makers. It is always difficult to judge between husband and wife, and after three hundred years it becomes impossible. From a review of all that had so far passed, an impartial judge would probably decide in Henrietta's favour. But it is interesting to find that, so far as later events could prove anything, they showed that Charles had the clearer insight, and that his remedy was the right one. For matters were rapidly working up to a final explosion, and a happy solution of all the difficulties.

Near the north-east corner of Hyde Park stood the famous gibbet of Tyburn, from which thieves and murderers took their last look at the roofs of a still distant London. But it was not only thieves and murderers who had perished here ; the spot was already revered by Roman Catholics as that on which a Protestant government had done to death so many heroic priests. One day in July, Charles was informed that his wife had made pilgrimage to the place, some said bare-footed, and knelt in the mud to offer prayers for the souls of the departed Papists. For the wife of a sorely pressed king, it was a wanton challenge, an unpardonable outrage on the public opinion he had most need to court. How far the story was true we do not know ; Henrietta denied anything beyond a per-functory stroll in the Park. But tales were flying around, growing as they flew, and Cæsar's wife must be above suspicion. Charles did not blame his wife, but he took her hand after supper, led her to an empty room, and locked the door upon them. Then he told her, as gently as possible, that her whole retinue must return immediately to France. What followed we cannot tell ; if there were tears and entreaties, Charles was unshakable, and they gave way to mad passion. Henrietta dashed her hands through the window glass and clung to the bars with bleeding fingers until Charles dragged her away. For out-side the windows, armed men were giving the French people the alternative of going quietly or being marched away by force. Charles had told Buckingham that he would have no more of the " mousers," as he somewhat ungallantly called a company including more *mesdames* than *messieurs*. When Henrietta grew calmer, she begged leave to retain a few favourites, and Charles granted the request. The remainder occupied Somerset House and withstood a fortnight's blockade before they bowed to the inevitable. Charles, very apprehensive of what King Louis might say, tried to soften the pill by making them a handsome present of over £100,000. Even so, they left unpaid debts in London, and they did a last service to the mistress for whose welfare they had pretended to be making all complaint. They sailed with a large proportion of Henrietta's jewels and garments in their trunks.

When these unworthy representatives of a great nation appeared in Paris, King Louis was in something of a quandary. Their dismissal was a breach of the marriage treaty, and they no doubt reported that they had done nothing in England to justify it. But Louis had just broken a marriage treaty with Spain in order to send his wife's Spanish retinue packing. He was in an excellent position for knowing that there are two sides to such questions, and he sent an able and admirable Frenchman, de Bassompierre, to find out how the land lay at Whitehall.

Bassompierre expected a cold welcome, and was not deterred when he got it. By patience and sheer force of personality he was able to get a grasp of the situation and suggest a settlement. Neither publicly nor in private letters did he take Henrietta's side. He told her she was the most at fault, and that anyhow she must make the best of things. He persuaded Charles to admit a smaller and better picked retinue from France, though he agreed that the Queen's household should remain predominantly English. He won, and deserved, the gratitude of all parties. Within a short time Charles was saying there was now no dispute between him and his wife except about which loved the other most. He even made peace between her and Buckingham, though he could not get her to take any interest in politics. In less than a year she had borne Charles their first child. It would not be long before she was writing home to say that she was the happiest queen, if not the happiest woman, in the world. So far as a mutual affection could triumph over other sorrows, she had no cause to withdraw the words until death took Charles away from her.

Charles had been cruel only to be kind. A single drastic and arbitrary act had relieved the pair from apparently irremediable unhappiness. It was the tragedy of his life that he could not do for England what he had done for his home, and never understood why he could not. For in studying the temporary state of Holy Acrimony into which the two had fallen, it must be remembered that Charles was simultaneously struggling with two great anxieties—the unhealthy relations growing up between Paris and Whitehall, the meeting, debating, and angry dissolution of his second Parliament.

The two were not unconnected. One of Parliament's grievances, which we have already mentioned, turned upon our relations with France. We must look at it a little more closely, for, besides the Parliamentary quarrel, it gave birth to a slander which dogged Charles to his grave.[1]

In the pleasant days when England expected a French alliance against Spain, King Louis had talked of attacking Genoa (practically a Spanish town), and had asked Charles to lend him English ships for the purpose. Since the plan was subject to alteration, the contract for the loan stipulated that the ships might be used against any enemy of France ; Charles presumed that all enemies were mutual. The presumption was false : Louis, faced with a rebellion of Protestant La Rochelle, forgot about Genoa, and demanded the ships for an attack on his own Huguenot subjects.

The position was almost Gilbertian. Louis declared that he could not march on the Protestant Crusade until he had crushed the Protestants at home. Protestant Holland, keener on fighting Spain than on religious niceties,

[1] See p. 296.

promised him the help of her navy. Catholic Spain was
encouraging the Huguenots. Charles was asked to follow
the Dutch example and join in crushing them.

Charles was perhaps a more scrupulous Protestant
than the Dutch. He certainly had a Puritan opposition
to reckon with, and it could block his supplies of money.
At the same time he needed French help, and he had signed
the contract. He could do nothing except hold things up
with every excuse and delay he could devise. He pleaded
bad weather, the unwillingness of the crews, defects in the
formalities, the need of a guarantee for the price of hire.
Buckingham even sent a message to his captain to intimate
that the King would be only too pleased if the crews would
mutiny and refuse to join the French fleet. The crews
loyally mutinied. By the time that this trouble had been
got over, and the ships, without their crews, handed over,
Charles had achieved his purpose. The Huguenot rebellion
was over, and Richelieu had signed a peace with La
Rochelle.

Then came the disastrous chance. Richelieu had a
thousand enemies among the great French aristocrats,
whose power he was planning to undermine. One of them,
sticking at nothing to discredit him, sent a hint to a certain
Marshal Toiras, commander of the royal troops near
Rochelle. When the Rochellois, secure in the knowledge
of the newly-made treaty, streamed out to gather the
harvest in the surrounding fields, Toiras turned King
Louis's cannon upon them, mowed them down, and set
light to the corn. Civil war blazed out again ; La Rochelle
closed its gates. The royal fleet sailed against the Protestant
city, and with it sailed seven English ships.

Such an incident could hardly improve the relations
between a Protestant and a Catholic nation. They were
soon imperilled by a further quarrel, and one with which
England has been familiar from mediæval times until the
year 1918. We had begun war with Spain by preying on
Spanish commerce and stopping neutral vessels from

importing contraband of war into the Spanish Netherlands.
French ships were towed into London and their cargoes
inspected by the Admiralty courts.   Contraband was
confiscated, a proportion of it went to a government sorely
tried for money, a proportion, too, to Lord Admiral Buckingham ; and contraband is an elastic term.   The inevitable
friction had been greatly increased by an incident for
which Buckingham was personally responsible.   The
St. Pierre of Havre, after giving a good account of itself,
had been released by the Court, and then stopped again,
for a further and stricter search.   Havre municipality was
talking of reprisals ; Paris demanded an explanation.   A
pretty quarrel was blowing up.

Meanwhile there was a European war, and, if France
would do nothing, England had a double burden to bear.
The news from Germany was ominous.   Mansfeld was still
far from the Palatinate ; King Christian needed English
gold to quiet his unpaid Danes.   The threat from the
South was growing.   Wallenstein had gathered an army of
unprecedented size, and was imposing discipline on its
motley regiments.   He told the Emperor they could be
fed and paid by violent requisitions on occupied territory ;
the system was to be a shade more orderly than Mansfeld's
indiscriminate pillage, and several shades more cruel in its
results.   As one of the Emperor's officials watched Wallenstein's troops file past, " God help the lands," he said,
" to which these men may march."   King Charles had summoned his second Parliament ; if he could get no money
from it, these men might march far indeed.

He was growing warier in this first harassed year of
kingship.   It suited him ill.   As with many men whom
nature intended to be high-minded and to expect high-
mindedness in others, disappointment and opposition
soured instead of widening his sympathy.   He still clung
to the belief that England was behind him and loyally
ready to pay for the war it had seemed to demand.   He
may have been right.   But he grew unnaturally suspicious

of his opponents in Parliament. A scheme was proposed for excluding the worst of them from Westminster. It was quite simple : six of them were appointed sheriffs ; a sheriff, tied to his own county, was ineligible for Parliament.

When a new Speaker waited on him at Whitehall, Charles may have imagined that he had been successful. He was treated to a ten-minute oration, fulsome with thanks about the Penal Laws, unnecessarily explicit about the blessings of monarchy and the abject unimportance of mere subjects ; Mr. Speaker was flattering about the King himself ("in whom greatness and goodness contend for superiority"), and ended with denunciation of Spain and hopes for the recovery of the Palatinate. To these hopes, Mr. Speaker declared, " the hearts, the hands, and the purses of all good subjects will say, Amen." He tactfully omitted to mention Cadiz.

It was Eliot that brought up the matter, and within two days. Eliot's name had not been put on the list of sheriffs : the Court did not fear him yet ; at Oxford he had even defended Buckingham's Admiralty, ascribing all deficiencies to the junior Commissioners. Now, to the surprise of all, he suddenly demanded an inquiry into the whole Cadiz business, " to discern the fault, to know the faulty." Then the House renewed its attack on Montague, reminded the King that they had only granted him his Customs for a year, inquired why our relations with France were so strained, and began to badger the members of the War Council to say how each of them had voted about the expenditure of war subsidies in King James's reign. Eliot was after bigger game ; taking his cue from a remark blurted out by the unimportant son of the great Opposition lawyer, Coke, he suddenly launched a grand assault on Buckingham. The House followed, voting impeachment ; it had found its leader. Eliot would use the Commons to pull down Buckingham, as they had pulled down Middlesex at Buckingham's nod.

Buckingham refused to be alarmed ; he was sure they

could never do it. When their "managers"—prosecuting
Counsel, as we should say—came to lay the charges before
the Lords, he sat opposite them, laughing. He was quite
sure he could answer their accusations. He did not fear
his many enemies among the Peers, though they would be
his judge and jury. He probably regarded the whole
business as a machination of jealous "grandees."

He had just received a letter from a disreputable
dependant of his called Sir James Bagg, who discussed the
situation in terms of the Peers' electioneering activities.
Bagg warned him against Lord Pembroke, who had just
added to his "means of placing divers burgesses" by
capturing Shaftesbury and Lostwithiel for his puppets,
and, Bagg suspected, Portsmouth. Pembroke, he says,
will be acting through these new members, not through his
recognized henchmen. As for Eliot, he has joined in because
" he can neither pay you your dues nor deserve your past
favours." He seemed to be working not so much against
Buckingham as against the King's authority : he is not
alone in this ; Buckingham must know already who else
is of this party.[1]

Bagg was an unpleasant creature, and perhaps it is
better to forget his jaundiced view of politics, and adopt
the conventional story of noble patriots impeaching an
unworthy favourite on grounds of high policy. The objection to Buckingham was obvious : every one knows that
vague and inescapable oppression that weighs upon any
body of men when they see at their head one who owes
his position, not to merit or capacity, but to personal
charm and the ability to use it. In a school, a regiment,
or an office, it is a just grievance : in the government of a
nation it may become intolerable. If there was envy and
faction among Buckingham's opponents, there was also
public spirit. The difficulty was to find precise accusations
which Buckingham could not answer.

[1] Bagg to Buckingham, *Calendar of State Papers*, Dom. Add. 1625-49,
dxxiii. 77.

The indictment was drawn up under thirteen heads.
Eight referred to events in the last reign. Buckingham
could not tell the Commons that they must have known
about those events when they supported him and his policy
a year or two ago. His answer was polite and almost
deferential : one suspects irony. " So great and so worthy
a body " as the Commons must be under a misapprehen-
sion, and Buckingham would remove it point by point.
He denied that he had accumulated too many official
positions. He was Admiral and Warden of the Cinque
Ports because, for administrative reasons, the two offices
could be more efficiently discharged by one man. All
his other titles were merely ceremonial and without political
significance, except perhaps the Mastership of the Horse,
which had enabled him to save the King a great deal of
money. He denied that he had bought any of them. He
had no need, with King James in giving mood : presents
to retiring predecessors were the custom. To the next
charge, that of extorting money from the East India
Company, he replied that he had, as Admiral, taken only
his legal share of the plunder accruing to the Company
from the sacking of a Portuguese trading station (he was
on thin ice here, the transaction had been less innocent
than he represented). He defied the managers to prove
that he had ever sold a place to any one. And he appealed
to charity and common sense on the charge of accumulating
lands and money, and advancing his relatives to power.
He had never solicited anything from King James, he could
hardly refuse the royal offers. It was implied that the
Commons were really attacking a dead king. It was true.
They were also attacking the system which made such
lavish grants to personal charm, and they must have our
sympathy for their attack. But it was a fairly easy one
to answer in a Court of Law.

Other charges referred to more recent times. The first
was to the undoubted growth of piracy during Buckingham's admiralty ; the Moors had recently established a

dépôt at Sallee, outside the Straits of Gibraltar, and their outrages now extended far beyond the Mediterranean ; war with Spain, civil war between Frenchmen, had increased the number of privateers. Buckingham could point to all these causes as beyond his control, could show that he had increased and refitted the Channel squadron, and suggest that if pirates escaped its vigilance, no man can control wind and wave. Secondly, he denied any intention to lend ships for use against the Huguenots. With less justice, he denied that he had alienated France by the staying of the *St. Pierre* ; he held an unfair advantage here, for the evidence was a government secret and beyond the Commons' reach.

Finally came an accusation superficially silly, but of evil implication. He was accused of interfering with King James's doctors, and increasing the King's last illness by unprofessional remedies. The appeal to sinister rumours was a trifle obvious.

The most curious thing about the indictment is an omission. Among all the criticisms of Buckingham's admiralty there was no word of Cadiz. Eliot had watched the damaged fleet crawl back into Plymouth : the spectacle had inspired his first speech in the new Parliament. Now he was strangely silent. The name of Cadiz, absent from the original charges, was mentioned thrice in the course of proceedings. A grievance was made of Glanville's secretaryship and loss of court fees, for Glanville was one of the " managers " ; Buckingham was blamed as the originator of the design, though it was sound in principle, traditional, and certainly in accordance with Eliot's own speeches of a year or two ago. Finally Eliot ended by taunting Buckingham with cowardice, because he had not given the supreme command to himself, rather than to a soldier of fifteen years' experience. Of rotten spars and tackle, mouldy provisions, and dishonest contractors there was no word. Eliot's enthusiasm for " discern the fault, to know the faulty " had evaporated. Indeed, Eliot was working with one of the faulty : among his fellow-managers was Robert Mansell, Nottingham's cousin and treasurer, who had resisted inquiry into naval abuses.

Nevertheless the accusations, pressed with all Eliot's burning rhetoric and a great deal of exaggeration, made a fair show. Behind them lay a great resentment at the system which made Buckingham's power possible. Behind them (if we may trust Eliot's own record) lay the feeling that had first sprung to life at the bedside in York House, when he realized that Buckingham was prepared to throw public odium on the Commons for their stinting of war funds. The Commons, under Eliot's leadership, were demanding the power to dismiss a minister of whom they disapproved. The Commons were feeling their way towards demanding the sovereignty of England.

It was in this light that Charles saw the impeachment : for him its essence was an attack upon the royal Prerogative. It came at the worst of all times, when he was in despair about England's unfitness for war, about his quarrels with Henrietta, about the growing breach with France ; and above all was the daunting emptiness of the exchequer. Money was owing to Mansfeld and King Christian ; without it they could not meet the Emperor's original army nor Wallenstein's newly raised hordes. Charles could not pay the debt. He was desperately trying to pawn the Crown Jewels, if Amsterdam could supply a moneylender rich enough and bold enough to take them. There was still a faint hope of a grant from Parliament, and Charles dared not stop the impeachment by a dissolution. He tried to put up smaller breastworks against the attack, asking the Commons to punish two of their own members for defamatory words spoken in the House. Then Eliot used the article about King James's medicine to make a direct hint that Buckingham was a poisoner : he might as well have implied that Prince Charles was an accomplice. Next day Eliot was in prison. Charles kept him there a week, telling the Commons it was not for words

spoken in Parliament but for an " extrajudicial " matter,
and so no breach of privilege. When the Commons
challenged the foolish plea by asking what that long word
meant, Charles had to let Eliot go, after trying in vain to
get him to implicate himself by a confession of disloyalty.

Charles was acting unwisely, but he commands some
sympathy in his battle with the Commons. He was protecting a friend from what he believed to be mere factiousness,
prompted by aristocratic jealousy ; he was protecting a
minister in whose hands lay the threads of all his policy ;
he was protecting a servant who was at least wholehearted
about the war, and for whom there was no obvious substitute. The crucial point was the feeling of the Lords, in
whose hands lay the decision of the impeachment. And it
was from among the Lords that there came an attack
which claims all our sympathy—the attack of an honest
man wronged.

Honest the Earl of Bristol undoubtedly was ; his whole
life shows it ; so does the florid, almost bucolic face which
Vandyke painted in the single picture, now at Madrid,
beside his own gentle and refined one ; even King Charles
might have acknowledged it but for the one fact that
Bristol hated Buckingham, and had reasons for his hatred.
Bristol had gone to Madrid, against his better judgment,
to negotiate for the Spanish match. He had seen Buckingham ride in to take the credit and ride out to break the
match. Still trusted by the Spaniards, Bristol had refused
the title and pension they offered him, and sailed for
England. Buckingham had kept him away from King
James by the order confining him to Dorset. There he
had stayed until King Charles's second Parliament. They
had sent him the usual writ of summons to appear, but
the Lord Keeper sent him a letter directing him not to
use it or come up to Westminster. Bristol, declaring, with
a happy irony, that he must obey the King's writ rather
than my Lord Keeper, arrived to take his seat. Charles
failed to prevent him. Bristol asked to be relieved from

the cloud of Royal disfavour or else brought to trial on some specific charge. Meanwhile he accused Buckingham of keeping him mewed up in Dorset for fear of what he might say. There was not the least doubt that the charge was absolutely true, and Bristol had chosen the most damaging moment to bring it. There was nothing to do except comply with his request and bring him to the bar on definite accusations.

They made a sorry show. King Charles had already told Bristol that his errors had been errors of judgment, not disloyalty. Now some attempt must be made to fix high treason on him : Bristol had mismanaged the negotiations deliberately, represented Spanish cunning as sincerity, advised Charles to become a Papist and revoke the Penal Laws. The indictment damaged no one but King Charles : even the pressure of necessity cannot excuse his allowing such libels to figure on a charge-sheet. Bristol countered with far more serious accusations against Buckingham's conduct in Madrid : he had there tried to make and then to break the match, to the peril of England's honour and safety. Buckingham might laugh at Eliot's attack. If he faced Bristol's with equanimity he must be a fool or a rogue.

He never had to face it at all. Charles, caught in the toils of ancient follies, knew himself beaten. Bristol was one day to be a Royalist, imprisoned by Parliament as an " evil counsellor." If only that day could have come earlier, if Charles could have shaken off the burden of his evil genius and accepted Bristol for his good angel, the whole pattern of his life might have been changed. The thing was impossible. All that was human in him yearned to save Buckingham from disgrace, all that was evil refused to acknowledge that, whatever the political necessities, he had done Bristol a grievous wrong. Meanwhile he could not yield without yielding also on a principle that was the keystone of his kingship. He could not accept the impeachment for what it pretended to be—an attack on the mal-administration of a favourite : he saw it only as a disguised assault on the ancient powers of the Crown, supported by jealousy, faction, and the basest insinuations, disloyally launched in the midst of war, and likely to paralyse the effort of the nation.

Charles sent a desperate message to the Commons demanding supply before any other business. Amsterdam had refused to take the Crown Jewels in pawn (Eliot made it a grievance that they had been offered), and the allies still demanded money. Charles said plainly that refusal would mean dissolution and unparliamentary taxation. The Commons were torn in two, and a long debate ensued. They could not know whether the country was behind them, or thought them unpatriotic obstructionists. Probably, as usual, the country was thinking mainly of crops and horseflesh. But Cambridge University had just defied the Commons by electing Buckingham its Chancellor; Royalist pressure and intrigue might not be the only reasons for the vote. Eliot and his friends were the victors in the debate; no money was to be granted till grievances were answered; and, as one member had said, Buckingham was the " grievance of grievances." Buckingham still pleaded that he could answer his accusers; Charles's agent in the Commons, sure that the charges were too flimsy to stand, asked for delay. " Not another minute," said the King, and sent for Black Rod. His second Parliament was dissolved.

Beneath the eye of the Almighty, four black smudges crawled across the tortured plains that had once been Low Germany. They were armies—two calling upon Him in the name of Luther and Calvin, two bearing on their banners the image of His mother and the emblems of His Pope. Behind them lengthened a trail of misery, burnt homes, and an innocent peasantry turned into hunted beasts. They drew near to each other. Mansfeld was the first to meet his fate, hurling his men in vain against Wallenstein's trenches by Dessau bridge. He fled to raise revolt in Hapsburg lands, to die a theatrical but not ignoble death among the Styrian hills. The Danes, un-

9

supported now, made a desperate dash for Bohemia. At Lutter, near the foot of the Harz, the Emperor's army caught them ; while the battle hung in doubt, some Danish regiments cried that they would fight no more until they were paid. Christian had spent his money, his nephew had sent no more. The army broke in rout and died in massacre. In a few months Wallenstein would have flattened out Denmark, his men would be staring across the Baltic and the North Sea.

" The whole round world," says the poet, " is bound by gold chains about the feet of God." But the devil also has his network of cords and pulleys. They bound Germany to Whitehall and York House and Christchurch, to Madrid and La Rochelle. They linked the little imps of jealousy and faction, dishonesty and muddle, to the great vampires who sucked their fill of Danish blood on the stricken field of Lutter.

CHAPTER EIGHT

DEFEAT

1626–28

IT was a perplexed England that faced the second winter of the new reign, and the King was the greatest source of perplexity. His original intentions had been uniformly excellent, their outcome uniformly disappointing. He had been eager to rule through Parliament ; yet he had failed to achieve any co-operation or even a reasonable supply of money. He had been enthusiastic about the war ; but his diplomacy, his allies, and his own venture had been unsuccessful to the point of catastrophe. It looked as if he was going to justify the schoolroom catchword, " a good man, but a bad king."

Such generalizations are always convenient, but generally misleading. Charles cannot be so simply disposed of. To begin with, he was not a particularly good man, in spite of several rather uncommon virtues. He had already commited a serious act of bad faith. There was in him a perpetual tendency to evade and equivocate—" squiborate," as one contemporary calls it—and to prefer the letter to the spirit. If a hasty temper is not necessarily a moral fault (" be angry and sin not "), it becomes so when combined with tardiness to acknowledge error ; many suns had gone down on Charles's wrath against Bristol. All these things told against the success of his kingship. They were only partly compensated for by his dignity and self-control, his intelligent and profound religion, his loyalty to a man once befriended, or a principle once embraced. The bundle of virtues and vices which had quarrelled with Henrietta and then won her lifelong affection was the same as that which failed to understand Parliaments and yet commanded the loyalty of the Cavaliers.

If there is any true distinction between public and private virtues, Charles was the last man to recognize it. He had a curiously mediæval strain in him which saw politics in terms of personal morality. The overwhelming fact in these early years was that he had pledged himself to help King Christian and the German Protestants, to maintain a feud with King Philip. The Commons prevented him from honouring that pledge, though it was with their encouragement he had taken it ; therefore there was something evil in the Commons.

He had warned them that, if they continued to refuse supply, he might have to resort to unparliamentary taxation. His first idea was an interesting one—to call together the electors in the shires and boroughs and ask them to vote him the money their representatives had grudged. This curiously democratic proposal was too novel or too hazardous for the official minds on the Council, and he was told it was impossible.

His next proposal was to ask his richer subjects for a free gift, as a sign of their " common care and affection." To prove himself sincerely in straits, he began a campaign of economy at home. The courtiers' pickings were docked, his own plate melted down and sold. The story would soon be going round that Henrietta kept her bedroom shutters closed in the daytime, lest visitors should see how ragged the sheets were.

It is easy to laugh at appeals to loyalty, unbacked by force. Nowadays, when national existence is at stake and men giving their lives in millions, we think it necessary to offer a rate of interest higher than the usual in order to induce men to lend their country money, and we try to pretend that they are patriotic in accepting the excellent bargain. Other ages have thought differently. The Athenians, for instance, ran a naval empire by relying on their rich to provide battleships and vie with each other in equipping them. All through the Middle Ages taxation retained an element of personal gift. We may even return one day to ideas of government based more on public spirit and less on fear or self-interest. But Charles's England was not ready for the Kingdom of God, and she was too old and too complicated to be ruled like a Highland clan. A few districts responded to the free gift : the general result was disappointing.

There were Tudor precedents for a Forced Loan, and Charles proclaimed one. He still tried to appeal to reason rather than compulsion. He asked the clergy to tell their congregations that Protestantism was in danger, and our reputation lost at Lutter ; if Wallenstein drove Christian from his own Denmark it would be the greatest dishonour " that ever this Kingdom was stained withall." He also appealed to lower motives ; our trade with Hamburg was in danger, Wallenstein might even swallow Holland and threaten England. He promised to call a Parliament in return for a hearty response. Meanwhile he clannishly expected unqualified support from his own officials ; the Lord Chief Justice was dismissed for refusing to pronounce that the Tudor precedents made a Forced Loan legal. His successor was Nicholas Hyde, uncle to the future historian Clarendon. Hyde had no patience with personal appeals and was eager to imprison the recalcitrant ; it was childish merely to summon them before a committee and scold them for their unpatriotic stinginess. But for a time the attempt continued and persuasion remained the only official method. It required a new danger to introduce a more drastic policy.

For more than a century, the chief axiom of our diplomacy had been that France and Spain were irreconcilable enemies, and that war with one meant alliance with the other. It had helped to ensure our safety, though Mary's Spanish alliance had not preserved Calais from French armies, and France had been too distracted with Civil War to help us against the Spanish Armada. But Charles was now faced with something entirely new, something fit to make Wolsey and Elizabeth turn in their graves. France and Spain were signing a treaty against us.

There had long been intense irritation between London and Paris. Charles, not without reason, considered himself duped by the French refusal to admit Mansfeld and join in the war with Spain ; he had ceased to trust any word from France. Louis had a grievance in the continued enforcement of the Penal Laws, and Charles was powerless to fulfil that bargain. His own counter-claim to champion the interests of the French Protestants pleased the English Parliament but infuriated King Louis. Now the shipping dispute was growing very serious. The delay in releasing the *St. Pierre* was followed by a selling of French cargoes before the courts had pronounced on them as contraband— an anticipation hardly excusable in a government desperately pressed for money, quite inexcusable as viewed through French eyes. Rouen began reprisals by an embargo on English ships, and other ports followed suit. The English merchants petitioned Buckingham for permission to recoup themselves by plundering French shipping. He refused them, and suggested to Richelieu that they should negotiate a new treaty, reconciling all disputes about contraband and prizes. But a single act, done behind Richelieu's back, made them irreconcilable.

The cardinal was not yet supreme in France, and he had one enemy only too glad to see his policy embarrassed and thwarted, an unscrupulous aristocrat who held the key position, the governorship of Bordeaux. The annual wine fleet from England lay in Bordeaux harbour ; we had not yet signed the treaty with Portugal which has secured us Portuguese alliance from the days of Queen Anne to those of George V, and taught us all to drink port wine ; we still relied on French wines to warm the inner man. Suddenly there came the news that the governor of Bordeaux had first exacted a large toll from our wine fleet and then confiscated all the cargoes. While

London raged at its losses and the prospect of a cheerless Christmas, Paris, regarding war as inevitable, added insult to injury by demanding that Charles should fill his home again with the full compliment of priests and Frenchwomen. And there was war.

Charles attempted to patch up peace with Spain, and Rubens was called out of his Brussels studio to negotiate. But Spain naturally demanded that England should abandon her Dutch allies, and Charles naturally refused ; among other things, Holland had just given him a new promise to punish the Amboyna murderers. But if any one expected a Franco-Spanish armada to sail up the Thames, he was quite wrong. Buckingham was far from a perfect admiral, but he could protect our shores. The first result of the war was to fill English pockets and relieve the aching needs of the Government with the plunder of French shipping. And it was England, with little more than a quarter of France's population, that did the invading. It was on a tiny scale. We have grown used to nations employing every ounce of strength in war, and forget the leisurely ways of our ancestors ; it sounds like a delightful dream, but we were for two years at war with two first-class powers, and operations were confined to the capture and recapture of a small island in the Bay of Biscay.

Events seemed at first to favour us. Spain, already struggling with the national decay which was soon to overwhelm her, had enough work to keep her armies afoot in Holland and Germany. In France, disgruntled aristocrats were sure they could raise forces against the hated Richelieu. Buckingham expected to do as Henry V had done before Agincourt, intervene in a French civil war, and with a more creditable motive ; for Charles proclaimed that he had no intention of conquering French territory. He was still the Protestant crusader, and his object was to succour the Huguenots, in open rebellion against King Louis. Richelieu had sworn to put an end to the political power of French Protestantism. He intended and persuaded Louis to secure religious toleration. But when that political power had been destroyed, King Louis's son and successor was to revoke the edict of toleration and destroy the Huguenots by persecution.

If an army went to France, it was clear that Buckingham must lead it. Eliot's taunt about Cadiz was too stinging, and success in the field might justify King Charles's choice of a minister. He was to show that he could do far better than Cecil, for all Cecil's experience. He consulted the experts at every turn, and their advice was not good. He had assembled an army considerably better than the disgraceful rabble of Cadiz. And he almost redeemed the strategical mistakes by his splendid energy and personal courage. Disaster awaited him, but not disgrace.

The first disappointment was our allies. Richelieu's aristocratic enemies made the feeblest of efforts. That middle-aged priest proved an excellent soldier ; he had only become a Churchman because family convenience demanded that it should be his elder brother who went into the army ; now he moved unimpeded armies towards La Rochelle and buckled on armour to besiege her. The city itself, later to do heroically, showed its worst side— in rebellion against King Louis, and yet half-hearted and undecided. One man accused the magistrates of being bribed by the King, another said the Rochellois had slavery in their bones. They could not make up their minds to admit Buckingham ; when they did, it was too late. Buckingham knew they would do so as soon as they realized that Richelieu meant business. Meanwhile he looked round for a base, and selected the isle of Rhé, a few miles from their walls.

The problem was not unlike that which recently confronted us at the Dardanelles—a forced landing with naval assistance, trench warfare, and the attempt to cut an enemy off from mainland supplies. The main difference was in the spirit of the troops. There were no rocky eminences to storm, no shell fire or machine-guns, only an inferior force of French drawn up to charge the landing-parties on the beach. But when Buckingham leapt into the surf, half the men refused to leave their boats to follow him. Some had even defied orders by remaining on board the ships. Buckingham had to scramble back and belabour them into action with a cudgel, and leap ashore again to meet the French charge. Met it was, and successfully. The English disembarked. Anne of Austria's lover had kept his word to King Louis: he had landed in France at the head of an army.

When the French came with a white flag to offer a large ransom for the bodies of their dead, Buckingham granted their request and refused their money. He forbade his men to enter the neighbouring villages for fear of pillage. Remembering what had happened at Cadiz, he saw their provisions landed and distributed with his own eyes. He risked his life to rescue a soldier marooned on a sandbank in the rising tide. When he rolled himself up in his soldier's cloak, to sleep under the bare sky, he had done more to fit himself for the leadership of England than in many years of courts and Parliaments.

The campaign became a siege. Toiras, commanding the French, found himself shut up in the fort of St. Martin, while the English overran most of the island, dug trenches round him, and blocked his approach to the sea with a boom. When the boom broke, they formed a cordon by stretching chains from ship to ship. Toiras was to be starved out.

The process was marked by an incident at which the blood runs cold. It was an occasional usage of war to drive into blockaded towns as many "useless mouths" as possible, in order to exhaust the supplies. Buckingham collected the wives and children of the garrison from a neighbouring village and marched them into no man's land. Toiras refused to open the gates; if he had no scruples about cannonading innocent harvesters in time of peace, he was not going to spoil war plans for a few women. And then (there seems no doubt of it) the English soldiers began to fire upon them. The French, vanquished in the fiendish contest, admitted them to the fort. There is no evidence that Buckingham knew what was going on ; at least one of his officers had never heard of it, and said it must have been the French who did the shooting. But it was surely Buckingham's business to know how his soldiers were amusing themselves, and he must bear the responsibility.

The siege lasted three months. Before its end, there was some doubt whether it was French or English who would starve. Buckingham had left King Charles to deal with the confusion and lack of money at home, and Charles was hard put to it to send provisions or reinforcements. His letters to Buckingham are full of unaltered friendship, and they contain one little note of affectionate admiration for Henrietta, still loyal and loving, though her husband and brother were at war. Buckingham's mother sent nothing but scoldings ; she had turned Catholic, rated him for taking God's name for his war on Catholicism, taunted him with England's refusal to pay for the Protestant Crusade. Kate had no politics, but wrote to urge her husband to follow the proverbial example of the staff officer and not expose his person. " It does not belong to a general to walk trenches," she said.

Then crushing news reached England. Toiras, at his last gasp, had sent out a message to arrange terms of surrender. That very night a wind arose and blew stiffly from the mainland. Down it came French provision ships, snapping the chains of the English cordon. Buckingham, roused by the sound of guns at midnight, rushed on board to avert disaster. But the ships were through to the fort, and immediately the wind died ; Buckingham's fire-ships, sent in pursuit, moved so sluggishly that the French could easily ward them aside. Three months' work was thrown away.

Wind, as well as muddle, had delayed the English

supplies and reinforcements ; they arrived at last, but nothing could be done. A desperate attempt to escalade St. Martin's failed. Meanwhile the one serious mistake of the campaign was bearing fruit. The small redoubt of La Prée, on the landward side of the island, had been left in French hands, perhaps for lack of men to take it. It had been no menace at first, but now Richelieu was before Rochelle with an army ; little by little, troops had slipped across until the redoubt held 6000 men. Buckingham must soon abandon the siege and re-embark for England ; he would have to do it in presence of a hostile army.

Buckingham's plan was excellent. His ships awaited the men close to a patch of land cut off from the rest of the island by salt-marshes, across which ran a narrow causeway. Once the troops reached this beach they could embark at leisure and in safety. To guard their passage thither along the causeway, Buckingham ordered his colonel-general and his sergeant-major-general to dig an earthwork. But he was a tired and dispirited man, no longer the splendid fighter, the unwearied inspector of detail that had sprung ashore four months ago. Inexperienced himself, he had hesitated to bully subordinates who were old hands at the game. It was even said that it was his officers who had caused all the trouble by refusing to attack the redoubt of La Prée, in spite of his orders. Certainly they had despised his hesitation as mere weakness, and treated many instructions with contempt. Now they were about to wreck everything. The earthwork was never dug. Nothing stood between the retreating columns and the watchful French but a screen of cavalry.

The Frenchmen charged. The cavalry became a panic-stricken mob, trampling their own countrymen under the hooves of frightened horses. The French slew and slew. It is said that pity and weariness stayed their hands and held them back while the last English, whom nothing but pity and weariness could save, stampeded across the causeway into safety. But when the ships sailed away from the hated island, something between a thousand and two thousand English corpses lay around the head of the causeway or had sunk into the salt-marsh. The Frenchmen marched away to join the iron ring that was closing round La Rochelle.

There were many excuses for failure, even for such failure as Buckingham brought home with him that winter : chance, the failure of allies, insubordinate officers, and the rawness of troops. But Buckingham made no excuses, and laid all blame upon himself. Charles tried to take it from him, saying the fault lay in his own failure to send supplies and reinforcements earlier. There was much truth in what both said. Neither had greatness, and it would have required a great general and a great organizer to lead England to military success at once after so many years of peace. Buckingham had done his best, with an outworn system and no adequate finance. A disgraceful fiasco at Cadiz had been followed by a failure from which he had won some credit, for all his mistakes. The next expedition might achieve the success that had been so narrowly missed. For there was no question of abandoning La Rochelle to Richelieu. Buckingham did not know when he was beaten.

By next summer a new fleet and army awaited his command at Portsmouth. Charles had called a third Parliament ; its story we must leave to another chapter ; but it had voted him a grant of money, liberal enough by former standards, insufficient for the war. There was still lethargy and mutiny and corruption, but Buckingham hoped to cure them while he prosecuted the war. Victory abroad would convince England, might even convince Parliament, that the King's cause was good. Of ultimate victory it was not in Buckingham to doubt.

Whether he could have done it, we shall never know. His days were numbered. For a time a strange melancholy fell upon him. He began to talk of making peace. Perhaps

he was affected by the muddle and inefficiency around
him which it was his business to cure before he sought
glory elsewhere. Perhaps he was suffering from the great
load of unpopularity which he affected to disdain ; what
is repressed is not always conquered. Bad news came
from the City. A creature called Dr. Lambe, whom
Buckingham may never have seen, had increased his trade
in quack drugs and magic philtres by boasting of the
Duke's patronage ; now the London mob had fallen on
Lambe and brutally lynched him ; men said it would be
Buckingham's turn next. A strange story was going round.
An old man from Leicestershire, bred on the Villiers estates,
had come up to tell him that three nights running he had
seen the Duke's dead father in a dream. He had been
charged with a message to the son : Buckingham must do
something to ingratiate himself with the people or look
for an early death. For an hour the countryman had
walked with the Duke, up and down Thames-side by
Lambeth Palace, while the servants watched them and
held the horses for their master's delayed hunting-party.
Buckingham swore that the fellow had revealed things he
could not have known without converse with the dead.
But if he was convinced, he hardly knew how to obey the
message : to the end he could not grasp how and why he
had incurred the hatred of so many good men. He remembered one of the charges at his impeachment ; perhaps
his official posts had wakened a reasonable jealousy ; he
signed away the Wardenship of the Cinque Ports. When
men had spoken to him of assassination, he had answered
that there were no Roman spirits left. It was not the
first mistake he had made about the English ; but it was
to be the last.

In a London garret, an out-at-elbows gentleman from
Suffolk sat reading political pamphlets and nursing a
wounded arm. His name was John Felton, and it was one
of his sorrows that he could not call himself Captain
Felton : favouritism or chance had passed him over in the

trenches of St. Martin.   Even his pay was £40 in arrears,
and he was weighed down with debts.   His reading told
him that Buckingham was a poisoner ; that Parliament had
named him as the cause of England's woes ; that all things
are lawful which are done for the common weal.   One
August day he left his books behind, strolled out to Tower
Hill and spent a much-needed tenpence on a butcher's knife.

He was as different from the vulgar criminal as any
man can be who plans another's death.   He called at a
church in Fleet Street to beg that prayers might be said
for John Felton, as for " a man much distracted in mind."
Then he set out to walk his sixty miles into Portsmouth,
and the waggoners who gave him an occasional lift did
not guess that their melancholy companion was about
to change the history of Europe.

At Portsmouth an ugly spirit was abroad.   A mutinous
sailor had been condemned to hang, and, though a reprieve
was made out, it was decided to frighten him by taking
him to the gallows first.   His comrades organized a riot
to rescue him, and almost mobbed Buckingham : the
sentence had to be executed.   Next morning, Buckingham
forgot the unpleasant incident in the news, brought to
his breakfast-table, that the siege of La Rochelle was
raised.   It was false, but Buckingham never lived to
know it.   As he left the table and went into the crowded
hall, a man slipped out of the dark passage, buried a
butcher's knife in his breast, and was gone again.   There
was a great hubbub.   Poor Kate, a babe within her and
near its birth, ran out of her room on to a gallery.   She
looked down on her husband's body, already laid out in
death.

Felton could have escaped.   He had only to pick up
his hat in the confusion and walk into the street.   While
men ran hither and thither, crying the Frenchmen had
done it, Felton mistook the word for his own name.   In
any case he was not one to shirk consequences.   He
stepped quickly back into the hall.   " I am the man,"

he said. " Here I am." It was with difficulty that they rescued him from instant death.

In the lining of his hat was sewn a paper so that, whatever happened, men should know his motive. The writing ended with these words :

" He is unworthy of the name of a gentleman and soldier, in my opinion, that is afraid to sacrifice his life for the honour of God, his King, and country. JOHN FELTON."

One wonders if there was a hint of self-doubt in that little phrase, " in my opinion," which so curiously mars the eloquent ring of the sentence. Certainly he was to change his opinion, though not his fortitude. When Dorset suggested torture to make him incriminate his accomplices, he replied that he had none, and that if they put him on the rack he would begin by incriminating Dorset. But his punishment was in his own conscience. While London made songs in his honour, he was confessing to abject repentance. The parson sent to attend him reported that his task was not to induce remorse, but to raise the prisoner from despairing of the possibility of salvation. Felton wrote to Kate Buckingham that " he could be content that his body should suffer exquisite torture to give her satisfaction," and the poor woman sent him her forgiveness. At his execution he asked that the hand which did the deed should be first struck off, but he was put to death without barbarity. A man much distracted in mind had gone to find peace in a less perplexing world.

Charles was at Southwick, a few miles out of Portsmouth, when Felton struck the blow. The messenger galloped up to find the household had finished breakfast, and was at morning prayers. He picked his way to where the King knelt, and whispered the tale of murder. The King prayed on. Not till service was finished did he rise and go to his room. Then he flung himself on his bed and gave free rein to sorrow, in a place where no subject could see that his King was of like passions with himself.

CHAPTER NINE

CUL-DE-SAC

1628–29

FIVE months before Buckingham died, Charles had called another Parliament. His Free Gift had failed, and Chief Justice Hyde was having his way with the Forced Loan ; recalcitrant gentlemen were going into prison. In some shires, the commissioners had disregarded the King's orders to assess only the rich " that so the poor may be eased and yet the business done." They were demanding money from comparatively poor men and pressing the unwilling into the army. When some refused to accept the press-money and be shipped for Denmark or La Rochelle, some of the King's Councillors wanted to hang the conscientious objectors : they were overruled and the whole business was stopped. But resistance was growing general, and it was embittered by the billeting of soldiers on the obstinate, by the pilfering of unpaid troops, and the biased decisions thereon of the military courts, enforcing Martial Law. Nothing but despotism on the continental pattern could have crushed the discontent. Charles lacked the power to establish even a temporary despotism. It is probable that he lacked the desire. He still thought the old machinery might work, and determined to give Parliament another trial.

Charles's third Parliament is justly famous. It struck at the roots of trouble by offering money while it prohibited unparliamentary taxes, and healed, temporarily at least, the great breach between Crown and Commons. If its last session could have closed as happily as its first, all might yet have been well.

The King had released, in time for the elections, all who were in prison for resisting the loan ; among them came Eliot and Wentworth and John Hampden. Pym had either paid or escaped assessment : he may still have been a poor man. A suggestion of excluding lawyers as certain opponents of the Crown was not adopted ; Selden took his seat ; Finch became Speaker ; with them was old Coke, risen to fame and fortune by using his vast learning and hectoring manner for the Crown, now hand in glove with the Crown's opponents. Finally, Huntingdon borough had returned the local squire, and St. Stephen's Chapel was to hear for the first time the voice of Oliver Cromwell.

In his opening speech, the King pleaded for quick decisions and timely supply. The Commons must act according to their conscience, but he, too, had a duty, and, if they would not help him, he must find other means. This was not a threat, for (Charles grew positively rude) he scorned to threaten any but his equals. Then he ended more graciously, called bygones bygones, and even hoped the Commons would show him what had been good in their " former counsels." He was sure that they would restore that co-operation than which " nothing could be more pleasing unto me."

The start was inauspicious. Coke proposed a Bill against arbitrary imprisonment. Pym's contribution was the framing of a petition for a general fast. Eliot attacked royalist clergy, announced that English liberty was in danger of destruction, and attributed all evils to Arminianism in the Church. No one talked of war funds, except one of the Court party, whose panacea was a large grant of moneys and a humble request to the King to abolish evils ; he asked, rather obscurely, whether there was not balm in Gilead. Then Wentworth rose and in one speech wrested from Eliot the leadership of the House. The most remarkable man of the generation had stepped into the centre of the stage.

Sir Thomas Wentworth came of an old family settled

10

in the West Riding, prominent since the Reformation. His father, Sir William, used to tell of a curious dream he had had soon after marriage : a man had appeared to tell him he would have a son " who should be a great and prominent man, and should then "—here Lady Wentworth woke her husband and cut the story short. Knowing its end, we may think she did well, though the old knight gave her a good scolding. Some time later, when they were staying at a house in Chancery Lane, she gave birth to Thomas.

He was sent to school, to Cambridge, to the Inner Temple. He was married to a Peer's daughter, and then (after the curious custom of the times) sent on his travels to France and Italy, with his wife left at home. Sir William died early, leaving him a parting message to keep faith with honest friends, fear God, govern his tongue, and " be pityfull to the poor." He also left him great riches and responsibilities, and Thomas Wentworth was trained for public life by the cares of a great estate and innumerable lawsuits. He also trained himself, methodically, sparing no pains. Deciding, like most wise men, that education can give no better advantage than understanding and skill in the use of words, he studied the best masters in English, French, and Latin, listened to sermons, analysed and answered political pamphlets. He spent long hours in perfecting his own letters. In an age of crabbed and cumbersome English, relieved all too seldom by a half-Shakespearean flash, Wentworth has style. Deeply moved, he could command a shattering eloquence. One of his letters, to be quoted later, will endure as long as words have power to influence the human heart.

He was soon to be accused of apostasy, but he had so far been unusually consistent. He had never applauded Buckingham ; he had always thought the war mere madness. He had one passion, to see England well governed ; one ambition, to have a hand in the governing. He had constantly applied to the Court for a post, and been constantly cold-shouldered. He had been jockeyed out of a position in local government by the intrigues of an evil-minded neighbour called Savile. He had quarrelled with the Commons over a disputed election, lost his seat at Savile's petition, endured a denunciation from Eliot, and secured re-election. He had missed the next Parliament by being appointed sheriff, faced prison for refusing to pay the Loan. Now he had come up to co-operate with Eliot and help the Court at the same time. He was not easy to work with. He was finicky about small matters, though direct and drastic in large. He was irritable, seldom in good health, painfully ill at the worst crises of his life. He kept a very tender side of his character for friends and wife and children. In public he was haughty to opponents : he hated clap-trap ; he hated fools. He said what he thought, and if others took offence, that was their business. He was a Yorkshireman.

His Parliamentary career was short, for his great work awaited him elsewhere. But he came at a critical moment, and was associated with the only constructive work of Charles's early Parliaments. In his first speech he won the confidence of the House ; he exaggerated the current evils, but he tactfully laid them to the charge of royal ministers who had torn up " the roots of all property " without relieving the needs of the Crown. He was soon to ensure that those needs should be relieved by a Parliamentary grant. Meanwhile there must be no more arbitrary imprisonment, no more billeting of soldiers, no more forced loans. Such were the foundations of the Petition of Right, one of the laws whereby England is England.

We used to boast that we lived in a free country. From the earliest times, our laws tried to recognize a certain sanctity in the individual upon which even Reason of State must not intrude. Nowadays the principle is threatened, rightly or wrongly, in the name of social well-being. In the seventeenth century, it was threatened by monarchy. Stinted by Parliament, the King's Government had de-

manded unparliamentary supplies; it had proceeded to
imprison and harass men in their homes for refusing; the
political battle had invaded the sphere of private rights.
Parliament had determined to raise a barrier against that
invasion by appealing to English liberty. By so doing
they fettered the King in the struggle and perhaps, since
he accepted the fetters, ensured his defeat. But it may well
be argued that England, losing her monarchy, fulfilled her
historic mission. In time of war we forget our principles;
at all times the poor man, in the grip of economic tyranny,
may find them something of a mockery. But they have
been a standard, a source of inspiration, and a centre for
appeal. In the last century, foreign countries looked to
us for the principles of liberty; if we can preserve our
heritage, they may look to us again.

The Petition of Right laid the foundations of the
tradition. It denied the Government's right to raise
unparliamentary taxes, to imprison or keep a man in
prison without showing cause. It forbade the billeting
of soldiers in private houses. It forbade the proclamation
of Martial Law.

It was not to be expected that the King would let such
a measure pass without opposition. He naturally suspected that its promoters aimed " not at the abuses of
power but at power itself." [1] Above all, it was an encroachment on his emergency Prerogative. He had every
justification in saying that the abuses were the result of a
double crisis—war, and the refusal of Parliamentary supply.
One of his friends in the Commons scored heavily against
old Coke, by quoting an opinion of his own, delivered in
the days when he was himself a servant of the Crown,
about the necessity for summary imprisonment. When
the Lords were drawn into the debate, Bristol, reconciled
now to the King, insisted on the Crown's discretionary
powers. Northampton foreshadowed Edgehill in a fiery
speech. There must be safeguards, he said, against

[1] D'Israeli, *Charles I.*

arbitrary power, but " when the subject's liberty is in question, I will creep on my knees with a petition to his Majesty in all humility. When the King's prerogative is in question, I will get upon my horse and draw my sword and defend it with my life and estate." Charles, believing his Prerogative to be very much in question, resisted to the last. Wentworth threw out a bait of money; over-riding Eliot, he persuaded the Commons to vote a subsidy, to be paid as soon as a settlement was reached: it was quite inadequate to the King's needs, but it was larger than the Commons were used to grant, and it was an earnest of that co-operation which was the blessed goal of debate. When the secretary reported it to the King, Charles asked how the voting had gone. " Carried by one vote," said the secretary, in a spirit of mischief; then he told the truth, that Wentworth had secured unanimity in the House; and it is said that tears started to the King's eyes.

He still saw the matter in a personal light. He wrecked Wentworth's first Bill and destroyed his leader-ship by asking the Commons to drop legislation and rely on his personal word that the evils should never be re-peated. He believed the Commons sincere in not wishing to destroy his Prerogative and begged for " a like charity " in believing that he cared for their liberties. " But for God's sake," he said, " do not spend so much time as to hazard the ruin of your liberties and my Prerogative by a foreign enemy." News of disasters abroad and the gallop-ing consumption in the Exchequer were driving him desperate. He kept the Houses talking all through Good Friday and spoilt their Easter holiday. Finally he tried to content the Commons with a promise to put the ancient laws into full force so that " his subjects may have no cause to complain of any wrongs or oppressions contrary to their just right and liberties."

It was an evasion, and a hopeless one. The Commons could not be content with so vague an answer. Eliot

began to talk wildly of the Government's disasters, Cadiz,
Rhé, the ravages of the pirates. A royal message put a
stop to such discussions. A feeling of helplessness settled
down upon the Commons ; their subsidy was unpaid, their
grievances unredressed ; every one expected a dissolution.
Some blamed Eliot for opening old wounds, all were in
despair for the future. They sat in silence, and many
burst out weeping. Speaker Finch, himself in tears,
hurried to Whitehall. Charles was at last convinced that
he was not opposed by a faction, but by the resolute will
of Parliament ; and Parliament refused to rely upon his
personal word. Next morning he called the Houses
together and addressed them. He regretted that his former
answer had not satisfied them, but he was " willing to
pleasure them in words as well as substance." The
Petition was read. The clerk replied to it, " *Soit Droit
fait comme il est désiré.*" That night the bonfires blazed
in London streets. Within a week, the Subsidy Bill was
passed and money at last began to flow into the royal
exchequer.

The settlement was shortlived. The Commons were
not in conciliatory mood. It may be argued that delay
and evasion had convinced them that the King was unfit
to enjoy Prerogative Power : it may also be argued that
the King had only evaded and delayed because he was
sure that a full and speedy assent to the Petition would
be followed by new and more questionable attacks on the
Prerogative. Certainly, within two days, Pym was engaged
in impeaching a clergyman called Mainwaring for a sermon,
printed, and licensed by the King, which represented it
as sin to oppose the Forced Loan. Charles had forsworn
Loans now, and Mainwaring had to admit error, pay a fine,
and be forbidden to preach at Court. Meanwhile the
Commons prepared a Remonstrance against misgovernment on Eliot's pattern. They quarrelled with the Lords
by changing the ancient form of money-bills so as to exclude
the assent of the Upper House : complaints were met with

equivocation and an answer (not unlike Charles's first answer to the Petition) which denied what it fulsomely pretended to grant. But such affairs were trifles compared with the struggle for the Customs.

For two centuries it had been the rule for Parliament to grant a Tonnage and Poundage Bill for life, early in each sovereign's reign. It had also been the rule for customs to be collected as usual until Parliament met and passed the Bill. Now the Commons had restricted their Bill to one year, in order to discuss its details. The year had long passed, they had done nothing to renew discussion. The King had continued to collect customs, pending their decision. They suddenly advanced a new resolution—that customs were an unparliamentary tax, and therefore illegal under the Petition of Right.

This claim will not bear a moment's examination. The Petition was slightly ambiguous in wording, but its intention was beyond doubt. It was directed against Forced Loans and the like, already of doubtful legality. It is highly improbable that any of the Commons thought of Tonnage and Poundage at all during its discussion. It is absolutely certain that the King had not contemplated surrendering his right to levy customs by granting the Petition. To claim that he had done so was a rather discreditable trick and a plain indication that certain people at least in the Commons did not want a peaceful settlement and co-operation with the Crown. Charles, willing to give the members time to reconsider their action, ordered a prorogation. Parliament broke up in July 1628 : it was to reassemble in January.

The intervening five months were some of the most important in the King's life. In August, Buckingham met his death. His name had been mentioned once or twice in Parliament, but there seems to have been an understanding that a second attempt at impeachment would mean a dissolution. Now he was dead, and with him went Parliament's most legitimate grievance.

With him died all chance of success in war. He had failed to relieve Rochelle a year ago. Lindsey, his successor in command, did even less. Richelieu had blocked the harbour-mouth with a dyke, and Lindsey could not induce the English ships to go within range of its batteries. La Rochelle surrendered to Richelieu and was generously treated. The political power of the Huguenots was broken, and King Louis respected their religion. If his son had done the same, one might say that King Charles had been fighting for nothing. Certainly his other quarrels were easily adjusted, and peace was made. Soon Rubens would come to England and negotiate a peace with Spain. The Dutch had captured a Spanish treasure-fleet and were beginning to despise our aid. The German Protestants were about to find a new saviour in Gustavus Adolphus, a surer paymaster in Richelieu. The war against the Hapsburgs went on, but without English intervention.

Europe might despise Charles for letting his subjects dictate to him, instead of establishing a despotism after the contemporary fashion. But no one abroad understood King Charles's problems. He had come to an understanding with Parliament, the feverish need for money was abating. So long as the Commons refrained from pressing their unwarranted claims about the Customs, there was life yet in the old system of government by King and Parliament. There were many hopeful signs. Buckingham was dead, and Charles was never to have a favourite again. Bristol was in favour at Court, as was Archbishop Abbot, recently under a cloud. The most powerful minister was Treasurer Weston, a moderate if uninspiring person. Time and chance were removing the worst consequences of King Charles's youth and King James's age. All might yet be well.

The Court had meanwhile obtained one recruit who was to prove the most important of all. Charles was so seldom blessed with an eye for the right man that this instance is worth recording. Three years ago, when it was proposed to exclude inconvenient opponents from the Commons by making them sheriffs, Charles had hesitated at Wentworth's name. " But Wentworth," he said, " is an honest gentleman." Now the time was ripe for an alliance. The Petition was passed, Parliament had granted the King money : Wentworth could not follow the Commons farther along the road they had chosen. He cared for nothing except good government : he cannot have wished to attack the King's right to levy Customs : he disliked Puritans : he disliked theological controversy. He had often petitioned for office under the Government. Now he became Baron Wentworth : he would soon be a Privy Councillor, then President of the Council for the North, Lord Deputy of Ireland, finally Earl of Strafford.

It has been said that he only accepted Court favour from motives of personal ambition, and that he waited until Buckingham's death had cleared the path to supreme power. It is quite false, for he took over his title and all that it entailed a month before Buckingham's death. The fact that this libel has been repeated, in Green's *Short History*, to the tune of 32,000 copies in one year, may help to explain the popular estimate of Wentworth, and of his master.

There is a tradition that one man was for ever antagonized by the so-called apostasy. The story tells of a meeting at Greenwich between Wentworth and Pym. Wentworth began to speak of the prospects of peace and co-operation between Court and Parliament, but Pym interrupted with the frankest expression of party spirit. All this fine talk could only mean that Wentworth was leaving his friends. " But," said Pym, " I will never leave you while your head is upon your shoulders." If the story is true, it was thirteen years before Pym accomplished his purpose.

There was talk of trying to buy over other members of the Opposition, and even Eliot's name was mentioned.

We do not know whether any offers were made. Pym and Eliot remained in opposition, and could generally command a majority. The King's servants in the Commons were feeble antagonists in debate. Wentworth's absence did not make for peace or moderation. The tendencies he deplored were soon to have free play ; they had perhaps grown stronger during the recess between the two sessions.

The King had done one provocative thing : he had repudiated Mainwaring's doctrines, but he had granted him a pardon and a new living. Otherwise he had attempted conciliation. He published a proclamation to discourage theological controversy in the Church, since it engendered bitterness and distracted the clergy from their more important duties. As the Commons complained of " innovations," by which they meant Arminianism, he forbade all innovations : the Church must work by its ancient Prayer Book. The Commons took the proclamation as a red rag rather than an olive branch. The King's attempt to enforce the Prayer Book rubrics in the interests of decency and an orderly ceremonial were to them Popish innovations. They pushed their doubtful claims to control Church government, assuring the King that they knew best how to obtain a godly and learned ministry. Charles had already raised the standard of godliness and learning among the clergy. The real question was whether the Church should grow more or less Puritan.

Even less successful were Charles's attempts to get the Customs question settled. Encouraged by Parliament's manœuvres and by the very human desire to pay as few taxes as possible, the London merchants had been resisting Tonnage and Poundage during the recess. Charles had their goods held in bond, until Parliament should decide the question. Conciliation could hardly go farther, in a matter affecting about half his ordinary revenue and threatening the very existence of monarchy.

It remained to be seen whether the Commons would

drop their dishonest contention that Tonnage and Poundage was barred by the Petition of Right. They did so,
but it was only to raise a more foolish claim. They discovered that one of the merchants whose goods were in
bond was a member of the Commons. They advanced a
new and startling argument that the property of members
as well as their persons must be free from interference,
even in a Parliamentary recess. They postponed all
discussion of principle, and summoned Customs officials
to the bar for daring to touch the goods of a " Parliament
man." If they had wanted to, they could hardly have
supplied Charles with clearer evidence that they were
defending the privileges of a close ring, rather than the
liberties of England.

As the debates proceeded, Eliot outbid Pym for leadership, and proceedings grew more melodramatic. There
was new talk of a Jesuit saved from execution by a royal
reprieve, of Arminian innovators promoted to bishoprics,
of Popish books licensed for the Press. The King, hoping
to cool hot heads, ordered an adjournment, then a re-
adjournment till " Tuesday come sevennight." Then
Eliot took the decisive step : he defied the order. He
rose to propose a new motion. Speaker Finch refused to
listen ; the House, he said, must adjourn itself at the King's
order ; he rose to go. Still Eliot persisted, though his old
friends would not support him, and Pym sat silent. Up
sprang Ben Valentine, member for Eliot's old constituency of St. Germans. He seized Speaker Finch and held
him down in the chair. With him was Lord Clare's son,
Denzil Holles. " Gog's wowns," said Holles, " you shall
sit till we please to rise ! " Scandalized members who
tried to release the Speaker were hurled back to their
seats. Never had St. Stephen's Chapel witnessed such a
scene. Eliot was talking about Popery again, and inveigh-
ing against the bishops. He suddenly suggested the
impeachment of the inoffensive Weston, in whom he saw
the ghost of Buckingham and " the head of all the Papists."

Then came a great knocking on the door ; the King had
sent a sergeant to remove the mace. Eliot had him sent
back and the doors locked. It was Black Rod who knocked
next, and with him was a guard to force the locks. While
they battered, Holles rose to put a motion of Eliot's proposing. Religious innovators were capital enemies to
King and Commonwealth : any man who had a hand
in levying Tonnage and Poundage was in like case : a
merchant who paid Customs was "a betrayer of the
liberties of England." Then the doors were flung open,
and Black Rod entered. The third Parliament was at
an end.

Charles had failed. The first breach with the Commons
had widened through three years : the Petition of Right
had only pasted paper over the crack, and now it was
irreparable. In a long and very able proclamation he
stated his case, not altogether unfairly. He claimed to
have expended all his energy on the war and every penny
he possessed, while the Commons disgraced England and
betrayed the Protestant cause. They had blamed all evil
on to Buckingham, but redoubled their efforts against
Royal servants when Buckingham was dead. They had
dealt unjustly with him in the matter of the Customs.
When they had at last voted a subsidy, their factious
example had encouraged the local assessors to collect it
dishonestly and corruptly, robbing the Exchequer. Meanwhile the Commons had interfered with the proper working
of administration, kept Customs officials hanging round
the House for a month, committed the Sheriff of London
to the Tower ; they had nosed their way among Treasury
officials, called the Attorney-General to order, destroyed
the prestige of the judges. Finally, they had fouled their
own nest by causing riot in the House. The " many
religious, grave, and well-minded men " in the Commons
had been " overborne by the practices and clamours of
the others." Delinquents would be punished. Meanwhile
let England, instead of magnifying her few grievances,

compare her happy lot to the misery of the Continent, trust her King to maintain Justice, Liberty, and the Gospel, and be thankful to God for " the great peace and quietness which every man enjoyeth under his own vine and fig-tree."

The threatened punishments were few and mild. It is sometimes said that the Tudors succeeded where the Stewarts failed because Tudor rule was based on the consent of England. But Elizabeth had had to imprison members of the Commons, and one died in prison, though he has never been acclaimed as a martyr to liberty. And the Tudors, finding their chief opponents among the Peers, had been able to kill the bolder of them in great number. Charles himself shrank from bloodshed, his opponents from incurring proved treason (though that had not saved some of Henry VIII's victims), and no one was put to death for politics until Parliament killed Strafford. It was Civil War and the Restoration which began a new age of executions.

Charles contemplated nothing extreme, and got himself into difficulties by trying to preserve legality and uphold the Petition of Right. The effort put him technically in the wrong and involved, for the second time, the dismissal of a judge. The prisoners, charged in Star Chamber with " conspiracy to bring government into contempt," were transferred to the ordinary law courts : they denied that any court had jurisdiction over things said and done in Parliament. Four were fined ; imprisonment awaited only those responsible for the last disturbance in Parliament, and submission, with an acknowledgment of error, meant release. Two refused to give it, and remained eleven years in prison ; Holles escaped abroad ; Eliot, most defiant and most high-minded, was released by death, no doubt hastened by imprisonment. Between Eliot and Charles there could be no peace. Eliot had been Buckingham's friend, and Buckingham had launched him on his career. He had turned against his patron, for good motives or evil, called him poisoner, attempted his impeachment. Eliot's death was the signal for one of the rare acts of cruelty in Charles's life. When young Eliot asked leave to take his father's remains to the family resting-place in Cornwall, his petition was endorsed with the words: " Lett Sir John Eliot be buried in the Churche of that parishe where he dyed." Eliot sleeps in the Tower, with Ralegh and Anne Boleyn.

And meanwhile the doors of St. Stephen's Chapel were locked, and for eleven long years they saw no debatings except in the parliament of spiders and of mice.

CHAPTER TEN

PORTRAIT OF A KING

1600-49

ENGLAND was to be ruled by her King. There was no law to compel him to call another Parliament, only ancient custom which he had decided for the present to defy. Some men thought he was merely waiting until circumstances changed and fresh elections were likely to provide a less obstructive majority in the Commons. Others suspected him of hoping that oblivion would creep over the whole idea of Parliament and open the way for despotism. Probably Charles had no consistent plan in the matter. But whatever his intentions, or even his character, they were still a puzzle to the majority of his subjects. England was ruled by an enigma.

The passing of three centuries, the ebb and flow of hostile prejudices, have obscured rather than cleared up the mystery. King Charles's character is still a matter of debate, far more so than that of his fascinating son. One may value Charles II high or low, one cannot doubt what manner of man he was ; but estimates of Charles I differ beyond hope of reconciliation. It is worth while going a long way round to arrive at some firm picture. It may emerge from a study of the King during his unparliamentary years.

The best side of him appears in his relations with wife and children. His quarrels with Henrietta were all forgotten ; they were fast friends as well as lovers. She had escaped a considerable danger, about the time of the French peace treaty. A child was expected, but something was going amiss. Henrietta's attendants attributed the

147

trouble to her insistence on walking everywhere, instead of taking a coach. Then she was badly scared by her dogs suddenly beginning to fight in her room. She was brought to bed prematurely. Charles implored the physicians to save her at any cost ; he might have another heir, never such another wife. The child came into the world, to live only two hours. But Henrietta was safe.

A year later, the heir was born. Henrietta was extremely proud of him, though she had to admit him dark and ugly ; and he was " very serious in all he does." Such was the first woman's appraisement of King Charles II, at the tender age of one. Her trouble with him later was that he refused to take medicine. Little Charles was to have two brothers and three sisters, and the whole family was united by a very strong affection. It is perhaps significant that jars did not begin to divide them nor Henrietta to show an unpleasing side of her nature until her husband was in the grave.

Charles was happy not only in his family but also in his relations with every sort of artist. There have been many kings who have patronized art from a sense of duty or ostentation, few to do so from real kinship and under-standing of artists.

He was fond of the theatre, but unfortunate in his period. Like so much else, the theatre had decayed during his father's reign ; there was a growing insistence on the inessentials of costume and decoration, and Inigo Jones was almost as important a figure as the dramatists. Ben Jonson survived through the first ten years of the reign, but his best work was done. Webster and Ford still wrote good tragedies, but they worked along a narrower, more morbid groove than Shakespeare. The comic writers lost gusto and virility without losing lewdness. They were still interested in the great emotion which makes men and women share a lifetime, and not preoccupied with the instinct that brings them together for a night. But they lacked the gay wit and adamantine style whereby the

Restoration dramatists were to make that instinct a matter of enduring artistic importance.

There were few great names in music : Orlando Gibbons died while composing music for Henrietta's welcome to England ; there were William and Henry Lawes, and a Mr. John Cooper, disguised, after the manner of his profession, as Signior Giovanni Coperario. But we boasted of being a musical nation, the standard of execution seems to have been high, and music was more of a habit among rich and poor than it has been in succeeding centuries. Charles, something of a connoisseur, did much to encourage good music in the churches. It was here that Puritanism was beginning to oppose it. Charles was perhaps all the less sympathetic to opposition for being excellently served in his own royal chapels and ignorant of the distracting effect of less able performers in the village choir. But, being the man he was, he could hardly fail to dislike the spirit which inspired the attack. It was to grow more powerful after his death, and end in the nineteenth century (it is hard to believe it nowadays) with one religious community expelling a girl for taking lessons in the piano.

But it is as a lover of painting that Charles remains really remarkable, and unrivalled among English kings. Contemporary rivals he certainly had, among them Richelieu and King Philip. Like them, Charles had agents all over Europe, and competition was brisk, though the prices paid were inconsiderable by the standards of a modern auction-room. At home his chief adviser was a Dutchman called Gerbier, who had once served Buckingham and attempted to educate Buckingham's erratic taste. It was to Buckingham that Gerbier wrote in praise of collecting pictures and against " those facetious folk who say it is money cast away on shadows. I know that they will be pictures still, when those ignorants will be less than shadows." Gerbier was himself an artist (besides writing on political economy, the science of fortification, and the education of the young), and he painted a miniature of

11

King Charles. Charles employed him also as an ambassador, at first to treat with Rubens, later with evil consequences : for Gerbier sold his master's secrets for gold.

The royal collection, in an age when reputations were
less fixed, was resplendent with famous names. Mantegna's
and Giorgione's recur often in the catalogue. The greatest
prizes were seven Raphael cartoons, still the property of
England.[1] But there is no doubt where Charles's heart
lay—partly with Correggio of Parma, more with the great
Venetians ; his collection of Titian and Tintoretto was
unequalled. Such a taste is perhaps characteristic of a
mind not so much interested in the world that is as in the
splendours of the world as it should be. But Charles was
founding an English tradition ; we have always cared more
for colour than for form, as well as shown more talent in
manipulating it ; for nearly two centuries after Charles,
most Englishmen looked on Venice as the centre of the
artistic world.

Most collectors hanker for the service of some living
artist, and kings can be choosers. James had employed
Mytens, not without great talents, though he could make
nothing of Prince Charles but a stiff picture of a stiff and
gawky youth. Now Mytens was growing old. Charles,
delighted with Rubens's visit to England as Spanish
ambassador, tried to get him to stay as Court painter, and
gave him an English knighthood. But Sir Peter Paul
was loyal to Brussels and to his distant employer. At
home in Madrid, King Philip had something of a monopoly
in Velasquez. Charles wrote to Franz Hals, but Hals
was unwilling to leave the merry and boisterous life which
so scandalized the trim burghers of Haarlem. But Rubens
had suggested a young assistant of his own, Henry Vandyke.

It was a lucky choice. Vandyke had been in England
before, and James had rather inconsiderately set him to

---

[1] Cromwell saved them when Charles's collection was sold up by
Parliament. They are at present in the South Kensington Museum.

copy other men's pictures. Now a specimen of his growing powers convinced Mytens that he was superseded, and he asked for leave to go home and end his days in Holland. Vandyke was given a pension, a knighthood, and a house at Blackfriars. But for two short visits to the Continent, he stayed there for all that was left of his short life. Seldom has there been such loving sympathy between artist and patron. If Vandyke idealized his subjects (and little Princess Sophia accused him of flattering Aunt Henrietta) it was to paint a pæan in praise of refinement, breeding, and intelligence. There is something frail but very lovely in the world that Vandyke depicted in his portraits. It is the world in which King Charles moved, perhaps dangerously isolated from ugliness and stupidity. It still remains for any one who wishes to see his friends and family, a few of his enemies, his own haunting and haunted face.

Vandyke was thirty-three when he came to Blackfriars ; he had only nine years to live. He had always had poor health and was harassed by poverty and worries. When Charles asked why his pension and earnings could not keep him out of debt, Vandyke replied that he soon got rid of money in keeping " open table for his friends and open purse for his mistresses. Charles's remedy was a characteristic one : he and Henrietta put their heads together and decided to bring their friend into the paths of thrift and virtue by marrying him to a Scotswoman— Mary Ruthven, of ancient lineage. When Vandyke's latest mistress heard of the betrothal, she tried, in revenge, to stab and disable that cunning right hand by which his genius expressed itself. She failed, and disappears into oblivion. But within a year of marriage Vandyke was dying. Charles offered £1500 to any doctor who could save him, but none of them could earn the reward. Vandyke's gentle spirit passed away from an England already threatened with the shadow of Civil War.

After Charles, Vandyke's best friend had been the Earl of Arundel. This strange and restless creature, proud and self-important, curiously erratic in his culture, was never quite at home in England, perhaps not quite at home upon this planet. He had been a friend of Prince Henry, but something divided him from Charles. His taste in painting was too catholic to be fashionable, but he may have taught the King to appreciate the Dürers he gave him, the inherited Holbeins, the one Rembrandt in the royal collection. But the two men differed in their view of art, as in their temperament. Indeed, it is a sign of the period that men were much in doubt as to what was art and what was not. Both Charles and Arundel had grasped the notion, by no means self-evident to the contemporary Englishman, that pictures have an intrinsic standard of their own, apart from their value as records or their place in a scheme of decoration. Outside the sphere of painting, Arundel seems to have been caught in the stream of the later Renaissance, somewhat muddied by its taste for the merely curious. Though Arundel had fine taste, he is probably more responsible than any other man for the habit of collecting things of no practical use and doubtful artistry ; he plays his part in the actions and reactions which gradually transformed the sparse dignity of Elizabethan interiors into the huddled monstrosity of the Victorian drawing-room.

While Arundel collected foreign curios, England was doing excellent work in applied art, and the adornment of the things of everyday life. There was a high standard in costume and furniture ; in Charles's reign, and probably through his influence, heraldic design took a last turn for the better ; silver-work, shedding its Elizabethan extravagances, enjoyed an Indian summer, with the melting-pots of the Civil War already grinning for its destruction. Charles seems to have been happy in the company of craftsmen. Sir Philip Warwick draws a delightful picture of his conversing with them, as with scholars and artists, willing to learn and yet shedding fresh light on their problems himself, never differing from them without a modest apology and a statement of his reasons for disagreement.

Arundel's search for oddities produced one find, not in Italy but on his own Shropshire estates. The curio is known to history as " Old Parr," and he was brought up to London for King Charles to see. Parr never knew how old he was, but the neighbours and parish authorities dated him 1483. In actual fact he seems to have lived upwards of 130 years, and he was still jovial. Even in the presence of this remarkable feat Charles appears to have been obsessed with its moral aspects. " You have lived longer than other men," he said to Parr ; " what have you done more than they ? " Parr, refusing to be put out, replied that he had got a wench with child when he was over a hundred, and done public penance for the deed. He told the King about the dissolution of the monasteries, which he remembered perfectly. Asked what his own religion had been through a century of reform and counter-reform, he replied that it had always been the religion of the Government. " I came raw into the world," he said, " and I count it no point of wisdom to be broiled out of it." But his common sense was not proof against the temptations of being a lion in London. Vandyke painted his portrait, and made an Old Testament prophet of him ; but in a few months he had gone out of the world, still raw. Dr. Harvey, discoverer of the circulation of the blood, was among Charles's protégés, and had the run of the royal parks for zoological research : now he was allowed to conduct a post-mortem on old Parr. He diagnosed " change of air " as the chief cause of death, but added a rider that the rich foods and late hours of London had something to do with Parr's belated demise.

Among such pleasant and curious paths we have perhaps strayed too far from the high road. A king's first business is to govern men. It is time to ask why this excellent husband and father, this patron of enlightenment, and friend of artists, had such ill-fortune in his kingship.

It has been assumed by those who study nothing but his politics that Charles was a stupid man—too narrowly stupid even to know when he was in the wrong.   This over-simplified theory has been made to fit the broad, political facts : it is applied to them unswervingly—though not without   difficulties — through   the   many   volumes   of Gardiner's great history.   It is hard to reconcile with all we know of the King's private life ; and there is another more serious difficulty.   It is contradicted by the recorded opinion of contemporaries.   Some hated him, a few, especially in his later days of suffering, came to love him dearly.   His enemies call him crafty and tyrannical, the less well-informed thought him frivolous and even cruel. No one suggests he was unintelligent.

The impression of those who met him is rather an opposite one.   He was shy, and men expected to find him stiff and uninteresting.   They spoke with him and found that the reverse was true.

It is probable that his mind, like his body, was late in developing.   It was said, when he was twenty-three, that the ride to Madrid had begun to make a man out of a back-ward youth.   Born to a position which demands quick decisions, he seems to have been cursed with the critical mind.   For a scholar and a lover of art, he writes a curi-ously uncreative style, always clear (in an age of tortuous English), but seldom pleasing and very seldom eloquent. He was always strong in argument, but particularly so in picking out the weak spots in an adversary's case.   It is possible that he saw, only too clearly, the weak spots in his own, for it had the essential weakness of everything uncreative.   He had no way of opposing the innovations of his enemies except by appealing to an ancient machinery of government which their manœuvrings were making unworkable.   If he felt such a weakness, he may also have felt that a king cannot afford to entertain such thoughts, and grown into a habit of crushing them down, and clinging desperately to the knowledge that his own intentions were

excellent, that events would one day justify them. The
suggestion is made for what it is worth. It would reconcile some apparent inconsistencies.

To say that he failed to recognize the signs of the times
is to beg the question. To say that he underrated the
importance of Parliament is to read history backwards.
On the Continent the signs of the times pointed to a decay
of parliaments, and it would have been a bold prophet
who could be sure that the English Crown would not
defeat its Parliament's claim to sovereignty. Indeed, it
is possible that Charles could have done so, but for a smaller
but a real miscalculation in Scottish affairs, due to ignorance
of conditions in Scotland. Parliament has now been sovereign for so long that we regard its advance as inevitable.
It would make for a fairer estimate of Charles if we could
forget the last three centuries of history and try to recapture
the atmosphere in which he lived. He shared his error—
if it be an error—with the greatest mind that this country
has produced. Shakespeare was only thirty-six years older
than Charles, and it was in Shakespeare's England that
Charles grew to manhood. Shakespeare wrote much on
political themes, yet he seems to see deliberative assemblies
merely as instruments used by great men for personal ends.
Charles, after an experience of three Parliaments, came to
a similar conclusion, and regarded those personal ends as
something it was his duty to resist. No doubt there were
other and better forces working alongside the evil ones, as
Charles himself expressly recognized. But he thought the
institution as a whole was more of a national danger than
an inspiration. He was perhaps wrong. But if the reader
thinks his view as groundless and as criminally ignorant
as it is sometimes represented, this book will have been
written in vain.

If there is something to be said for Charles's general
principles, contemporary evidence supplies one excellent
reason for his many practical mistakes. Clarendon and
Bulstrode say that, though his judgment was sound, the

King distrusted it himself, and yielded to the opinion of minds inferior to his own. Enemies say the same. St. John told a Presbyterian friend that "the King had an unhappiness in adhering and unweariedly pursuing the advices of others, and mistrusting his own." Cromwell is more brutally frank ; if Charles had trusted his own judgment, he said, he would have fooled them all.[1]

It is perhaps permissible to follow the modern fashion and trace this weakness to a very early source. Charles's childhood was an unfortunate one. He was cursed with a stammer, for years he was almost a cripple ; the comparison of his own lot with that of his luckier brother would help to destroy self-confidence, while an innate fastidiousness and love of virtue isolated him in James's vulgar, boisterous, and immoral Court. The death of his brother, the departure of his sister to foreign lands, coincided with the coming of a new fear—the fear of a great responsibility, looming nearer as his father grew old. Then Buckingham dawned upon him, splendidly self-confident ; a rather lonely heart opened up to an undreamt-of affection, a new hold upon life. His idol was far from flawless, but Charles's nature, desperately loyal, refused to acknowledge the flaws, and turned bitterly against those who tried to make the most of them. When they became too obvious to be ignored, Charles had already formed the habit of relying on outside advice. The shock of his friend's murder confirmed his opinion of his adversaries' wickedness, but could not make him self-reliant. He was by nature hasty. Many men have attained real greatness by acting solely on impulse. But Charles, cursed with the analytical mind, could not trust his own impulses. The moment he began to act, he began to doubt ; he drew back, listened to conflicting advice, floundered into contradictions, into apparent or real dishonesty. His whole mental and moral equipment was that of the scholar, the counsellor, the critic. In quieter times it might have seen him through a happy and

[1] Carte's *Ormond*, ii. p. 12, See Hume, vii. 519.

prosperous reign, until he bequeathed a not ill-governed kingdom to his adroiter, self-confident, less scrupulous son. It could not fit him to deal with the peculiar problems of his times. It destroyed English monarchy.

One more thing is needed to complete the picture. Charles has been accused of a lack of imagination, and the criticism seems unjust. Humour he certainly lacked, and the balance that goes with humour ; he was a Scotsman. But it might be truer to say that he was actually betrayed by an excess of imagination, especially in the days when he rode to Madrid to heal the strifes of Europe or, a few months later, pictured himself as the champion of Protestantism. When hard facts cured him of such dreams, his imagination began to play on a romantic conception of the Church and of himself as its rejuvenator. It is the one dream of King Charles which was and is a reality. If he could have seen modern England (with all its faults) plentifully supplied with churches in which a well-educated clergy worships God in the words of his beloved Prayer Book, more regularly and with greater ceremony than his own age permitted, he would ask indignantly why any one counted him a failure. It is the literary fashion to-day to sneer at the whole institution, and to talk loudly of empty churches without going to see how surprisingly full many of them are. The phase may pass. Meanwhile England has a Church and a ministry and sacraments ; the humble can always find what they seek ; and if the indifferent should one day turn back to the tradition upon which our whole civilization rests, they may be glad to find that tradition unbroken and surviving in forms which King Charles consecrated by his life-work and cemented with his blood.

CHAPTER ELEVEN

UNPARLIAMENTARY

1629-37

WHEN a king of Charles's virtues, vices, and aspirations begins to govern without Parliamentary check, the choice of ministers for Church and State becomes a matter of crucial importance. It was partly Charles's fault, partly his misfortune, that, apart from Laud and Wentworth, he was served by men of mediocre ability and uninspiring character. The majority of them do not seem to have been any more capable or honest than the men who exercise power in our own times. King James's rule had not been the sort to bring talent or virtue into places where it is noticed, and it had put a high premium on dishonest intrigue. It was said of Charles by one who knew him that "no temptation could dispose him to a wrongful action, except it was so disguised from him that he believed it to be just." The judgment is perhaps over-charitable. But certainly there were at Court too many experts in the fashioning of such disguises.

The department most free from these tamperings was the Church. Its nominal head was Archbishop Abbot, a man of strong principle and sterling worth, but inclined to lethargy, devoid of all charm and rather barren of intellect. He was nearly seventy, and very suspicious of anything reminiscent of Rome. Charles, unable to see eye to eye with him, was already relying on Laud, whom he had made Bishop of London. Laud's influence was all for a tightening of discipline in the Church, for enforcing regularity, efficiency, and certain not very extreme forms of ceremonial; men must kneel to receive Communion, the table must be at the east end (not in the nave for people to use as a hat-rack), and the clergymen must wear surplices. This campaign, and its political implications, is too important to be summarized here. We shall hear more than enough of it later.

Of the lay ministers, Weston the Treasurer was the most important. He had been a time-serving courtier of King James and a client of Buckingham : Charles accepted him for his ability with " resignation " rather than " affection." Henrietta detested him. He was unpopular, partly because his wife was a Papist ; he tried to make up for it by exacting strictly the Penal Law fines. He curried favour and insulted men by turns ; he was terrified of those he had offended. He was something of an old woman. Clarendon tells a good story of Weston promising to befriend a certain Mr. Cæsar, scribbling a memorandum about him and dropping it into his pocket ; weeks after he suddenly found a dirty scrap of paper marked " REMEMBER CÆSAR," and, failing to recognize his own writing, imagined that some amateur soothsayer was warning him against a plot of assassination ; he had barricaded his house, armed his servants, and proclaimed a state of siege, before he discovered the mistake. It is only fair to add that he used to tell the story against himself in later years.

Short of Middlesex, he was probably the best man who could be found for the routine of his unpopular office. With no Parliamentary subsidies, Charles had to " live of his own," and his own was meagre. Courtiers' pensions were cut to the bone ; many who had ruined themselves by lending money for the war were repaid slowly and in part only. It was an age of insufficient or nominal salaries, when officials and ambassadors expected unofficial pay in the form of monopolies or a grant of Crown lands. Many had grown rich in King James's time, and they still adorned Charles's Court, and kept the standard of extravagance woefully high. Holland and Carlisle astonished foreigners with their lavishness. The latter had absorbed much Crown land from King James, and married into the wealthy family of Percy ; his wife, Lucy Carlisle, was the reigning beauty of Charles's Court and knew how to spend. But to new courtiers, Charles could give little. A few made money by trade, some lost it in the same way. Most of them starved for luxuries and envied the established fortunes. Only Lord Treasurer Weston managed to build up a new one himself.

Weston had also a hand in the King's foreign policy, perhaps the worst blot on Charles's reputation as a ruler. It had no consistent principles except the now hopeless hankering to recover the Palatinate for his sister's family and a slowly growing recognition that France and Holland would soon be more powerful enemies than Spain. There was even a proposal to join Spain and help her reconquer the Dutch provinces. But nothing could be done, and Charles only humiliated himself while he painfully learnt the lesson that Europe could afford to despise a king without money and without an army. Nor were Charles's methods above the very low standard of contemporary diplomacy. It was one of his envoys, Sir Henry Wotton, who defined an ambassador as " a man sent abroad to lie for his Government."

The real need it was not in Weston, perhaps not in any one, to supply. The English Crown must remain a cipher abroad and in jeopardy at home, so long as an increasingly modern country was tied to a mediæval system of finance. Even Parliamentary subsidies were assessed on an anti- quated system, perfectly unfair in incidence, and giving every opportunity to assessors with an itching palm. In a time of rising prices and growing prosperity, a subsidy yielded less and less. Charles protested against the system, James had tried to get the whole finance of the country overhauled, but, quarrelling over details with the House of Commons, he had achieved nothing.

Now that Parliamentary grants had ceased, nearly

half the revenue came from Tonnage and Poundage.   The
merchants made bones about paying customs and appealed
to the late controversy in Parliament ; for a time some
refused to trade at all.   But growing prosperity and the
prospect of great gain soon dissuaded them.

The other half consisted of fines on criminals and
Roman Catholics, the so-called " tenths and first-fruits "
contributed by the clergy, and the proceeds of Crown
Lands.   The mediæval kings had held a large proportion
of English soil, granting it away to reward friends or
conciliate opponents, and recouping themselves from the
lands of those who died childless or were condemned for
treason.   James had made lavish grants, and there had
been no civil wars to extinguish the landowning families,
no attainders for treason such as had enriched the Tudors.
Only poor Ralegh died for treason, and he left nothing
but debts.

If Charles was tied to a mediæval system of finance,
he was determined to use every expedient which it suggested.   He revived an old law forcing all men of considerable income to accept knighthood, and pay the appropriate
fees.   He began to reclaim all the forest land that had
been filched from the Crown since the early Middle Ages.
His servants and the lawyers carried out the process
harshly and defiantly, and he must be blamed for not
checking them.[1]   Titles that had held good for three
centuries were now called in question ; there was a constant
oscillation between the letter and the spirit of the law,
according as either might favour the case for the Crown.
Some of the sufferers became strong Parliamentarians,
and among them were the richest and most powerful in
England.

Finally, there was ship-money, the most notorious and
yet the most defensible of King Charles's measures.

England needed a fleet.   Her coasts and her trade were
at the mercy of pirates, Moorish or Christian.   Our safety

---

[1] D'Ewes (2. 136) puts all the blame on the judges and juries.

was threatened by the new navy that Richelieu was building in France.   The Dutch were already strong at sea ; they were carrying on war in our neutral waters, driving Englishmen from their ancient fishing-grounds, even landing to dry their nets in England and shooting at any one who tried to disturb them.   To such a situation the mediæval notion, that naval protection was merely a matter for the coastwise districts, was quite inapplicable.   Inland towns had naturally resisted the attempts to tax them for the upkeep of the navy : it was seventy years now since Hull had tried to make the Yorkshire manufacturing towns contribute, thirty-five since she had succeeded, thanks to the Council for the North.   Charles took the decisive step : he turned ship-money, a local and sporadic levy, into a general tax on the whole country.   There was opposition, first in London where it was least excusable, later in inland shires.   But it died down or was overcome. Hampden was not yet ready with his protest.

One point about ship-money is often missed.   It was used to build ships.   The accounts are extant and they show that, apart from one small loan to the military garrison of Berwick when the Scots invaded, every penny raised during the reign went to the navy.   It was not spent wisely—too much on laying down new vessels, like the magnificent *Sovereign of the Seas*, not enough on ensuring efficiency and honesty ; the sailors were still shockingly treated.   But ship-money laid the foundations for a real renaissance in the navy, overdue since before the Armada. If the firm of Blake Brothers, Bridgwater merchants, grumbled at the amount of ship-money they had to pay, its senior partner may have been glad in later years that King Charles had provided him with so many stout ships to lead against Van Tromp.

It would have been a hard matter to enforce ship-money, forest enlargement, or the knighthood fines without the support of the lawyers.   As a body they had begun to come round to the King's side after the dissolution of the

third Parliament. Coke had gone into retirement at Stoke
Poges, and died there in 1634. But Noy, an opponent of
the Crown, was bought outright and became Attorney-
General, merely asking what his salary would be. Speaker
Finch, whom Holles had held down in the chair, became a
royal partisan and was to be Chief Justice. Others followed,
and it became the fashion in the Westminster Courts to
see how far the law could be wrenched in the King's favour.
Charles probably lost more than he gained from his fair-
weather friends, most of whom deserted him again in the
day of need. Meanwhile they made his cause unpopular
by parading their partiality and coupling many a sound
legal judgment with provocative speeches about an illimit-
able Prerogative and the wickedness of resistance.

One grievance against the Crown they never surrendered.
They remained jealous enemies of the Prerogative Courts.
Star Chamber they dared not attack, nor the Archbishop's
High Commission, to which came not only ecclesiastical
cases but many matters of inheritance, marriage, and
public morals. But they maintained the old war with the
Council for the North, and they had many allies.

The Council for the North had fallen on evil days. Its
cheap, swift decisions still attracted litigants, and it decided
cases on a system distasteful to Westminster. Westminster
and its judges on circuit retorted with writs of prohibition,
calling cases out of the Council's jurisdiction ; and they
were winning in the contest.

Two things hampered the Council. It was not only a
law court, it was also the instrument whereby the Crown
kept the northern gentry active in their local duties, as
did the Privy Council in the rest of England. It had to
see that they levied rates upon themselves and administered
them efficiently on roads and bridges, the militia drills, the
relief or employment of the poor. It had to supervise the
decisions of justices of the peace, stop unjust enclosures of
common land, detect fraud, and prevent forms of profit-
making that were damaging to the community. In pro-

portion as it was active, it was unpopular among the rich. In the West Riding, where clothiers were destroying their own trade by fraudulently stretching the cloth (France had began to prohibit its import), the justices refused to court unpopularity by enforcing the law, and the Council had to take the odium on itself.

Secondly, internal corruption was at work, greatly increased since the Elizabethan tradition of officialdom gave way to Jacobean scandals. One President of the Council fixed a kind of tariff by which men could buy a seat at his board and recoup themselves with bribes. He had found on his land deposits of alum (needed by the clothiers), and handled the production in truly modern style. A monopoly was purchased and a company formed to exploit it with high prices ; when it ceased to pay, the shareholders put the business into so-called Government hands and drew salaries, while the losses fell on public funds. Finally, the Council for the North came into the hands of the Savile family, country gentry with clothing interests, at feud with the Wentworths. The alum scandal continued, reinforced by corrupt bargains with the Papists in the matter of penal-law fines. The Saviles had obtained Buckingham's ear, and though Buckingham does not seem to have shared in the plunder, they did as they liked.

There was one person both willing and competent to set matters straight, and that was Lord Wentworth. He was soon to have a seat in the Privy Council, and the result was a series of orders making for good government and the protection of the poor.[1] Meanwhile he was warmly welcomed at York as President of the Council for the North. In his inaugural speech he challenged the lawyers' writs of prohibition as a " bleeding evil " from which the Council was slowly dying. He appealed for a truce to local feuds in the name of decent government. He assured his hearers that the Crown was their best safeguard against

[1] See Gardiner, vii. 160.

local oppression. Perhaps some memory of his father's last words strengthened that side of his nature that was always "pityfull to the poor." " I do here offer myself," he said, " an instrument for good in any man's hand. He that useth me most hath most of my heart, even to the meanest man within the whole jurisdiction."

Wentworth might beg for a truce to old feuds, but the North was not likely to respond, and he was soon making new enemies on all sides. He had most of the qualities that attract enmity—a hot temper and a haughty manner, inflexible honesty, contempt for laziness, hatred for every backstairs way of making money. " Justice without respect for persons " has been called his motto. The work was tough, for the North was a curious mixture of the modern and the primitive. On the one hand the clothing interest of the West Riding was against him. On the other were turbulent noblemen like Lord Eure, who got into debt and refused his creditors satisfaction until Wentworth brought up artillery from Scarborough to enforce their claims. There was Sir John Bourchier, an old alum profiteer, who had to be imprisoned for breaking down the King's fences on land recently adjudged Royal Forest. Wentworth persuaded the King to release him after six months. In eight years, Bourchier was giving hostile evidence at Wentworth's trial ; in sixteen he had put his signature to the death-warrant of King Charles.

Wentworth went on his way. He stopped a campaign of slander against himself, made successful sallies against the encroachments of the Westminster courts, supported the levy of ship-money, knighthood fines, and forest enlargement, bullied the gentry into doing their work. He accused them of " observing a superior command no farther than they liked themselves, and of questioning any profit of the Crown . . . which might help it to subsist of itself." If he made friends to balance his enemies they were not among the rich and powerful. We only know

12

that when his wife died, the whole city of York extended its sympathy and wore "a face of mourning." But Wentworth cared little for popularity or unpopularity. The next work to which the King appointed him was to earn him more enemies still.

Such were the men, some bad, some good, through whom Charles governed his kingdom for eleven unparliamentary years. Their virtues and vices must be his responsibility. No doubt they did many things without his knowledge, exceeded instructions, and, especially in the law courts, became *plus royaliste que la roi*. No doubt he often wished he could find better men to work for him. But there is no doubt of his general approval ; he always resented the suggestion that subordinates, not the King, were responsible for Crown policy. Loyalty or obstinacy made him protect his servants, as he had protected Buckingham long after his predecessors would have thrown him to the dogs. It is the tragedy of his life that, when the crisis came, he had to sacrifice the noblest of all his servants, and the manner of that sacrifice did him more harm than good.

Dr. Johnson, sacramentally speaking the last of the Cavaliers, said that a Government should be judged by the provision it makes for the poor. From such a test Charles's Government emerges with great credit. The poor law established by Elizabeth seems to have worked tolerably well, especially in relieving the infirm and disabled. It received a new vitality in King Charles's reign from the energy of his Privy Council ; it extended, with excellent effect, the provision for finding employment for the ablebodied. The whole system fell to pieces during the Civil Wars. Cromwell revived its efficiency for a time, but a harsher and more irresponsible spirit was already growing. The Puritan triumph coincided with the extinction of that mediæval and Catholic spirit that links poverty with saintliness and makes its relief a religious duty. By the time the Restoration came to continue the weakening of central government, poverty was well on its way to becoming a crime.[1]

In order to ensure that the gentry should attend not only to poor relief but to all their duties in central government, Charles checked their growing habit of living in London houses and becoming useless figures in a useless " Society." Those who held no Court appointment were driven back to their estates and their work by heavy fines.

At the same time Charles maintained his predecessors' policy of forbidding jerry-building in London, and even the repair of old houses with cheap materials. A petition from his first Parliament for the relaxation of this rule is one of the few that he met with a direct negative. More interesting, in view of the future, was the incident of the Dutchman who erected a mechanical sawmill in 1634, and was told to take it down again, as it was creating unemployment among the sawyers. Two other measures link Charles's reign more directly with our own. He was the first to license a regular service of London cabs, though noise and congestion soon forced him to limit them. He founded the Post Office, by turning the royal system of dispatch riders into a public post and instituting regular mails to Scotland, Plymouth, Holyhead, and the Continent. When we grumble for our penny post we might remember that our ancestors in Charles's reign had to pay nearly a shilling for each hundred miles.

There is one instance in which Charles set his face against an ancient horror, apparently growing worse in Protestant countries, certainly intensified by King James's peculiar views. The persecution of witches was perhaps the most hideous feature of contemporary life, and James, bitten with superstitious terror in his Scottish youth, encouraged the practice in all his kingdoms. Most men believed in the reality of witchcraft and the duty of stamp-

[1] See E. M. Leonard, *Early History of English Poor Relief,* and M. James, *Social Problems during the Puritan Revolution,* pp. 15–20.

ing it out : [1] many women confessed, apparently under no pressure, to Satanic intercourse. But others, undoubtedly innocent, were abominably tortured into confession : others, protesting innocence, were convicted on evidence shamefully flimsy and patently prejudiced. Against one batch of seven poor wretches in Lancashire, a boy had been allowed to bear witness who afterwards confessed that he had done it to save himself from a scolding for being late in bringing the cows home. The women were denied counsel, and one complained that a high wind outside and the noise of many spectators prevented her even hearing the evidence against her. Before the Privy Council heard of the case, three of the victims had died in prison and one was dying. The remaining three were brought to London, admitted to an interview with the King, and provided with a pardon. They seem to have been kept in prison, perhaps to save them from lynching by the people. A year later the Bishop rescued two more from condemnation and death.

Charles made a bolder and more general stand against an institution peculiar to extreme Protestantism—the Puritan Sabbath. It was generally agreed that nobody should work on Sunday : the Puritans were trying to see that nobody should play. They pointed to the amount of drunkenness and ribaldry that Sunday entailed, they even got one judge to defy the King's orders, prohibit Sunday " wakes " or festive gatherings, and order clergymen to read his prohibition in church. The judge was severely reprimanded. Meanwhile Charles republished " The Declaration of Sports " which his father had written but practically retracted. It forbade any one to discourage people from dancing, archery, " leaping, vaulting, or any such harmless recreation." Charles pointed out that Puritan activities were justifying the Papists when they

---

[1] Any one who has read of the poisoning and child murder among the witches of Paris in Louis XIV's time will agree that there was something in the orthodox view.

called Protestantism a religion of gloom ; that whatever the rich might think, the poor had only their Sundays for recreation ; that nothing could so increase drunkenness on Sunday as the prohibition of sports. His opponents had to win a civil war before they could have their way. They are perhaps innocent of later follies, and that boxing of the compass on the Fourth Commandment which denied any pleasure on Sunday, but doubled the servants' work with vast family luncheons. But there is still a witness against the Puritans in the youths who kick their heels in mischievous idleness and tell each other smutty stories at the street corners and village greens of what was once Merrie England.

The ideas that Charles attacked had many sincere if narrow advocates. A few were glad to suffer for their faith. Whether it was wise to punish them is very doubtful : it is often represented as the worst mistake Charles made. Undoubtedly the whole business is often exaggerated.[1] Branding and mutilation were the ordinary instruments of local government. J.P.s used them constantly to punish the poor. Much of the opposition to Charles's policy arose from their use against the well-to-do and the educated. Even so the cases are far fewer than is generally implied. In fifteen years there were barely half a dozen.

The first was Dr. Gill, a schoolmaster at St. Paul's, who had said, with libellous detail, that Charles was fitter to be a Cheapside shopkeeper than a king. He lost his orders as a clergyman and his place at school. He was condemned to be fined and have his ears cut off, but these sentences were immediately cancelled, and the King signed a free pardon. Gill was followed by Dr. Leighton, whose book (printed in Holland to escape censorship) was held to suggest civil war, and certainly referred to bishops

---

[1] For a really unpardonable instance of misrepresentation, I recommend the reader to a certain incident in Mr. Drinkwater's play on Oliver Cromwell.

as " the trumpery of Antichrist " and to Queen Henrietta as " a daughter of Heth." He was sentenced to fine, imprisonment, branding, and the cropping of both ears. Again there seems to have been an intention to remit the corporal punishment, but Leighton defeated it by escaping from prison. He was recaptured and half the sentence executed.

Finally, there was William Prynne. He had been warned before for his controversial writings, and in 1634 he brought out a colossal tome called *Histriomastix*, a wholesale assault on the theatre. He was accused of libelling the Queen, then busy with preparations for a new play at Court. His sentence was the same as Leighton's ; it was executed in full ; it seems barbarously extreme. It is clear that the Court was not only striking at a libeller but at a whole system of thought—if it can be called thought—which represents not only acting as a mortal sin, but also dancing, keeping Christmas, lighting bonfires, and even " dressing up houses with green ivy."

The sentence did not, at the time, seem to be a mistake. Its brutality was not in question : Prynne had urged similar punishments for actors, with hanging for those who persevered in their wicked profession. There is no evidence of popular indignation, and Prynne's fellow-lawyers declared their approval of the sentence by inviting Charles and Henrietta to a play at the Inns of Court. The only protest was against the humiliation being inflicted on a man of position, because " neither his academical nor barrister's gown " could save him. Nevertheless, it is generally a mistake to provide opponents with a martyr. Prynne had some of the stuff from which martyrs are made : he was to persevere, to be arraigned again and suffer, amid great indignation, with two companions, before he ended his curious life as keeper of the Tower archives, antiquary, and friend of Charles II.

Meanwhile the King had three kingdoms to rule, and six or seven millions of men. If he punished a few Puritans, the ghastly executions of Catholic priests were dying out, while most of Europe was still alive with persecution.   For one reason or another, we were at peace, while the Continent was racked with the most terrible of all wars. The wealth of England was increasing steadily.   Whatever Charles's motives, his unparliamentary government was resulting in attempts to distribute that wealth with some approach to fairness, certainly to demand a *quid pro quo* from the rich in the form of service to the community. There was opposition, and men jibbed at the yoke, some for evil motives, some on high principle.   There was no sign of general disloyalty, still less of civil war.   Three things must happen before that danger could threaten— in Ireland, in Scotland, and in Lambeth Palace.

CHAPTER TWELVE

THREE KINGDOMS

1633–35

GEOGRAPHY plays cruel jokes on mankind, and perhaps its cruellest was to place the English and Irish on adjacent islands. It may have been necessary for us to conquer Ireland ; it has been easy to achieve a partial conquest ; sometimes, with greater effort, we have made it complete. Before the resultant hatreds can die away, we are confronted with the insoluble problem of governing a people whose idea of government, whose sense of right and wrong, differs radically from our own. Assuming our own standards to be superior, we have generally attempted to enforce them. We have recently abandoned the attempt after seeing the situation go from farce to the deepest tragedy. The seventeenth century refused to make such a surrender, though its task was harder. Tudor conquest and repression had been unscrupulous and unspeakably savage, leaving terrible legacies of hatred. Psychological divergences were more pronounced, and the colour of contemporary politics made religious difference more mischievous. The conquerors, assuming that they represented a higher civilization, thought that they had nothing to learn from Ireland. The best of them could see no way to help her but by forcing her to become English. The worse were making this doubtful task an impossible one by demonstrating how greedy, how unscrupulous, and how surprisingly cruel an Englishman can be. The jest was at its grimmest.

The official remedy for Ireland's woes was " plantation," the destruction of tribal ownership, the substitution of private property on the English model, with a high proportion of English landowners. It was an unwise method for recommending a higher civilization. A learned Victorian once described English land law as " the most unmitigated nonsense ever put together by the perverted ingenuity of man." But perverted ingenuity enabled us to jockey Irishmen out of their land and replace them by honest, god-fearing Protestants. The process affected huge districts, reducing thousands to beggary or dependence. And England sent over too many Protestants who had neither honesty in them nor the fear of God. The black sheep of respectable families, the leaders of disreputable ones, became the landowners of Ireland.

For there was money to be made by the ingenious. Richard Boyle, a clever lawyer of shady reputation, had landed in Dublin with a hundred pounds and was now Earl of Cork, holding more land than any one in Ireland. He had even found profit in the Protestant Church. While the vaults of Dublin cathedral were wine and tobacco shops, and its Communion table a seat for servants and apprentices, while another church was a stable, another a tennis court (with the parson as marker), Lord Cork had bought up a large number of curacies, appointed curates at £25 a year, and kept £275 apiece for himself. He had put a relation into Lismore bishopric, and farmed its revenues, paying £100 and pocketing £5000. He drew £500 a year for repairing the cathedral, and the cathedral was ruinous.

The double process of robbing the Irish of their land and the English Church of its money was going on in a country barely recovered from the Elizabethan method of reconquest—systematic starvation of whole counties, and no quarter for those who surrendered. Some would have pushed the business to its logical conclusion, the extinction of the Irish race. King James had tried to reintroduce Christianity into the hardened hearts of the settlers, and perhaps he did a little good. But his governors could hardly expect to rule with gentleness and scrupulous legality. Of Lord Deputy Falkland, left as a legacy to Charles, there were ugly stories. Charles ordered an inquiry into his method of "planting" Wicklow; he was told that the lawyers had indicted a Wicklow magnate for conspiracy; that some of them hoped for a share of his land; that they had extracted their evidence from condemned felons by a promise of pardon, and from one unwilling Irishman by the simple expedient of putting him on a red-hot grid. Falkland, perhaps innocent himself, protested against inquiry and was removed. There was delay in finding a successor. One peer refused the work; he had been in Ireland before. Then Charles sent Wentworth.

Wentworth had just married again, and he liked his work at York, but he accepted the post. He made conditions—a free hand, no backstairs work at Whitehall, no places or pickings for courtiers. He brought two Yorkshiremen with him, one, Wandesford, to be the only Englishman for whose death the Irish raised a keening. He found the resident officials "a company of men the most intent on their own ends that ever I met with." The Government was Protestant, and it was strangling the Protestant Church with corruption. It had no right in Ireland but the right of conquest, and it was letting its army go to rack and ruin. Its revenue depended largely on trade, and trade was at the mercy of local pirates. Wentworth crossed the Irish Sea in safety, but the pirates got £2500 worth of his baggage. Lord Cork met him on the quay, all smiles and courtesy. Wentworth went up to Dublin Castle, reviewed the situation, and rolled up his sleeves.

The castle was mildewed and ruinous. The kitchen poured smoke into his study. Here he sat and watched an old lean horse outside the window, cropping the meagre grass while its legs sank slowly into bog; from time to time it struggled free and tried a new place. Wentworth was rich, and he built himself a new wing ; a careless Irish servant-girl left a scuttle of live coals under the stairs, and the new wing was burnt to the ground. Wentworth was finicky about writing materials, and decent paper could not be bought in Dublin. He was a heavy smoker, and Irish tobacco was vile. His health was bad, his hair was growing grey, his shoulders stooped with too much office-work. But for the company of two little daughters he would have grown " very melancholy." He tried to cheer himself with a truly Irish hospitality, but could make few friends. He was discovering what scandals lay behind fine clothes and smiling faces, and he had come to cure them.

He made enemies by the score. The most dangerous, as time would show, was the City of London, which held great lands in Ulster under the terms of a recent plantation. Wentworth found those terms unfulfilled, and confiscated the land.

With Cork there was no chance of his agreeing. Cork was religious in his own odd way and believed that " it had pleased the Almighty, by His Divine Providence," to bring Lord Cork to Ireland. On his own estates he was a good landlord, developing, building, educating ; Cromwell was later to say that with a Lord Cork in every county there would have been no troubles. Wentworth saw only a heavy, paunchy man with unpleasantly drooping moustaches,[1] who had made a fortune out of other people's misery and was enjoying it, self-satisfied, in defiance of principle and decency. He managed somehow to avoid an open quarrel, even while he exposed Cork's peculations and wrested back some of the plunder of the Church. With another colleague, Mountnorris, he lost his temper completely. Mountnorris was a corrupt official, who would one day be secretary to Henry Cromwell. He had a mean habit of fleecing the young gentlemen of Dublin at cards.

[1] An anonymous portrait of 1631 is preserved at Marston. It is reproduced in Miss C. F. Smith's life of *Mary, Countess of Warwick.*

He was detected in considerable peculations. At the Council board he was an intolerable bore. Luckily he could not stay in the same room as a cat, and Wentworth used to get rid of him by bringing cats to Council. At last Wentworth could stand him no more. Some injudicious words of Mountnorris, uttered months ago, were construed into a charge of mutiny—for Mountnorris held a military commission. He was found guilty, and the regulations allowed no penalty but death. Wentworth immediately assured him there was no intention of executing the sentence. Indeed, this strangely contradictory despot ruled Ireland for seven years with a minimum of bloodshed. Mountnorris was released after a short imprisonment. But the sentence had implied dismissal from office, and Wentworth was hampered by him no more.

Meanwhile debts were being paid off, and the annual deficit became a surplus. Piracy was put down, trade flourished, the Ulster flax-industry was founded. The army became an army again, Wentworth's own troop being a model to the rest. The men were paid and provisioned, instead of " fetching in every morsel of bread upon their swords'-point," at the expense of peaceful citizens. The Church began to revive, Wentworth rating bishops for allowing the bloodsuckers to plunder them, and trying to make the parsons learn Irish so that they could talk intelligently to the Papists they were supposed to convert.

While Wentworth did all that energy and honesty could achieve, the real roots of the trouble lay untouched, and in places they struck deeper. A succession of Wentworths might conceivably have made Ireland English and Protestant and prosperous. One can only guess how much that is of benefit to humanity might have perished in the process. But there was only one Wentworth ; he had only seven years in Ireland, and he thought of her mainly as a pawn in the great game that involved three kingdoms. Wentworth was an Englishman ; his purpose, though honest, was an English one, and nothing that came from seventeenth-century England could cure the deeper evils of Ireland.

His methods varied from the unscrupulously drastic to the tyrannously unjust. In his own words, he found " a Crown, a Church, and a people spoiled. I could not imagine to redeem them from under the pressure with gracious smiles and gentle looks." The plea is good, but not quite good enough. He bullied and manipulated the Irish Parliament, and punished juries for verdicts given against the Crown. He broke one definite promise given by King Charles, the one promise that might have healed the breaking hearts of Irishmen—that titles to land should be no more disturbed. They had granted taxes on the understanding that this, among other " King's graces," should become law : it was the one reform that Wentworth stopped. His excuse was that existing titles based on robbery must be revoked in the name of justice. But he used the opening to plan a new plantation in Connaught. Its objects were economic development, spread of Protestantism, garrison against invasion. The same motives had been alleged to justify the worst rapacities of his predecessors' time. The new plantation was never carried out, but its planning was a direct breach of the royal pledge. Wentworth and Charles must share the guilt.

Charles has often been blamed for a rather guarded and unfriendly appreciation of Wentworth's work. Certainly he still held back the Earldom for which Wentworth petitioned, and he did one worse thing (though he promised never to repeat it) in allowing a large sum of Irish money to go into the pocket of a courtier. Two things must be remembered. Wentworth, as events were to prove, was one of the most dangerous of all servants, and Charles may well have been wise to suppress in public any enthusiasm he may have felt for his work. Secondly, Charles lived for years under a constant bombardment of grievances against Wentworth's high-handed honesty, of

Weston's intrigues to thwart him, of Henrietta's ill-concealed dislike and disapproval of his person and ideas. When Wentworth came home for his one holiday, knowing courtiers doubted what his reception would be. He read a long report to an impassive King. As he proceeded, Charles grew more encouraging and ended with unqualified approval. For the next few days, Wentworth was the lion of the Court.

Two friends he had always had, and his correspondence with them, across the Irish Sea, was his one link with the more refined life to which he had been accustomed. One was Lucy Carlisle, whose beauty and brains gave her great influence. But a cold nature and disloyalty in her friendships made her an inspiration rather than a source of comfort.

His other friend, whose influence with the King may have done much to balance that of Weston and Henrietta, was Bishop Laud. His correspondence with Wentworth was naturally full of congratulation on the rescue of the Irish Church. But the bond between the two went deeper. They had the same mind in their different work. Both took " Thorough " for their motto, both detested lethargy, inefficiency, and self-seeking. They summed up their hatreds in the nickname " Lady Mora," my Lady Delay, with which they christened Weston. Weston died, but in other forms his spirit was still active. They thought it mere weakness in the King that allowed Lady Mora to clog his administration. They were perhaps right, though they may have underestimated the task of expelling her. They may also have underestimated that grain of worldly wisdom in Weston's methods and the King's tolerance. Without Lady Mora as passenger, Laud and Wentworth might have made the chariot of State roll with half the friction and twice the impetus. Aiming at the stars, they might have landed their master even sooner in the ditch.

The two were as different in origin as in outward aspect. Wentworth's face, dark, proud, and dynamic, is unmistakably an aristocrat's ; Vandyke gives all his sitters the same lovely hands, but with Wentworth's he may have been accurate, for even Henrietta commented on their beauty. There was nothing aristocratic about his friend. Twenty years before Wentworth's birth, a respectable clothier's widow in Reading married a second respectable clothier, and their only child was William Laud. He was sixty before Vandyke painted him, and even Vandyke cannot hide the resemblance to a provincial schoolmaster with a faint air of surprise at the wickedness of the world. He was more learned than his friend, as befitted his calling ; a professorship he founded at Oxford still testifies to his interest in Arabic. He was of tiny stature, inclined to fuss, inclined to be irritable. He was one of the few great Churchmen who never commanded the affection or allegiance of women. He was something of a saint, while Wentworth had some very human failings. He was utterly ignorant of the courtier's art. He never forgave himself a sin of his youth, when he presided at the marriage of a divorced woman to please a patron. He cared less than Wentworth for ease or money, and shared his hatred for slackness and self-seeking, his love of order and discipline. Both looked to the Crown as the safeguard against all evils : neither wished it to be above the law or act with arbitrary tyranny, but, while Wentworth always believed that Parliament could be led or driven into the service of good government, Laud referred to it as " that noise." In a sense, the Crown betrayed them, because, though they did not realize it, only despotism could have made their programme possible, and Charles refused to be a despot. Neither could see any divergence between the interests of the Crown and the interests of the English people, and both died for their narrow but not ignoble faith. Wentworth's work perished with him, and for two centuries England was a paradise for all he hated. Much of Laud's remains to this day.

The Roman Catholics maintain that a country which

breaks from Rome has taken the first step on a road that ends with the rejection of Christianity. One cannot argue with people who think in centuries and particularly in future centuries. But one can recognize the peculiar perils of Protestantism : they were underrated by Laud's contemporaries, who felt that political oppression of Papists and envenomed denunciations of Rome would preserve them from reconquest, and were unconscious of the opposite danger—the possibility that the great message of Christianity might be so confused with dialectic, so watered down to suit individual tastes, as to be powerless in a later generation. Laud thought in a more disciplined, perhaps a narrower way ; we are in violent reaction to his ideas to-day, and can see little except the failure of their exponents to adjust themselves to the pressure of modern problems ; but they are worth examination in the light of different conditions.

It is sometimes forgotten how far back his roots stretched. His father could probably remember Reading as a mere adjunct to a great monastery. He himself lived thirty years under Elizabeth. He went up to an Oxford resounding with barren disputes between cliques of self-satisfied Calvinists. While Sublapsarian argued with Superlapsarian and agreed only in denouncing the Scarlet Woman of Rome, the bishopric of Oxford was unfilled, and my Lord Essex pocketed its revenues. The English Church had reformed doctrine ; but while Rome reformed these incidental abuses that had brought the Reformation to a head, England was full of ruinous churches, drunken and loose-living parsons ; the poor could not understand theological controversy, and their souls were being lost by sheer slackness and corruption. It was to be the cardinal error of Laud's life that he always identified slackness and corruption with all forms of religious dispute and all revolt from orthodox Anglican doctrine. He never understood the later Puritans : he knew there was much that was merely lazy and stupid in their dislike for ceremony ; he did not realize that there also was burning conviction. When he became commander of the Church Militant, he could not tolerate arguing in the ranks : all were agreed on the fundamentals, and dispute about minor matters (whose decision was beyond the limits of the human mind) bred dissension and even mutiny in the face of the enemy. He never pretended to have an exclusive message from God, and hated the Pope for making such a claim. He argued against the persecution of opinion and the forcing of any man's conscience. He insisted only on an outward uniformity of conduct and ceremony (again as in a military body). He knew from personal experience that religion means not only religious ceremony, almsgiving, and the service of the poor, but also the striving for truths behind and beyond the Prayer Book, the plumbing of depths no words can express, the wrestling with God's angels. But these things he kept to himself and could fit into a ceremonial framework. He was culpably unsympathetic towards men who had to share them with others, who were hindered by outward forms from pushing out into the depths, who were slowly suffocating in the orderly atmosphere he created.

He had been hated at Oxford. Even his attack on Rome was an unfashionable one. He had made the interesting discovery that Christendom was not divided between Rome and the Protestant rebels, but contained Greek and Coptic Churches,[1] as old as Rome, as tied to ceremony and yet strongly anti-Papal. He wanted to fight the Pope with his own weapons, and was dubbed a Papist for his trouble.

He was fifty before any one noticed him. Then James and Buckingham picked him out and employed him against the Popish controversialists who had converted Buckingham's mother. His arguments were sober, charitable, but, to a Protestant, unanswerable. They made him Bishop of St. David's ; Charles translated him to London

---

[1] He later established a Greek undergraduate at Balliol—who taught Evelyn to drink coffee, for the first time in England.

13

and made him Chancellor of Oxford.   He converted the University from extreme Calvinism, and made it a Royalist stronghold.   He became the motive force of a campaign to make the clergy more conscientious, more energetic, better educated.   Archbishop Abbot was Calvinistic and also a slack organizer, but he knew that nine-tenths of Laud's programme was overdue.   One did not need to be a High Churchman to dislike hearing that one church was used for cock-fighting, and in another a dog had run off with the bread from the Communion.   Records show that at this time Laud's attack was almost all directed against disorders and slackness, rather than Puritanism.[1]   Laud's own cathedral of St. Paul's was ruinous ; booths and houses clung to it like parasites ; porters used the nave as a short cut, and the whole building was a promenade for the idle, a noisy stand for City bargainers, a haunt of pickpockets. Laud had it stripped and repaired.   Inigo Jones designed the necessary additions :   very odd his classic columns must have looked supporting the ancient Gothic.   Londoners began to treat their cathedral with respect, to use their increasing wealth on the restoration and beautifying of the City churches.   Within a dozen years St. Paul's was to stand neglected again while the City killed Laud and waged war upon his master.   Then Cromwell offered it to the Jews as a business centre.   Eight years after his death it was in ashes, and Wren replaced it with a glory beyond Inigo's dreams.

Old St. Paul's was still in the repairer's hands when Charles received an invitation from the Scottish nobles to come and be crowned in Edinburgh.   Laud went with him ; together they took a look at the Scottish Kirk ; and they did not like what they saw.

There was little lack of zeal or efficiency, but there was a lack of uniformity.   The services, too, had none of the beauty and dignity which Charles thought necessary to religion.   The kirks were bare and ugly, wearing with

[1] See Gardiner, x. p. 224.

pride the wounds inflicted by the Reformers on their fabric : not Reformation, said Laud, but deformation.

The organization of the Kirk was a compromise of sixty years' standing. The nobles had prevented John Knox from abolishing bishops, but had forced them to hand over a large proportion of the episcopal revenues, destroying their self-respect and their influence with the people. Meanwhile the bishops' power was limited by the system of grouping several parishes under a " presbytery," or committee of elected elders, controlling the appointment of ministers and the morals of their flock. This discipline was backed by the General Assembly of the Kirk, manned by nobles and laymen as well as clergy, and exercising a Papal power of excommunication. Aristocratic rapacity had extended beyond monastic and episcopal lands and seized on the parish tithes. The nobles had resisted Royal control more successfully than in most European countries ; they still enjoyed a local power of life and death ; now they had secured a right to make their tenants leave crops ungarnered to the weather until the landlord chose to collect his tithe. King James had tried to strengthen the bishops' position and appealed to the nobles to surrender their ancient rights. " He might as well," says Gardiner, " have lectured a gang of smugglers on the propriety of respecting the interests of the Revenue." James also annoyed the more Protestant instincts of the nation by his " Articles of Perth," of which the most obnoxious was the rule that men must kneel to receive Communion. For beneath and even among the aristocrats there was a sincere and extreme Calvinism which every man must respect and no government could outrage without great danger.

Charles began his reign with a bold stroke. The power of the nobles was reduced in the Edinburgh Parliament : some of their spoil was resumed to the Crown and devoted to ecclesiastical purposes : tithe was restored to the Kirk. Their black rage was softened by a certain amount of

compensation. The " Articles of Perth " were slightly modified. Some Scots at least could have Communion served
to them while they sat : their Kirk was financially independent : their farms were freed from a wasting burden.

However angry at the time, the Scottish nobles gave
Charles a royal hospitality when he came to be crowned
ten years later. It is even said that the debts they con-
tracted accounted for some of the later troubles. The
elaboration of the coronation service, the " Popish "
embroidery of the altar cloth caused a good deal of gossip.
But Charles received a rousing welcome from his countrymen when he rode round the Northern Kingdom. Whether
the little old man with the black cloak dogged him from
Dunfermline Palace we do not know. He certainly had a
narrow escape from drowning in the Forth at Burntisland,
and busybodies rushed round to find out what witches had
raised the storm.

It is interesting to speculate what reputation he might
have left, had death found him at Burntisland. He had
certainly failed to achieve popularity in England, and was
neither hated nor loved. He had failed abroad, partly
through his own fault, partly through Parliament's shabby
treatment. But he had done much for Scotland and
chosen the best available governor for Ireland ; he had
encouraged much needed reforms in the English Church,
and done something to keep the rich to their duties to the
community. The tone of public life had risen from a very
low depth during his ten years. A fine taste had encouraged every form of beauty and enlightenment. The three
kingdoms were finding a new prosperity.

It was not to be. Charles had before him a little more
happiness, many years of anxiety and suffering. He must
live to see the ruin of all he loved, the killing of his servants,
the exile of his wife and children. He must become a legend,
loathed and execrated by many, but inspiring in others a
tremendous, a not quite explicable devotion.

CHAPTER THIRTEEN

Ominous

1635–38

CHARLES returned from Scotland in a hurry. He was only just in time to welcome a new arrival into the world, the little prince who would one day be James II. At the same time an old man, honest, lethargic, a little muddled, was passing away in Lambeth Palace. When Laud appeared at Court, still ignorant of Abbot's death, Charles greeted him with a surprise. " My Lord's Grace of Canterbury," he said, " you are very welcome."

Some idiot in the Queen's train offered Laud a Cardinal's hat as an inducement to bring England Romewards. The Pope had sent an envoy to treat for reunion, and Mr. Secretary Windebank was given the work of conducting the hopeless negotiations. When the offer to Laud was repeated, a few weeks later, Laud remarked drily that Rome must first be other than it was, and went on with the campaign he was now free to conduct. Its first aim was still order and efficiency, and if it had stopped there all might yet have been well. But it went on to offend powerful interests, not altogether unjustly : it alienated some very admirable souls of whose allegiance any Church might be proud ; it associated itself with a certain form of government, shared in and increased its unpopularity, and brought Church and Crown crashing down together.

Laud was quite fearless. While he bullied parsons for slackness and insubordination, he insisted on the rich paying heavy fines for their adulteries and high-born ladies doing public penance in a white sheet. Meanwhile he was trying to free the Church from lay control.

All but the highest nobles were forbidden to keep private chaplains in their houses, and Laud attacked the system whereby rich individuals or private corporations supported " lecturers " and preachers in competition with the parish priest. Some lecturers held meetings of their own, some stayed in the vestry while parson read the service and then emerged to do the showier work in the pulpit. And their discourses were apt to be very Puritanical in tone ; and if they did not speak of politics, every one knew that some at least had very definite views.

Here indeed was the whole crux of the matter. Laud's Church was an " established " one : its head was the King : it could not avoid encouraging his friends and reviling his enemies. Even international Rome has frequently found its servants tying themselves to a political party. Protestants are in worse case, Luther throwing all his influence into the scale of German princes and abusing rebels with an un-Christian ardour, Calvin tinged with the political ideas of Geneva, a republic menaced by kingly and ducal neighbours. The English monarchy had led the revolt from Rome and absorbed the Pope's authority ; it was inconceivable that the Church should not be used for monarchical ends. We have seen the end of one such alliance in our own day : the rulers of Russia, using their Church to support a tottering government, have fallen and destroyed all Christianity in their fall.

Laud could see no stay but the Crown for helping the Church to remain independent of aristocratic or popular control, and transmit to posterity a tradition undiluted by passing fashions. It must not, as have some disestablished churches, change its doctrine and discipline to suit the tastes of those who pay for its upkeep and sacrifice expert opinion to the amateur, centuries to a single generation. There had been too much of this in the recent past. " I could have been as gracious with the people as any," said Laud, " even the worst of my predecessors, but I ever held it the lowest depths of baseness to frame religion to serve turns." But Laud's master was a struggling king, in need of support. Laud did not realise that Royalism was a passing phrase, for every one likes to think his own views are part of the changeless stuff of the Universe ; but his enemies accused him of framing religion to serve the King's turn, and the charge is absolutely unanswerable.

The bias showed itself first in the control of appointments. Laud had long ago made a kind of Crockford's Directory of the Clergy, and marked each name P. or O., Puritan or Orthodox. The P.'s were seldom dismissed, though frequently rated. It was rather that men of a certain cast of mind knew that there was no welcome for them and certainly no promotion in the English Church. The prohibition against controversy and preaching on " curious points of doctrine " was relaxed, and relaxed in disfavour of Puritanism, in favour of the Royalist. Some care was taken to prevent the preaching of submission to arbitrary despotism, but Mainwaring, who had told a congregation to subscribe to the Forced Loan, had now become a bishop. Meanwhile the Puritan prayer-meetings were prohibited in private houses, in fields, and woods. Baxter, later to be chaplain to a Roundhead regiment, tells us how such proceedings of Laud's turned him from his previous loyalty to Church and Prayer Book. He knew many excellent Puritans, and thought that " those who silenced and troubled such men could not be genuine followers of the Lord of Love." The same Church which broke up their prayer-meetings, censored their books, and rewarded their opponents in the pulpit. Many were emigrating to America (Laud thought of prohibiting them, but cancelled the order), and there were among them enough men to set up a state based on principles which were perhaps farther from those of the Lord of Love than ever Laud's had been. The intolerance on both sides makes one wonder whether the problem was not for the time insoluble. It is interesting to find that the first step to a solution was already being taken, and on American soil,

The little colony of Maryland, sent out by Charles, probably as a refuge for the Papists he was forced to oppress at home, decided to adopt what a contemporary Parliamentarian called "that grand Chimæra, Liberty of Conscience." Their Parliament made it law, all Christians become equal, and it proved no Chimæra.

At home Laud's policy provoked considerable resistance. Congregations fought against the removal of the Communion Table to the east end and its railing-in. Individuals broke stained-glass windows. Brave Prynne was still in prison, but still writing. He contrived to get a book printed without licence, attacking the Declaration of Sports, bishops and their political power. He was pilloried again, and lost what was left of his ears ; lawyer Finch savagely suggested that he should also be branded on the cheeks. Beside him stood two companions, both condemned to ear-cropping—a clergyman called Burton for preaching two fierce sermons against ceremonies, and Bastwick, a doctor, who had published a scurrilous attack on bishops and " every limb of Antichrist." The London crowd had, this time, nothing but cheers and encouragement for their bravery, and Prynne met many demonstrations of sympathy on the long journey that took him to rigorous imprisonment in Lancaster gaol. Laud refused to sit among their judges, " because the business hath some reflection on myself." But he spoke at the trial, refuting the prisoners out of their own Calvinist authorities. Some men said that Laud was using an official position to wreak a private spite. It was an unjust charge, but it was partly Laud's fault that it could be made—and believed.

No one can doubt that the bishops were growing seriously unpopular with large classes, especially in London. If one had to point to any single reason for the downfall of King Charles, it would be to the policy which concentrated all grievances into one and presented a single target to shafts whose dispersion might have made them comparatively harmless. The united front may be an admirable thing, but it can be very perilous, when retreat at one point endangers all the line, and the least compromise anywhere is a blow to the prestige of the whole. Charles had never disguised his government's sympathy with Laud's religious ideas ; he was now beginning to make increasing use of bishops in political offices.

Scottish bishops became ministers of state. Their promotion angered the nobles, their hold on men's respect was small. Charles only knew that they had fewer axes to grind, owed their position to himself, shared his general view of life. Meanwhile he advanced Laud, already powerful on the Council. When a colonial committee was formed, Laud was one of its members ; when Weston died, the Treasury was put into commission, and Laud was among the commissioners, Bishop Juxon another.

Laud's work at the Treasury was always honest and often wise. He even took the popular side in the great Soap Question, which Weston left as a legacy. Privileges had been granted to a new company, almost amounting to a monopoly ; the Government was to be paid handsomely from the profits ; Weston, it was discovered too late, had also made a bargain for the benefit of his private pocket. The old soapmakers raised a rumpus, all the more easily because some of their rivals were Papists. Papists had contrived Gunpowder Plot, so Popish soap would burn and blister the hands. A solemn court of inquiry met, containing the Lord Mayor, the Lieutenant of the Tower, and sundry other bigwigs, and they solemnly sat and watched two washerwomen attack two bundles of dirty clothes. To London's rage and Laud's annoyance, the verdict was for the new soap. Two years later its manufacturers, unable to make headway against public opinion, were nearly bankrupt. The Treasury was out of commission, and in Juxon's hands, and the soap privileges were transferred. The rare alliance of London with lawn sleeves had triumphed.

Meanwhile more serious resistance was growing. Soon

after Prynne's punishment, John Lilburne was whipped through the streets for denying the jurisdiction of Star Chamber. The Ship-Money Writ of 1636 provoked a more general quarrel. Charles asked the opinion of the judges, and ten of the twelve replied that he was within his rights to levy it. The judgment was felt to reflect merely their dependence on the King. Lord Saye decided to defy it, and persuaded a friend in a neighbouring county to do the same. For some unexplained reason, the second was made the test case, and the name of John Hampden immortalized. And thus a lawsuit about a matter of 31s. 6d. (seven guineas, as we should call it) became the battle-ground for two theories of government, two contrasted philosophies of human life.

Probably at Lord Bedford's suggestion Hampden had chosen as his advocates Robert Holbourne and Oliver St. John. The latter was the more powerful. He waived the plea that precedent only warranted the collection of ship-money in coastwise counties. He allowed that the King alone could decide when England was in danger for need of a fleet. But he argued that in such an emergency the King must call Parliament before levying ship-money, for Parliament was the only safeguard of the rights of property. This argument, sound politics perhaps, seems to us an extraordinary plea in a law court. But every one knew that this was no ordinary lawsuit.

The Crown lawyers proved that precedents sanctioned the levy of ship-money without Parliament's consent, their opponents that it was only an occasional, not a regular tax. They argued that the King was claiming a tiny sum in order to safeguard the nation's wealth ; Hampden's lawyers showed that such a principle sanctioned all illegal taxation. The latter indeed made it look as if ship-money was not a mere expedient for increasing the navy, but a prelude to despotism based on arbitrary taxation of every kind. They have imposed their view on the majority of historians. Finally, Holbourne outbid St. John with the extreme claim that Parliament, not the King, was the judge of national danger. The Attorney-General countered by declaring that all questioning of the King's authority was in itself a national danger. They were outside the region of private law : the custom of centuries, the sharing of sovereignty between Crown and Parliament, had broken down : where sovereignty was to lie in the future was a question to be decided not by the flapping of legal gowns, but by the brandishing of sword and pike.

The judges gave their decision, two by two, over a period of months. Of twelve, two were for Hampden on technical grounds, three on grounds of principle. Seven were for the King. Finch came last, and did a deal of harm ; he boldly declared that even an Act of Parliament limiting the Prerogative was null and void.

So barren and dangerous a victory could hardly strengthen the Crown ; it certainly helped to bring his enemies together. Their leaders had not lost touch with each other since the doors of St. Stephen's Chapel were locked behind their retreating backs.

Pym had taken no part in the rowdy scenes with which Eliot's friends brought Parliament to its close. Within a year he had found new employment in the City, as secretary to a company whose objects were the development of some most unpromising islands near the coast of Honduras. " The Company for the Plantation of Providence, Henrietta, and the Adjacent Islands " was founded in 1630. It lasted some ten years, and numbered among its directors the Earls of Essex, Warwick, and his brother, Holland ; Lords Saye, Brooke, and Mandeville (later Manchester) ; Sir William Waller, Mr. Oliver St. John, and probably John Hampden. It only needs St. John's cousin Cromwell to make the complete staff of a Roundhead army.

The company was not a success. Providence had been nothing but a dépôt for smugglers and buccaneers, and to that it continually reverted, in spite of its directors' attempts to turn it into a settlement of godly and discreet

Puritans.   The colonists were ordered to send home a half-
share of agricultural profits, but the crops were all failures.
They were meanwhile warned against drunkenness and
bad language, told to burn their cards and dice, and restrict
themselves to " chess and shooting " : one wonders what
language the islanders used when such instructions arrived.
Godly chaplains were sent out, and proved less godly than
the directors hoped : one taught his flock to sing catches,
and this, it was whispered (though the horrible rumour was
denied), on the Sabbath day.   An attempt was made to
revive agriculture by importing negro slaves : the traffic
in them, soon to be a vast business, was generally defended
on the ground that it helped to convert the heathen ; but a
Providence settler who questioned the right to possess
slaves still in a state of " strangeness to Christianity " was
told that his objection was " groundless."   But nothing
could make the colony prosper.   The shareholders, in
truly modern style, assured each other that all that was
needed was more capital.   They produced it, sunk it in
the business and lost the lot—Brooke as much as £20,000,
Pym nearly £16,000.   The whole venture ended in the
island reverting to buccaneering and a Spanish expedition
coming to clear away the nuisance.   Don Juan Diaz
Pimienta had a sharp fight of it, but the English surrendered,
400 being shipped back to Europe while 350 negroes
remained in Spanish hands.

Officially the directors met week after week at Lord
Brooke's house in the City : the same men, if local legends
are true, foregathered at Saye's castle of Broughton, and
at Fawsley in Northampton, the home of Hampden's
cousin Knightley.   It is scarcely conceivable that even
at Brooke House they talked only of business (though
business included the friction with Laud at the colonial
board over the appointment of chaplains).   It is more
likely that they also planned their campaign for English
liberty.   One is tempted (though it is grossly unfair) to
quote Dr. Johnson again.   " Why is it," said that pre-

judiced old gentleman, " that we hear the loudest yelps for
liberty from the owners of slaves in America ? "

It is unfair for more than one reason, partly because the
first protest against slavery (before the Quakers', before
Johnson's toast, " Success to the next negro rising in the
West Indies ") came from the Puritan Baxter. But it is
perhaps permissible to draw attention to facts which show
that Charles's opponents were not merely high-souled patriots
but also ordinary men of business and (as we shall see)
party politicians with every trick of the trade at command. These facts have been suppressed in the popular
histories, while space is given to every sordid intrigue
that went on at the King's court. There may be some
value in retelling the story without such suppression
and without more praise of what has been overpraised
already. It may help us to realize that we are dealing
with men of flesh and blood, and not with " historical
figures." Charles's opponents were not particularly bad
men. Their attitude to Roman Catholicism is the hardest
thing for us to understand, and here it was Charles that
was above his contemporaries, not his enemies beneath
them. Probably few of them worked consciously for an
extension of their economic power over the poor, or saw
that such would be the result of their triumph. Few
were religious hypocrites : Hampden's famous saying,
" If it were not for this reiterated cry about religion, they
could never be certain of keeping the people on their side,"
does not necessarily imply hypocrisy. The best of them
must have regretted an alliance with the enemies of culture
and refinement ; Prynne and Milton are odd bedfellows.

Their common ground was the demand for a new
Parliament and the concession of whatever demands it
might make. It is doubtful if any one foresaw how
extreme and and even contradictory those demands might
be. Only Charles was sure that each concession would
make way for a new demand, until the Crown he had been
born to guard was reduced to impotence : it is not easy to

prove him wrong. His financial expedients, at which the opposition expressed such indignation, were aimed at making him independent of Parliament, until an unusual crisis demanded unusual expenditure. There was a chance that, before it arose, the benefits of Royal administration and the pressure of the Church would convert England to the King's point of view and weaken even the opposition in the House of Commons. The crisis came too soon ; it was about to arise in Scotland ; and it provided the opposition with a magnificent opportunity.

For a long time there had been talk of a new Prayer Book for Scotland. Charles spent years over its composition, months over the form of its printing. Laud gave his advice, the reluctant Scottish bishops were asked to revise it. Meanwhile Scotland decided how to resist its introduction. The best way was naturally to represent it as " Popish." When it appeared, there was little to justify such an accusation, and some men were even driven to point at the ornamental capitals which Charles had inserted in the text, as reminiscent of a monkish missal. And it was hard to meet Charles's plea for uniformity as an answer to the Papists' jeer at a Church which did not know its own mind. But it was easy to raise Presbyterian feeling against a book compiled by bishops, and national feeling against one concocted in London. Charles's real and unpardonable mistake was to unite against himself the spirit of Wallace and John Knox.

In the summer of 1637 some one tried to read the new service in St. Giles' Cathedral, and there was a riot. It is sad that accuracy compels one to reject the story of Jenny Geddes hurling her stool at the bishop and crying, " Will you read Mass in my lug ? " If a stool was thrown, it was probably by a shopkeeper's widow called Mrs. Mean. It was even suspected that some of her fellow-gossips were 'prentices disguised in skirts. They were put outside, and the service proceeded to the tune of splintering windows.

It is not likely that Charles had any conception of the greatness of his danger, but as news came from Scotland that riot was fast becoming revolution, men noticed that he began to wear a tired and harassed look, to hunt less often, to forsake his tennis. At Court, the Fool Archie blamed Laud for the trouble ; he had always disliked and ridiculed the little Archbishop. " Who's the fool now ? " he asked Laud, when news came in from Edinburgh ; and off he went to get drunk in a tavern and call Laud a monk and a traitor. Arraigned for his words before the Council, Archie pleaded " the privilege of his cloth." But he lost his place and would have been whipped but for Laud's humane intervention. He retired to his native Westmoreland, begot a bastard, grew respectable, married, and died rich, twenty-five years after his master.

His successor was called Muckle John, and his task must have been a hard one, in a Court overshadowed by coming doom. Things were not improved by the arrival of an unwelcome visitor—Henrietta's mother, Marie de Medicis. Richelieu, who had risen by her favour, had long found her impossible and expelled her from France. Now she petitioned for an invitation to London, and, when Charles refused, came without it. "*Adieu, ma liberté,*" sighed Henrietta, but Charles could hardly show his mother-in-law the door. They welcomed her royally, and she settled down at St. James's, to scold and give bad advice, to intrigue against Richelieu, to intrigue against Parliament, to intrigue, Italian fashion, merely for the sake of intriguing.

Meanwhile the King's opponents were rousing themselves on every side. The Scots were writing to England and sending abroad for aid. Richelieu's agent was eager to foment the trouble ; Richelieu said it needed no fomenting. Within two years of the Edinburgh riots, Scotland was at war with herself and with England. Within four, Ireland was in rebellion, the Long Parliament sat in London, and the King's servants were in prison or exile or the grave. The hunt was up.

CHAPTER FOURTEEN

First Blood

1638-40

A TRULY despotic government has one great advantage over its opponents ; it can strike quickly, before they collect their forces, or even their thoughts. Charles had no such advantage. His position was based solely on the loyalty and duty of his subjects ; he had no army, not even a proper guard for his palace ; his police system had not changed since Shakespeare created Dogberry. He had a few firm friends, a few undoubted opponents. But now that the crisis of his life approached and the Scottish trouble precipitated all trouble, he had no means of distinguishing friend from foe, the loyal from the time-servers and traitors. The secrets of his Privy Council were sold, his palace was honeycombed with spies : it is even said that he had to take precautions against Scottish servants who ransacked his pockets in the night. His own agents were less successful, though his enemies found at least one secret paper had disappeared, to turn up in the Government's possession. Meanwhile treachery and rebellion clothed themselves in the phrases of fulsome and deferential loyalty. The air grew thick with lies—lies nicely calculated to estrange King and Parliament and People. Some of them are still current, though the most potent of all has not borne scrutiny. It is not possible to believe, as many honest men were induced to believe, that Charles contemplated the weakening of Protestantism and the introduction of Popery. Yet, but for that slander, it is doubtful if Charles could have been defeated.

As soon as it became clear that the Scottish riots were

a serious matter, Charles sent the Marquis of Hamilton north to gain time and, if necessary, to make concessions. Hamilton was a bad choice, not very wise, not very loyal to his master. And time was just what the Scottish opposition needed. They set up a provisional government, quaintly called " the Tables," representing nobles, gentlemen, clergy, and townsmen. One of their spokesmen was a minister named Alexander Henderson, who had already sent a very reasonable protest to Charles ; he did not assert that the Prayer Book was indisputably Popish, and rightly emphasized the grievance that it had not had the sanction of Scottish Parliament or Kirk Assembly. The emphasis was soon to be shifted, for home consumption ; Henderson presided over the signing of the Covenant. A document fifty years old, in which King James and his nobles had pledged themselves to resist the then real menace of Popery, was disinterred from the archives : a few paragraphs were added in which professions of loyalty to Charles were mixed with the assertion that religious " innovations" (done by his order) . . . " do sensibly tend to the re-establishing of the Popish religion and tyranny." Henderson stood in Greyfriars' Churchyard, as he stands to-day in the Victorian steel-engravings that adorn the walls of a thousand God-fearing Scottish homes, and watched noble and townsman and peasant sign the ingeniously constructed document upon a tombstone. There were similar scenes all over the Lowlands. Practically all the aristocracy signed, even Montrose, the bold hunter, the cunning swordsman, the scholar, and the poet, who would one day be a thorn in Covenanters' sides. Only Montrose's cousin, Napier of Merchiston, was far-sighted enough to refuse ; he was an honest man and a Royalist, although his father invented logarithms. Other recusants were bullied and threatened in the streets as Papist dogs ; recalcitrant ministers lost their livings. Charles had never attempted the hopeless task of forbidding controversial preaching in Scotland ;

14

now the pulpit thundered against him. One Glasgow preacher declared that he " was sent to them with a commission from Christ to bid them subscribe," and the appropriate name of this particular blasphemer was Mr. Cant. The result was most satisfactory. Half a million Scotsmen (nearly half the nation) from every Lowland region except Royalist Aberdeen, signed a document implying that their King was trying to force Popery upon them.

Charles refused to believe that a people could be so united against him. His concessions came slowly, too slowly to rally the moderate men to his side, and powerless to affect the extremists. He abandoned his Prayer Book, rescinded King James's "Articles of Perth," practically destroyed the political power of bishops, and granted a Kirk Assembly to discuss settlement of all grievances. The Tables called it, but used an obsolete and illegal system of election in order to pack the parliament of the Kirk with laymen. "Not a gown among them," reported Lord Hamilton ; "many swords and many more daggers."

It was at this Assembly that the King's most obstinate enemy declared himself : Argyle joined the Covenanters. Archibald, Earl of Argyle, was head of the vast Clan Campbell, hated and feared by the other Highlanders, commanding an army of 20,000 men. He himself had lived as a townsman and politician. Long ago he had come to London, and, while his own father warned the King to lock him up in prison and keep him there, Charles had tried to secure his friendship by doing him a good turn. It is difficult for any but a Presbyterian to speak of Argyle without prejudice, doubly difficult after a glance at his portrait, with the foxy, squinting eyes and pendulous nose. His advocates claim that he was a consistent, sincere, and able defender of the aspirations of contemporary Scotland, but they cannot deny that he was unscrupulous, callous, vindictive, and a coward of the first water. He was to be Montrose's life enemy, but now Montrose was in his party and marching to attack the Northern Royalists. He succeeded in breaking their power. The Covenant was supreme in Scotland.

Charles had long been preparing for war ; his main plan was to blockade Scottish ports with the navy, and the Border with English militia : meanwhile he asked Wentworth to send Irish troops to Scotland, attack Argyle's lands, and rally what loyalists could be found. He had also taken one step by which he has incurred, not altogether unjustly, a terrible odium : he had asked, unsuccessfully, for the loan of Spanish troops.[1]

The problem was becoming a military one ; its issue depended on three armies now afoot in Charles's kingdoms : and the King saw every advantage in his enemies' hands.

The most efficient were Wentworth's Irishmen, loyal, well-paid, and trained over a period of years. But they were few in numbers, and there were two objections to their employment. Ireland was a conquered country ; to denude it of troops was to invite rebellion ; all Wentworth could do was to promise help when he had had time to recruit new regiments. Secondly, the majority of the soldiers were Roman Catholics : by using them at the decisive point, Charles would give a handle to the most dangerous of calumnies. Indeed, the Irish troops were immensely valuable to his enemies, used as a bogy. Rumour multiplied their numbers and ferocity, and honest Englishmen lived in terror of having their throats cut by imported hordes of Papist savages.

The second army was that of the Covenant, apparently well-paid, provisioned, and equipped, and including a number of Highlanders to whom war was the routine of life. It also included a high proportion of Scottish veterans from the German wars. It was commanded by the little crook-backed Leslie, who had served thirty years in the Swedish ranks and been knighted by Gustavus Adolphus. He was cousin to a Covenanting Peer, and had been recalled

---

[1] One cannot be sure whether he already knew that the Scots had asked help from Richelieu.

from Germany, slipping through the cordon of English ships. He was a mere soldier of fortune and probably cared little for the Covenant. But his men cared much ; they were under strict discipline ; they knew, or thought they knew, for what they were fighting.

On the other side of the Border lay King Charles, looking at Leslie's encampment through a new-fangled telescope. Henrietta had begged him not to go in person, and indeed the danger was no imaginary one. The troops began by showing great enthusiasm, but there was a woeful lack of trained and experienced men. To reinforce the northern militia, Charles, always the mediævalist and always penniless, had summoned his Peers according to the ancient custom, to pay for their land by military service. Partly as a result of this, partly through Court intrigue, Charles had hampered himself with Arundel, Holland, and Essex as commanders. The first two knew nothing of war ; Arundel was soon to profess disgust at all politics, retire to continental picture galleries, and leave England to its fate ; Holland, a mere courtier, was to change sides thrice during the Civil War and bring nothing but money to either ; Essex, probably still loyal, possibly in correspondence with the Scots, would soon be a convinced Roundhead. The worst feature of the situation was the lack of money. The army was paid and provisioned largely by the generosity of the King's friends, by a gift from the clergy, and by a loan that Henrietta had contrived to raise among the English Catholics : for these long-suffering loyalists knew that the dark sky would grow darker above them with the triumph of principles such as inspired the Covenant.

Charles decided on negotiation. He began with a proclamation which the Scots promised to read publicly in their camp and then read privately in a tent to a few officers who knew its contents already. He declared that he had come to clear himself " of that notorious slander . . . that I shut my ears to the just complaints of my people of Scotland." He promised to submit political

grievances to a Parliament at Edinburgh, religion to a
Kirk Assembly. The Scots could not meet his argument
that the late Assembly had been elected on an illegal
system and under considerable pressure. They promised
to dissolve the Tables, and restore the royal castles they
had captured in Scotland. Both armies were to disband.
Such was the treaty of Berwick, broken as soon as signed.

The Scots put it about that Charles had promised to
ratify anything and everything that Parliament and
Assembly voted. Meanwhile they insisted on excluding
the bishops from their seats. They then abolished episcopacy altogether. Charles consented to this as a provisional
matter, but refused to accept it as a permanent arrange-
ment. They replied by reconstituting their Parliament,
denying his right even to prorogue it, and insisting that
the royal castles should only be handed over to commanders
approved by themselves. " There is a Scottish proverb,"
wrote Charles, " that bids you put two locks on your door
when you have made friends with your foe."

The usual justification for the Scottish breach of faith
is that King Charles could not be trusted, that there was a
real fear of his revoking all concessions, admittedly reluctant,
as soon as he had military strength. It would be a better
reason for not signing a treaty than for breaking one
already signed. And there is no trace of renewed preparations to coerce Scotland until the Scots had made it quite
clear that they were not going to abide by the treaty.

If rebellion means anything, then Argyle and his
friends were rebels. They were twisting the agreement
of Berwick into a revolutionary instrument more potent
than their army. And that army, disbanded now, could
spring to life a good deal quicker than Charles could raise
forces to punish them. Unpunished rebellion is a con-
tagious thing, and there were plenty of English malcontents learning from the Covenanters how a King may
be reduced to impotence. Charles could rely on no one.
Hamilton had long ago got a foot into the Covenanting

camp. Half the English nobles were indifferent. It was
said that the Berwick negotiations had been hurried on
because the great lord Pembroke wanted to get home to
his hunting and hawking.   There was only one man whose
loyalty and serious purpose there could be no doubt, and
that was Wentworth.   It might be dangerous to employ
him in England, for Yorkshire and Ireland had taught
him drastic methods, but there are times when nothing
matters so much as loyalty and energy, and Charles sent
for Wentworth.   Wentworth obtained at last his long-
sought Earldom, and took the name of Strafford.   He
was a sick man, he was tired, he had eighteen months to
live : but it was not sickness that killed him.

His first advice was bold : a Parliament must be called.
The King must end the eleven years' grievance, the King
must have money.   Charles accepted, not without trepida-
tion : he suspected that there would be some members at
least in active correspondence with the Scots.   Strafford
hurried back to Dublin, held an Irish Parliament, and
bullied it into voting a large sum of money and voting it
unanimously.   There was much enthusiasm and many
hard words for the Covenanters.   If Strafford found one-
tenth of such loyalty at Westminster, his advice would be
abundantly justified.

At the English elections there was great canvassing
and many accusations of bribery and pressure.   But
when the Houses met, no one knew what to expect.   The
opposition opened a long catalogue of grievances, the lead
being taken by a gentleman with the scarcely credible
name of Harbottle Grimston.   He was seconded by
Edmund Waller the poet, a cousin of Hampden's.[1] Waller
attributed all evils to the " intended union between us
and Rome," and compared England under recent taxation
to Job when " it pleased God . . . to take all that he had

---

[1] He was to do some of the most remarkable feats of coat-turning during
the next twenty years.   His last and best was to follow up a eulogy of
Cromwell with rhymed rejoicings, three years later, at Cromwell's death.

from him." To Waller himself the comparison was un-
apt, for he was a very rich man, had married a City heiress
worth £40,000, and had probably not paid £100 in taxes
during the last ten years. Pym was more sensible, and it
was upon his list of grievances that the House went into
Committee : it included the relaxation of the Penal Laws ;
the preaching of absolutism from pulpit and Bench ; the
excesses of the Prerogative Courts ; the dissolution
and intermission of Parliaments, and the infringement of
their privileges ; Tonnage and Poundage, knighthoods,
monopolies, forests, ship-money—every expedient whereby
Charles had secured a revenue independent of Parliament.

For a week Charles allowed the committees to talk
unhindered. But the longer they did so, postponing
the discussion of war funds, the bolder would the Scots
become. He appealed to the Lords, showing them a
letter, discovered in Edinburgh, asking for King Louis's
help. The Peers showed less indignation than he hoped,
but they sent a message to the Commons suggesting that
it was time money was debated : even from this twenty-
five dissented, among them Essex, Brooke, and Saye.
The Commons described the inoffensive communication as
a breach of their privilege to be sole controllers of finance.
Charles sent them a direct message, offering to abandon
ship-money if they could vote some other method of
maintaining the navy, and demanding funds for war.

The test of Strafford's experiment had come, for upon
the Commons' answer hung the whole question, raised for
the last time, whether King or Parliament could work
peaceably together. On it hung also the history of England. And it is just at this point that our knowledge of
what happened becomes most scanty and untrustworthy.

What may be called the Royalist version is based
mainly on Clarendon. Clarendon was then plain Mr.
Hyde, an eye-witness and protagonist, and so far from
being a Royalist as yet that he was soon to help in the
impeaching of Strafford. His account is simple and

intelligible, though it involves one great difficulty which
prevents its being accepted in full. It depends on personalities rather than political principles and, largely on
that ground, has been dismissed as worthless.

The key position was held by old Sir Harry Vane, the
king's secretary and his spokesman in the Commons. He
undoubtedly hated Strafford : he was accused of wishing
for a dissolution on personal grounds, because he was
afraid that the Commons would attack a mischievous
monopoly from which he drew much profit : he was soon
to join the opposition, and, incidentally, to earn its contempt. It was his duty to lay the King's proposals before
the Commons. After a long argument in Council, Strafford
persuaded Charles to ask for about a million and a half
pounds : to ask more, Strafford believed, would be to
court refusal. Vane was given his instructions according
to Strafford's opinion. Next day Vane arose in the
Commons and asked for well over two millions. It is
possible (though there is no scrap of evidence) that the
King and Vane had had another meeting and decided to
throw over the Council's opinion. Even now the Commons
did not regard the sum as impossible. Glanville, Buckingham's old enemy, begged them to grant it, with tears in
his eyes. Discussion arose, some thinking the amount
excessive, some disliking a bargain with the King over
ship-money, some wishing to include in the bargain the
King's ancient right to make counties pay " coat and
conduct " money—that is to provide food and clothing for
the militia. Before discussion was ripe, Hampden rose to
move for an immediate answer, yes or no, to the King.
Hyde, convinced that this was a dishonest move to force on a
deadlock, proposed further debate until the minor issues
were clear and, meanwhile, a vote that the House intended
to grant the King some money. While some members cried
for Hampden, some for Hyde, Vane rose to say that debate
was useless : the King would have his full demand or
nothing at all. The House adjourned still undecided, and

Vane hurried off to the King to recommend a dissolution, as there was no hope that the Commons " would give a penny."

There is one great weakness in the story, which prohibits its full acceptance. Vane may have done something dishonourable, but if his treachery had been so blatant, it is inconceivable that Charles should not have detected it within a few weeks and dismissed him. But Vane remained in royal service for another eighteen months.

The other story throws all responsibility on Charles. He is accused of plotting with Vane, behind Strafford's back, to make further debate impossible and give an excuse for dissolution. There is no evidence for this, but it is suggested that he thought the matter of " coat and conduct " money a critical one, that he may have heard that one member was questioning the legality of the press-gang, and wished to silence all such speakers by a dissolution. Or again, it is suggested that the King had heard of Pym's proposal for a petition that a new treaty should be made with the Scots, and dissolved the Houses to prevent so much encouragement being shown to rebels.

The odd thing is that there is a second eye-witness's account, coming from a decided Parliamentarian, and it leaves everything in doubt. Rushworth, clerk and historian to the Parliament, was later secretary to Fairfax and Cromwell. His statements are generally very accurate, but contemporaries accused him of false emphasis and the deliberate suppression of facts. He took full notes of the early debates, of Pym's speech, of Waller and the good Sir Harbottle. When he comes to the crucial moment he is practically silent. He merely says that the House debated the King's message and was dissolved : no word of Pym's petition, no word of " coat and conduct " money. It is dangerous to argue from silence, but for all Rushworth tells us, every Royalist contention might be true, the House loyal, Hampden cunning, Vane a deliberate traitor.

The Short Parliament had lasted three weeks. If we can only guess at the causes of its failure, the results were apparent and disastrous. Clarendon says that as soon as Charles learnt how things lay, he bitterly regretted the dissolution and even asked whether it could be reversed. His opponents were in high feather. Clarendon met St. John an hour after, and was surprised to see the lawyer's gloomy face wreathed in smiles. St. John was glad of the dissolution : the Short Parliament had been too con- ciliatory and " could never have done what was necessary to be done—as indeed it would not, what he and his friends thought necessary."

If his Parliamentary experiment had failed, Strafford was determined to carry on vigorous war with the Scots. He thought Irish troops could be brought over. An English army was reassembling on the Border. One enthusiastic young officer wrote home, " We care not to aske " what happened in Parliament, if the rumour of strong reinforcements were true. But reinforcements cost money and the Commons had granted none. Their refusal seemed to Strafford to create a situation justifying the most drastic methods. An attempt to debase the silver coinage, as in modern fashion, was blocked by the merchants. Charles had long been angling for money from abroad, and was now marrying his daughter to a Dutchman in the vain hope of assistance : he can hardly have guessed that her son would one day lead over a Dutch army to dethrone James II. Henrietta wrote to the Pope for money, and was brought up short by a demand that Charles should first declare himself a Catholic, in secret if necessary. Strafford was plaguing the Spanish ambassador for a loan, and bullying the City merchants. The latter consented, then found out that there was a Jesuit in prison and unhanged, and demanded his blood as the price of their money. Charles had difficulty in saving the wretched man's life. Short of such a ghastly bargain, there was little left undone to raise money for the war.

The new army was levied largely in the southern counties, many of the men were Puritan, none had any quarrel with the Scots. Discipline was poor ; the officers debated whether the Petition of Right, forbidding Martial Law, prohibited the hanging of mutineers ; meanwhile mutineers were beginning to murder their officers. One, a Roman Catholic, was martyred outside Wellington Church for refusing to join in Protestant worship. London provided a series of riots, tore down the Communion rails in churches, and tried to lynch Laud. A man was hanged, another—for the only time in the reign, the last time in English history—was put on the rack. The riots stopped, and London grew suddenly quiet.

Strafford had planned to invade Scotland, but it was the Scots who invaded first. Six peers, Brooke, Bedford, Essex, Mandeville, Scrope, and Warwick, had written to promise them help " in a free and legal way." The Scots wanted more unqualified support before they moved, and the Peers refused to set their hands to anything that made them liable for treason. But Savile, now acting as their secretary, blandly forged their names and sent a satisfactory document to Edinburgh. Thus encouraged, the Scots began to march with Leslie at their head. They carefully avoided giving offence in England, and paid for everything they took. They routed the King's ill-paid, ill-disciplined levies at Newburn Ford. They occupied Newcastle.

The King was beaten. He summoned his Peers to York and began to treat with the Scots. The first thing to be discovered was Savile's forgery. One might imagine that it would mark the ruin of his career. One would be wrong, for his career was just beginning. The victims of his forgery found it had been too fruitful to be punished. They had their signatures burnt, but the fruits remained. The next discovery was that the Scots were in no hurry to get things settled ; they only wanted to stay in England and be handsomely paid for doing so. In other words, penniless Charles must call a Parliament and do all that it told him to do, just so long as the Scots cared to remain.

Such was the upshot of the two years that had passed since the riot in St. Giles'.

There are some who attribute it to the new Prayer Book, withdrawn a year ago, to Charles's mishandling and "duplicity," to the righteous indignation of the Scottish people. Others are suspicious of the curious neatness with which everything worked to the conclusion desired by his enemies, the independence of Scotland under the control of Argyle and his friends, the calling of an English Parliament, embittered by a recent dissolution, with a Scottish army to back its demands. Then, and for fifty years after, there was endless talk of collusion and a deliberate engineering of the crisis. Charles had the rooms of Brooke, Saye, Pym, and Hampden searched for incriminating evidence, but nothing was found. Documentary evidence is still lacking, and one may say that the culprits committed little to paper, or that they had time and motive enough during the next twenty years to cover their traces. On the other hand, one may dismiss the whole thing as an evil-minded suspicion. The important thing is that the Long Parliament was about to sit, that its demands would be irresistible so long as Leslie kept his men in England, that Leslie did not go home until the power of the English monarchy was crippled for ever.

The Long Parliament sat for nineteen years. It outlived the only man who could legally dissolve it, as it outlived Strafford and Pym, Laud and Essex and Cromwell. Proscription and civil war, co-option and "purges" at the point of the Cromwellian sword, radically altered its nature : Cromwell himself destroyed its House of Lords and expelled its Commons with a file of musketeers ; but a ghost survived and came to life again. Of the members who trooped to Westminster in the autumn of 1640, there were one or two who lived to see that last session held in an England which had forgotten Pym and was waiting to give enthusiastic welcome to a second Charles, to adorn itself in ribbons and periwigs, to applaud Nell Gwynne, and provide matter for Mr. Pepys's Diary.

CHAPTER FIFTEEN

UNJUDICIAL

1641

THERE had been two petitions for the summoning of the Long Parliament—one from the Scots, one from twelve English Peers. Now that it was meeting, there was little doubt that the Commons would have Scottish support; but twelve Peers were not the House of Lords, nor was that body at the orders of Saye and Brooke, Mandeville and Essex. It soon became clear that the Lords were to be the deciding factor between King and Commons. For impeachments were in the air.

Charles summoned Strafford to London, promising that he should not " suffer in person, honour, or fortune." Strafford saw only one way in which Charles could keep his promise : they must stop opponents from an impeachment by carrying the war into the enemies' camp. Impeachments had always started from a majority in the Commons, but Strafford urged the King to arraign certain persons on his own initiative for treasonable correspondence with the Scots. He had seized Savile's messenger. He may have had evidence against some fellow-Peers, even against Pym and Hampden. But Pym struck first.

Strafford reached London on the evening of November 9. On the morning of the 11th the King held a review of soldiers at the Tower. In the Commons some one began to talk of a Popish plot. Pym rose, asked that the doors be locked, and demanded Strafford's impeachment. In a long speech he denounced him as an Apostate, the Counsellor who had ruined the Kingdom. He even reflected on his morals, and there must have been loud laughter in the

London taverns, where it was whispered that Lady Carlisle had been Strafford's mistress, and was now gracing Pym's bed. No doubt it was pure slander, but she was soon to be hand in glove with Pym.

Next came an Irishman called Clotworthy, an old enemy of Strafford. He was sitting for a small Devon borough, though no one could quite make out how he had managed it ; " by the contrivance and recommendation of some powerful persons," says Clarendon, " . . . that so he might be enabled to act this part against the Lord-Lieutenant." His evidence was vague and hearsay, and some members thought it insufficient. The House even wandered off (ironically enough) into a discussion on the Penal Laws, until Pym recalled them, insisted on immediate impeachment, and gained his point. Pym carried up the message to the Lords, begging for summary arrest. Strafford strode into the House—perhaps, at the eleventh hour, to accuse his accuser. The Peers shouted to him to withdraw. Black Rod conducted him to the door, and soldiers to the Tower.

While they prepared the charges, the Commons sent to release Prynne and his fellow-prisoners, and summoned Windebank to their bar. Windebank fled to France. They impeached Laud, too old and too brave to fly ; he joined Strafford in the Tower. Finch anticipated attack by coming to the Commons two days before Christmas and defending his work with the usual aggressiveness and great ability. The Commons impeached him before adjourning for their Christmas dinner. But Finch was dining at The Hague.

There were now vacant places to fill. Bristol joined the Council, but with him came Essex, Saye, and Bedford, while St. John became Solicitor-General. It has been suggested that Charles was making a feeble attempt to conciliate opinion. It would be probably nearer the mark to say that he was acting under a very considerable pressure. The new Councillors brought with them the forger Savile to sit at the Board. We know only too much nowadays about the foisting of rascals into a place of honour, and it is not surprising to find Savile was soon to obtain a peerage.

The Commons now proceeded with a money bill to pay the Scots—£4250 a day was their figure—and with a bill for Triennial Parliaments. If the King issued no writs for three years, elections must proceed without his leave. It would put Government, said Charles, "almost off its hinges," but he had to sign.

His best chance was that the Lords would defy the Commons and find Strafford innocent. By an unlucky chance, Arundel was senior Peer and President of the Court. Arundel was honest, but an enemy of Strafford, and honesty was to be sorely tried in the coming weeks. The trial was to go forward in Westminster Hall, before a huge audience. Ladies thronged the seats ; the baiting of England's greatest man was one of the sights of town. A Scottish commissioner was disgusted at the way the audience chattered and sauntered, brought in their meals, and swilled beer and wine from the bottle. Charles had been put in a little box, hidden with lattice-work to prevent him overawing the judges ; he tore down the lattice with his own hands. The prisoner was brought in, stooping, crippled with illness, and in great pain. His enemies hoped he might spoil his case with such bursts of rage as had terrified Yorkshire squires and Irish officials ; but they were disappointed. He submitted himself humbly to his peers, not doubting their justice. "His behaviour," says a Parliamentarian, "was exceeding graceful, and his speech full of weight, reason, and pleasingness." Denied counsel to speak for him, he occasionally consulted the lawyers at his side. His private secretary, Radcliffe, might have been more useful, but he was out of reach ; Clotworthy had seen to that by starting a prosecution against Radcliffe in the Dublin law courts. But Strafford alone was more than a match for his enemies. For twelve years his great power of brain, his penetrating exactness, had been busy in the service of the King ; now he turned them to the task of saving himself from a dishonourable death.

Many of the charges were ridiculous, mere " flym-flam," as he called them, and some the prosecution dropped hurriedly. Pym argued that though no single one was sufficient, yet the sum of all amounted to High Treason. Such an argument is bad law, but it is a fair plea in a political crisis—on the one condition, that each charge can be proved beyond dispute. There were few indeed that Pym could bring within any distance of proof.

The first was a lie—that Strafford had extracted from Charles unusually despotic powers for the Council of the North : Strafford's Commission as President did not differ materially from that of his predecessor, now supplying evidence for the prosecution. The second, that he had intimidated justices, could only be substantiated by mis-dating and probably misquoting an angry remark he had made in Court.

The Irish charges were more serious. There was no doubt that Strafford had broken the law, and there was no lack of men, Cork and Mountnorris among them, to supply evidence against him. Strafford pleaded the con-ditions of Ireland to a Westminster as ignorant of them as it has always been ; he roundly asserted that there had been more justice and even legality in his time than in that of former governors ; he strenuously denied that any-thing he had done could possibly amount to High Treason. Finally, he appealed to the benefits Ireland had gained by his rule. Pym ridiculed them : if the revenue had in-creased, Strafford had pocketed the surplus (Strafford showed that he had actually lost money, not gained) : if churches were built or restored, there had been no spiritual edification (much depended on Puritan Pym's idea of edification) : Strafford had appointed a groom to be parson of two parishes (the " groom " was an M.A. of Dublin, and his double stipend amounted to £150) : one of Straf-ford's bishops had just been detected and executed for unnatural vice (Strafford pleaded he was not omniscient, and a clergyman applying for a bishopric would hardly confess to sodomy). And it was High Treason that Pym had to prove.

Finally, there were the charges relating to the last eighteen months. Strafford had betrayed the King by engineering the dissolution of the Short Parliament, counselling the continuance of ship-money and the raising of other unparliamentary revenue ; he had urged aggression against Scotland, and the reduction of England by Irish troops : when war with Scotland came, Strafford had deliberately betrayed the King's army to defeat at Newburn Ford. The last charge was too ridiculous to be pressed. To approve ship-money, sanctioned by the judges, was hardly treason ; and Strafford had fought against the dissolution of Parliament.

When Strafford had replied to the several charges, he pleaded, in final defence, that such as the Lords considered proved could not possibly amount to High Treason. The only dangerous accusation was that relating to the Irish troops. Sir Harry Vane charged Strafford with recommending at Council that they should be used against the disaffected in England ; Vane said that he had taken notes of his words, but the King had ordered him to burn them. There had been six other Councillors present : Laud was now in prison, Finch abroad ; the other four denied that Strafford had given any such counsel.

The impeachment was breaking down. It was useless to plead that the details of the evidence were immaterial, because Strafford was a notorious enemy of Liberty. Even if it were true, the Lords were a Court of Law and they were there to see justice done on strict proofs. There was one remedy for Strafford's enemies to adopt : Pym eschewed it, and the proposal came from Hazlerig, Lord Brooke's brother-in-law : the Commons must drop the impeachment and substitute Attainder. No judicial procedure was necessary, no examination of evidence. The Lords ceased to be a Court of Law. The Commons must

15

simply vote a Bill declaring Strafford to be a public danger
and induce the Lords to pass it.   It had been a favourite
Tudor method for using subservient Parliaments to remove
an inconvenient nobleman : Hazlerig was stepping into
the shoes of bluff King Hal.

In the ensuing debate Bristol's son Digby deserted his
former friends.   He had voted for impeachment by judicial
process, but he could not stomach this Attainder, this
creating of a new crime, calling it treason, and then killing
a man for former breaches of the new law.   Such a precedent would make bloodshed the end of every political
disagreement, even, Digby insinuated, of every private
feud.   The House threw him a sop (blackening its own
case in the process) by voting that the attainder of Strafford must not be considered a precedent.   It is significant
of the state of political feeling that at such a crisis barely
half the House had troubled to attend.

The Lords were indignant.   They had just quarrelled
with an outrageous demand from the Commons, that new
charges should be brought and Strafford allowed no time
to collect evidence for their refutation.   They now refused
to drop the trial.   Pym and Hampden persuaded the
Commons to let impeachment and attainder proceed side
by side.   But a grave error had been made, and the Lords'
eyes were beginning to open to what was really going on.
Something must be done to destroy the majority in the
Lords which would certainly block the Attainder, to restore
a shaken faith in the Commons' honesty of purpose, and
save Pym and his friends from a disgraceful fiasco, perhaps
from political ruin.   Pym had two cards up his sleeve.

Sir Harry Vane, on whose testimony so much depended,
had a son and namesake.   Young Harry and Pym now
came forward with a curious story.   Long ago Vane had
got hold of his father's keys and used them to rifle a certain
cabinet, covered with red velvet.   There, he said, he had
found the Council notes, since burnt, had read how Strafford advised the King to bring over Irish Papists " to

reduce this kingdom," and taken a copy of the words. Six months ago, with the burden of his secret still oppressing him, he happened to be talking to Pym about the " sad condition of England." He had opened his heart to Pym. Pym now felt the moment had come to show the Commons young Harry's copy of his father's notes.

The story was an exceedingly fishy one, and the whole business was suspected to be an elaborate comedy. Old Harry blustered and swore he did not know what his son had been doing. He may have been speaking the truth. But it is a little difficult to see why, if there was any foundation for the story, Pym had kept it to himself until this decisive moment. It is still more difficult to forgive Pym for the argument he based upon it. To prove High Treason, two witnesses are necessary to each fact : the elder Vane had taken the notes, the younger had copied them, and that made two.

So much for impeachment and the marshalling of evidence. The Lords were hardly likely to be impressed. And Strafford had already said that if he used the phrase " this kingdom " he had meant rebellious Scotland, then under discussion at Council. But for the attainder no evidence was necessary. The Peers might yet be frightened or persuaded into voting Strafford a public danger. Essex had said, " Stone dead hath no fellow," St. John that " it was no foul play to knock foxes and wolves on the head." But Essex was not the House of Lords. Not a third of that body was in favour of Strafford's execution. Something must be done about the other two-thirds. Pym played his second card, and it was the ace of trumps.

It was put into his hands by the treachery of an officer in the King's army. No army is a natural lover of Parliaments, and this one was discontented, ill-paid, and tired of watching large chests of money proceed along the Great North Road to keep Scottish rebels in comfort. One such load, £50,000 of cash, had been designed to pay the King's army and then suddenly diverted to the Scots' camp by

an order from the Commons.   Here was good material for
a Royalist plot among the soldiers.   Carefully planned,
resolutely handled, it might save Strafford and restore
the King's authority.   The slightest mishandling would
destroy both.   Unfortunately it was in the hands of Queen
Henrietta and her indiscreet friends.

She had long forgotten her antipathy to Strafford—
perhaps by concentrating attention on his beautiful hands ;
she had been holding midnight colloquies with Pym and
Hampden at the backdoors of Whitehall.   Candle in hand,
she smiled and begged and bribed ; she thought she was
helping Strafford.   Now there came to her some army
officers : two happened to be poets, John Suckling the
disreputable lover, and Davenant, who used to boast that
his father kept the inn where Shakespeare stayed at
Oxford on his journeys home, that his mother had been
great friends with Shakespeare, that poetic talent is
hereditary—and rare among innkeepers.   Other accomplices were the Queen's secretary, Jermyn, a peer or two,
and the unpleasant creature, young George Goring.   The
plot developed into a project for bringing the army up to
seize London, and establish a military despotism.   In this
form it was suggested to Charles.   He would not hear of
it.   The most he would allow was a plan to rescue Strafford
from the Tower by military force.   Goring misliked such
a paltry conclusion : he misliked it still more when the
conspirators refused to make him lieutenant-general.   He
went and told Bedford and Mandeville of the whole design.
It was April 1, but they believed him.   And they told Pym.

Pym bided his time for a month.   He waited till the
morning when a small party of soldiers was sent to the
Tower to demand admission in the King's name.   The
Lieutenant of the Tower was a Scot, possibly a friend of
Pym's : he kept the gates shut.   Meanwhile Pym was
speaking in the Commons ; he produced a Protestation
against Popery, drawn up, with the help of a Scottish
commissioner, on the lines of the Covenant ; it was signed

in the Commons and sent out to the City, where it received 20,000 signatures. Twenty thousand Londoners believed that the Papists were about to cut their throats, and armed mobs of shopkeepers began to mass in the streets. Pym had told the Commons that there was a Popish plot on foot to " overthrow this kingdom." Then, three days after the incident at the Tower, Pym disclosed what he had heard from Goring. The House locked its doors ; when a gallery began to give way under two unusually fat members, some one cried out that there was a second Gunpowder Plot. The City trained bands were summoned to protect Parliament from Papists, and marched to Covent Garden before they were told that obesity, not Guy Fawkes, had caused the alarm. Pym was embroidering Goring's story with suggestions of a French invasion to help King Charles ; as Richelieu was Pym's well-wisher and, as some whispered, his paymaster, there was a nice irony in the tale. Parliament asked for the ports to be stopped up, and appointed a secret committee, headed by Pym, Hampden, and Clotworthy, to investigate the danger. In the atmosphere thus created, the Lords began to debate the Attainder Bill.

The stopping of the ports had let loose a thousand unemployed sailors in the streets, and the rioting became very dangerous. At the beginning of the trial, the crowd outside had " saluted " Strafford, " and he them with great humility and courtesy." Now they were besieging Westminster, threatening Bristol for his obstinate impartiality, and Digby for speaking against Attainder, posting up a list of the fifty-nine " traitors " in the Commons who had voted against the Bill. The Court believed that the whole feeling had been artificially worked up. It detected Lord Pembroke encouraging a mob to shout against Strafford. One of the rioters confessed that " the Parliament men had sent for them." And it was curious that one crowd had vanished to their homes at a mere word from the House of Commons. But when the

Lords met to debate the third reading of the Attainder Bill, their coaches were besieged by armed mobs crying for Justice and Execution. The streets were unsafe for any who believed the two words were not synonymous. Of 150 Peers, about a hundred were accustomed to arrive for debate. On this crucial day, only 46 entered the House. Eleven brave men voted against the Bill. It was passed. Pym had succeeded.

His defenders say, and with reason, that in a crisis a politician must not be too scrupulous; that Strafford was a traitor to English liberty, if not in English law; that he had to be destroyed in order that a new England might arise. There is much truth in such contentions, as well as much ignorance. But if murder was done for the sake of liberty, it was only such liberty as comes from the transference of sovereignty into the hands of Parliament, of committees, and of public petitions. It was just these things that were defaced in the process, just these on which was laid a curse that has never been lifted. If the atmosphere of Parliament to-day is curiously repellent to a casual onlooker, it is to be remembered that its victory was sealed by the blood of Strafford and of the hundreds of men for whose death the unjudicial murder suggested a model.[1]

---

[1] The Commons' vote might prevent Strafford's attainder being quoted as a legal precedent, it could not prevent the evil example. The next fifty years were to be filled with wild accusations of " Treason " and horribly frequent executions, the worst being those connected with the so-called Popish Plot, when Shaftesbury had perfected Pym's methods.

Strafford himself warned the Lords of the danger : " Except your Lordships' wisdoms provide for it, it may be the shedding of my blood may make way for the tracing " (? hunting) " of yours. . . . If such learned gentlemen as these " (the prosecuting counsel), " whose tongues are well acquainted with such proceedings, shall be started out against you ; if your friends, your counsel, denied access to you ; if your professed enemies admitted to witness against you ; if every word, intention, or circumstance of yours be sifted and alleged as treasonable, not because of a Statute, but because of a consequence or construction of lawyers, pieced up in a high rhetorical strain, and a number of supposed probabilities—I leave it to your Lordships' consideration to foresee what may be the issue of such dangerous and recent precedents."

Meanwhile, there was one organ of government over which Pym had no control. The Bill had passed the two Houses : it was not law until it received the signature of King Charles.

Charles had attempted to rescue Strafford from the Tower : his failure had been disastrous. He had seen Pym privately, twice ; we shall never know what passed between the two men, but it was thought that Charles offered him high office to save Strafford's life, and that Pym refused. Finally, he had adopted Lord Saye's advice. After the Restoration, when Saye had fished successfully in twenty years of troubled water and earned the nickname of " Old Subtlety," it was believed that Saye's suggestion was made with intention to betray. It was simple and sounded reasonable : it was recommended by Bristol and Savile. Charles must summon the two Houses to a conference, admit that Strafford was guilty of many " oversights " and " misdemeanours," and promise not to employ him again ; but he must tell Parliament that they were using a charge of High Treason to kill a man who had committed no treason. Charles did so, taking occasion to deny that Strafford had suggested the use of the Irishmen in England or had ever counselled despotism. It is impossible to doubt that an acceptance of the King's offer would have helped to save England from the terrible woes that ensued. But both Houses professed indignation at it as an attempt to interfere with the course of justice.

Charles still hoped to save his servant's life, wrote promising to do so, in spite of the " strange mistaking and conjuncture of these times." Now the House had passed their Bill. On Saturday morning it lay awaiting the Royal signature. On Sunday evening it was still unsigned. Outside the windows of Whitehall a mob still roared for Strafford's blood. To refuse assent could hardly save him from their violence. The Constable of the Tower had openly boasted that he would execute the prisoner with

or without the royal warrant.   It was not Strafford's life
that was at stake now, it was King Charles's honour.

He had been accused of every fault, never of deserting
a servant.   He had supported Buckingham in the teeth of
terrible storms, he had supported men wiser and better
than Buckingham, as well as men more foolish and corrupt.
He had taken on himself the consequences of their actions.
Now he was asked to assist in destroying the wisest and
best of all.

The Lords came to beg for his signature.   The Queen
was weeping before his eyes ; what counsel she gave, we
do not know, but she and her children were in certain
danger from the bloodthirsty crowd.   The lawyers gave
their opinion and they echoed Pym ; no single charge was
treasonable, but the sum of all might amount to treason.
The Council met and was more honest ; it refused to pronounce on Strafford's guilt, but a king " must be more
tender of the safety of the kingdom than of any one person,
how innocent soever."   The Bishops came, and twisted
religion to urge signature " even for conscience' sake."
Their natural leader was in the Tower now, but one can
hardly doubt what Laud's counsel would have been.   As
it was, only two were worthy of their Master : Ussher
from Ireland, Strafford's friend ; Juxon, who was to be
at Charles's side when it was his turn to tread a scaffold.
Men might talk of political consequences, reinterpret the
law, wrench religion from its hinges.   Still the King's mind
was dominated by one thought—" This man hath done
nothing worthy of death."   It was a strange fate that
put such a man as Charles in the place of Pontius
Pilate.

Perhaps he would never have done it but for Strafford's
letter ; it had been six days in his pocket.   It is too long to
quote in full, though there is hardly a phrase in it uncharged
with tragic meaning.   When we grow weary of the " thrills "
of modern fiction, we might do worse than read again
Strafford's last letter to his King.

" May it please Your Sacred Majesty,—

" It hath been my greatest grief in all these troubles, to be taken as a person who should endeavour to represent and set things amiss between Your Majesty and Your People, and to give counsels tending to the disquiet of the Three Kingdoms. . . .

" Nay, it is most mightily mistaken ; for unto Your Majesty it is well known my poor and humble advices concluded still in this—that Your Majesty and Your People could never be happy, till there was a right understanding betwixt you and them ; and that no other means were left to effect and settle this happiness, but by the Counsel and assent of Your Parliament. . . .

" Yet such is my misfortune, that this Truth findeth little credit ; yea, the contrary seemeth generally to be believed, and myself reputed as one who endeavoured to make a separation between You and Your People. Under a heavier censure than this I am persuaded no gentleman can suffer. . . .

" This bringeth me in a very great strait ; there is before me the ruin of my Children and Family, hitherto untouched, in all the Branches of it, with any foul crime. Here are before me the many ills which may befall Your Sacred Person and the whole Kingdom, should Yourself and Parliament part less satisfied one with the other than is necessary for the preservation both of King and People. Here are before me the two things most valued, most feared by mortal men, Life or Death.

" To say, Sir, that there hath not been a strife in me, were to make me less man than, God knoweth, my infirmities make me. . . .

" But, with much sadness, I am come to a resolution of that which I take to be best becoming me, and to look upon it as that which is most principal in itself . . . the Prosperity of Your Sacred Person and the Commonwealth, things infinitely before any private man's interest. And therefore in few words, as I put myself wholly upon the

Honour and Justice of my Peers . . . so now, to set Your
Majesty's Conscience at liberty, I do most humbly beseech
Your Majesty for the prevention of evils which may happen
by Your refusal, to pass this Bill, and by this means to
remove—praised be God, I cannot say this accursed, but,
I confess,—this unfortunate thing, forth of the way towards
that blessed Agreement which God, I trust, shall ever
establish between You and Your Subjects.

" Sir, my consent should more acquit you herein to
God than all the world can do beside. To a willing man
there is no injury done. And as, by God's grace, I forgive
all the world, with a calmness and meekness of infinite
contentment to my dislodging soul, so, Sir, to you I can
give the life of this world with all the cheerfulness imagin-
able, in the just acknowledgement of Your exceeding
favours ; and only beg of Your Goodness you would
vouchsafe to cast Your gracious Regard upon my poor
son and his three sisters. . . .

" God long preserve Your Majesty.

            " Your Majesty's most faithful and humble
                        Subject and Servant,

                                    " STRAFFORD."

Late on Sunday evening, Charles called a second Council.
Their opinion was unaltered. Charles must do the unpardonable thing, the thing for which he never forgave
himself until the day of his own death. He gave way.
He excused himself by saying that his wife and children
must be saved from the mob. He promised, next day, to
sign the Attainder.

When they told Strafford, the iron self-control that had
prompted his letter broke down for an instant. " Put not
your trust in princes ! " he exclaimed bitterly. But when
a friend suggested that Charles might satisfy the Opposition
and save his servant by offering to abolish bishops, he
replied that he would not " buy his life at so dear a
rate."

Charles sent a last letter to the Peers, begging, though the Bill was law, for a remittance of the death penalty ; even delay, he added, would be a charity. The postscript was fatal, it suggested that a last attempt of rescue might be contemplated. Charles may have intended one, or he may merely have hoped that certain people would change their minds. But the Lords were obdurate : they professed themselves alarmed for the Queen's safety. " Stone dead hath no fellow."

They refused Strafford leave to see his friend Laud, unless he petitioned Parliament : Strafford would have no more to do with Parliament, for he was now before " an Higher Court, where neither partiality is to be expected nor error feared." They refused him leave for private execution inside the walls. Friends were expected to attend a friend's execution ; the " patient " claimed their prayers and encouragement. Strafford had to face serried thousands of his enemies. But as he passed out to Tower Hill, Laud's hands were stretched through the window-bars to bless him.

He told the crowd he forgave all enemies, with heart, not lips : it had been his " ill-hap to be misconstrued." The executioner prayed for the customary forgiveness for himself : for " you and all the world," said Strafford. He was laying down his life for peace and goodwill in England, and he was not the man to spoil the sacrifice with last-minute rancour.

He was a soldierly man and without fear. His calmness steadied others in the ghastly business at which none could have been expert : it was twenty years since Ralegh had been beheaded. A single stroke released his " dislodging soul " to its rest.

Two tales remain to be told. At the crisis of the trial it had been noticed that Pym faltered, searched his notes in vain, stood silent and ashamed for quite a time. His friend the Scottish commissioner attributed it to an act of God—" to humble the man." The great poet Browning has suggested that it was rather remorse for an old friend and comrade. The two theories are not incompatible, and perhaps the Scotsman was right.

The second is a trifle. On the night of the execution, a number of gentlemen sat drinking in the Cross Keys Tavern. They argued whether Strafford had died a Christian or no ; one suggested that he was a Papist, one a Puritan, another an atheist. "Why trouble ye us with this damned fellow ? " said a certain Mr. Lambert. "He is as sure damned as I will break this glass ! " He threw the wineglass up in the air. It hit the ceiling, it hit the wall, it hit the floor. But it did not break.

CHAPTER SIXTEEN

APPEAL

1642

A DISASTROUS chain of events had led Charles to the humiliation and dishonour of Strafford's death. Its first link had been an attempt to assimilate Scottish worship to that of England ; now it looked as if his opponents would make a converse error. Pym's majority in the Commons was already threatened by the question of the bishops. Some members wanted the Church to remain an " established " institution, controlled by experts independent of laymen, dependent on the Crown. Others were embarking on a course that could only end in remodelling her to match the Presbyterian Kirk. As always, the question of principle involved a question of money. England had escaped proper taxation for years. It was taxed now, but the burden might be lightened by abolishing bishops and confiscating episcopal revenues.

For the moment the attempt, resisted by a strong minority in the Commons, was blocked by the Lords, who refused even to exclude bishops from the Upper House. The only agreement was on the subject of diminishing the Royal Prerogative. Parliament first established its position by forcing Charles to renounce the right to dissolve it without its leave. All his expedients for financial independence were voted down, ship-money, knighthood, forest enlargement, unparliamentary Customs dues. Then the Prerogative Courts were swept away, Star Chamber, the Council for Wales, the Council for the North, High Commission.

No one can doubt that they had been arbitrary instruments of monarchy. High Commission had handed Prynne over to Star Chamber for his cruel sentence : it had persecuted Puritans with fines and reprimands. It has been calculated that such activities represent about 5 per cent. of its cases. The remaining 95 per cent. were not begun on its own initiative, they were brought before it by any one who preferred High Commission to the ordinary courts. One such case may be set beside Prynne's. Two poor men accused a merchant of adultery. They forfeit sympathy by asking blackmail. The merchant rushed them before Quarter Sessions and had them condemned to such floggings that one " lost his voice and almost his reason," the other died under the lash. The survivor appealed to High Commission.[1]

Of the Council for the North we have already spoken. Its abolition, says Dr. Reid, was " highly profitable to the judges and lawyers," but " established a judicial system which, at least in the North, amounted to an absolute denial of justice to poor men."

If such were some of the remoter results of the landslide that was now destroying English monarchy, there was no doubt of its immediate cause : an army of Scots was still encamped in England. Parliament had no particular use for it now that Strafford was dead and the Prerogative in ruins ; and it was extremely expensive. Pym, prefiguring the confiscations of the Civil War, proposed to pay the Scots by seizing the estates of " those who had caused the mischief." He even suggested a Forced Loan on London, but for this amazing attempt to take a page out of King Charles's book he was called to order by the Commons. The obvious remedy was to send the Scots home.

Charles had a notion that he might make use of them, now that they had become a burden on their former paymasters. He announced his intention of visiting Scotland. Parliament could not prevent him, it could only send

[1] *Cal. of State Papers.* Dom. 406. 75. ? 1638.

commissioners to watch his movements. Bedford.
Hampden, and Saye's son, Fiennes, followed the King
northward. Three months after Strafford's death, Charles
was reviewing Leslie's army at Newcastle ; next day he
rode into Edinburgh.

He had long distrusted the double-faced Hamilton :
" very active," he called him, " in his own preservation."
His adviser was now Montrose, a man of great and versatile
genius. He was to show himself the greatest soldier of
the age, greater than Cromwell, as Cromwell's admirers
confess. He was something of a poet. He was an acute
political thinker, and his thought was now leading him to
the conclusion that only Royal Prerogative could prevent
the design of Argyle and his friends " to stand and domineer
over the People in an aristocratick way." For the present,
Montrose counselled conciliation and Charles was endlessly
conciliatory. He assented to every Bill, he distributed
offices to his late opponents, he ratified Presbyterianism
in the Kirk, and even listened to hours of Presbyterian
preaching. He was warmly welcomed everywhere.
Hampden and his colleagues might well grow nervous. But
the Scots had no intention of helping Charles against the
English Parliament. If Charles had hoped to collect any
evidence about collusion between Hampden's friends and
the Scots (for impeachments were still in the air), he was
disappointed. He began to grow weary of finding every
concession followed by a fresh demand, every friend of
Argyle's getting a Government post. He was soon to
receive a hint that he was not wanted in Scotland.

Edinburgh was still mediæval in its ideas of public order ;
the great lords kept large and quarrelsome retinues, and
lived in a world of armed intrigue, back-alley murder, and
open battle in the streets. In this atmosphere arose " the
Incident " : its non-committal name indicates that no one
knew what happened or whether anything happened at
all. What was supposed to be happening was a plot to
murder Argyle and Hamilton.

They accused Montrose and, by implication, King Charles, stirred up all kinds of rumours, and added verisimilitude to them by running out of Edinburgh. Charles rode to Parliament and begged, with tears in his eyes, for an open investigation; it was refused, for matters must be sifted in secret. For days he argued. " However the matter go," he said, " I must see myself cleared " ; a secret inquiry was " a private way to Hell." Parliament refused his request—" just and reasonable," as he truthfully called it. His credit in Scotland was ruined, whatever support he had gained was destroyed. When Argyle returned in triumph, he had to give him a pension and a Marquisate, Hamilton a Dukedom, Leslie, the illiterate soldier, the Earldom of Leven.

On top of everything came the news from Ireland. Strafford had hinted at danger, and even suggested that his own arraignment might prove the signal for rebellion. The deputies who succeeded him were a stupid soldier and an adventurer grown rich by evicting Irishmen from their land. Strafford had been high-handed, but he had been honest and well-intentioned; his successors were neither. Six months after his death, England heard that the Papists had risen and slaughtered three hundred thousand English —men, women, and children—with fiendish barbarity.

It was not the truth, though the truth was sufficiently appalling. The Irish had determined to reverse the plantation of Ulster by evicting English intruders. Some of their leaders had tried to do it without bloodshed, some had not cared. There was much deliberate murder and some bad atrocities. Many of the English had been stripped of clothing as well as land, and died of starvation and exposure. Perhaps ten thousand had perished thus, five thousand been deliberately killed.

The blame has been laid partly on Charles, but the charge is unproven. He had been corresponding with the Catholic Lords who later joined the rebellion. They were grumbling that the Scots had secured Presbyterianism by rebellion, while Ireland's religion was still proscribed. It is probable that Charles promised them some form of toleration in return for support, and they may have twisted this into an argument that rebellion would have the King's sanction.

This hypothetical accusation of blundering was embroidered at the time into a story that Charles had ordered a Papist massacre. The evidence was supplied in curious fashion. There is still extant an order, signed in the King's name, requiring the Catholics to seize Protestant strongholds. It is dated October 1, 1641; it is sealed with the Royal Seal of Scotland; it is a palpable forgery. No one knows who held the seal on October 1, for it was passing from a retiring Chancellor to his successor. Whoever had charge of it that day has a great deal to answer for; but he had struck a shrewd blow at the King's reputation.

It is a curious feature of many Revolutions that all their permanent results are achieved in a few months or even weeks, with little or no bloodshed. There follow years of agony, while extremists and reactionaries struggle with each other, and then a settlement on the former basis. It was so with England in the middle of the seventeenth century. By the end of 1641, our constitution was, roughly speaking, that of the 1660 Restoration. The years between produced nothing but evil memories.

Charles had accepted the new settlement; no doubt he resented it in private, but there is little sign of any plans to overthrow it. Meanwhile Pym was losing his unquestioned majority in the Commons; his friends among the Peers were in the minority again, the two Houses were at odds over the bishops. A balance of powers, each impotent against the other, might possibly have given England peace.

That hope was destroyed by the Irish rebellion. The problem became a military one again. Charles was active and urgent about the necessity for crushing the Irish

16

Papists. The Commons professed a like enthusiasm, but
they showed themselves as dilatory and grudging as could
be ; while they bickered with the King about money and
recruiting and army appointments, the flame licked up
Protestantism in Ulster and spread through the length
and breadth of Ireland. They can hardly be blamed.
They were quite sure that Charles would use any army he
obtained to reverse all that the Long Parliament had
done. He probably had no immediate intention of so
doing, but no one could calculate what might happen when
a victorious army returned home in a year or so from re-
conquered Ireland. There was no calling Strafford from
the grave, but Pym and Hampden and Essex might join
him there. A situation had arisen with which no constitution could deal. Men had utterly ceased to trust one
another, there was no stability, no assurance that achievement might not be followed by defeat. And Parliament
had fixed the penalty of defeat : it was death.

The struggle for army control was complicated by the
struggle over the bishops. A considerable Royalist party
was forming in the Commons. London was inventing the
nicknames of " Roundhead " and " Cavalier."

Cromwell was beginning to become prominent in the
Commons, though he was nearly shouted down for a disappointing speech about the bishops. He saw no necessity
for bishops to be so rich. He contradicted the argument
that to abolish them was to undermine the class-system.
Bishops could go, while the gentry remained the gentry.
Cromwell was in Pym's camp, with his kinsmen Hampden
and St. John. He was slow to recognize that another was
forming.

The split was defined by the Grand Remonstrance, a
vote of no confidence in King Charles's government, or his
sincerity in maintaining the concessions wrung from him.
Cromwell told Falkland there would be little trouble in
getting it passed. It was noon when the final debate began,
embittered by bad news from Ireland and rumours of a

second Army Plot.[1] While the light lasted, the talk went on, and when darkness came the candles shone on angry faces. The Royalist minority claimed the right of a minority to register a public protest of disagreement; one of them was sent to the Tower for pressing the claim. Swords, still scabbarded, were brandished between the debaters; at one time it looked as though they would be drawn and St. Stephen's Chapel witness the first battle of the Civil War. But a peaceful vote was taken—159 Ayes, 148 Noes. It was four in the morning, but the Remonstrance had passed. Falkland had the laugh of Cromwell. " I will take your word for it another time," said Oliver, and he added that, but for the majority of 11 votes, he would have sold up his property and emigrated to America. " So near," says Clarendon, " was the poor kingdom to its deliverance."

If there were so many Royalists in the House of Commons, there were more outside, and they were growing impatient with their King. Even Laud, in the diary he still kept in the Tower, had written that the King who let Strafford die was " a mild and gracious prince who knew not to be, or to be made, great." Suckling, before that, had told Charles that all his troubles came from lying down in the position prescribed by law, and allowing his enemies to walk over him. It is the kind of advice that every king must listen to, must occasionally follow, according to the demands of circumstance. Charles had resisted the temptation, or lost the opportunity, put it which way you will. Now he would abide by the constitution; the Commons had wrenched it out of shape for the present; time might bring a remedy.

Henrietta was indignant and impatient with her husband. She was intriguing for money from abroad, for

[1] This one had no foundation in reality, except a document circulated among the troops, suggesting that they should prevent and punish any one who raised mobs to overawe Parliament and endanger the life of King or Peers.

a promise of troops if actual rebellion broke out. She was still hoping for help from the Pope, though Charles refused to give any encouragement to the hope that he might secretly turn Catholic. She increased and justified the suspicions of Parliament, infinitely strengthening its position. She made the position of her fellow-Catholics terribly dangerous. Parliament had already insisted on a priest being hanged, drawn, and quartered at Tyburn, as in the good old days when Elizabeth reigned, instead of a milksop with a Papist wife. How far Charles was implicated in Henrietta's foolish games it is difficult to discover. Certainly he should have found means to stop her. She was surrounded by gallant officers and rowdy bullies who did not mince matters when they spoke of " King Pym " and his colleagues. She began to wonder whether she was married to a man or a constitutional maxim.

Then came news that moved even Charles to action. Rightly or wrongly, it was reported at Whitehall that Pym and his friends had met in the City, discussed Henrietta's intrigues, and decided to impeach the Queen.

There was nothing for it but to strike first, arrest Pym and his friends, and try them for High Treason. Charles picked on Lord Mandeville, soon to become Earl of Manchester by his father's death. The choice was probably unwise and he soon concentrated on five members of the Commons—Pym, Hampden, Hazlerig, Holles, and Strode. The charges were drawn up ; if they could be proved, they amounted to a treason far blacker than Strafford's. The members had conspired to subvert the Constitution by destroying regal authority and seizing " an arbitrary and tyrannical power over the lives, liberties, and estates " of Englishmen ; had invited the Scots to invade England ; had deliberately cast " foul aspersions " on the King in order to alienate the people's affections ; had raised mobs to overawe and put pressure upon Parliament, destroying its ancient freedom.

It had long been a principle that a charge of High Treason justified any reasonable precaution against the accused and overrode lordly or parliamentary privilege. No impartial Parliament could have denied this, no Englishman would have hesitated to put it into practice against an unpopular, for instance a Popish, form of Treason. Yet when Charles ordered the sealing up of the members' private lodgings to stop the destruction of incriminating evidence, the Commons arrested his officers. They promised Charles to detain the accused men to answer their accusers (we shall see how they kept their promise), but said they must appoint a committee to debate whether their arrest would not be a breach of parliamentary privilege. One can imagine the results of such dilatory proceedings in a case like Gunpowder Treason ; and it was a civil war that was at stake. Charles decided to act. He would arrest the members himself.

Needless to say, the plan was betrayed, for no secret was safe at Whitehall. There was a fatal delay, possibly due to a lingering scruple in the King's mind, to fear of a fiasco, to mere irresolution. A morning was wasted. The members must be arrested at the afternoon session. Still Charles doubted, and Henrietta fumed. " Go, you coward," she said, " pull those rogues out by the ears or never see my face again ! " Charles went. But she had already destroyed his slender chance by telling Lucy Carlisle of the design, and Lucy had slipped a message through to Pym. A Frenchman, posted perhaps by the French ambassador, was watching in the street for Charles and his following : some three or four hundred men, army officers and others, came at his heels. The final warning reached Pym in plenty of time. The five members got into a boat and disappeared downstream to the City.

One of them, Strode, was for staying to face his trial, but he was over-persuaded. One cannot help wondering why Pym did not follow Strafford's example and rely on the justice of the Peers. There is not the slightest indication that Charles intended anything but a strictly legal trial— indeed anything else would have been madness. We are generally told that Pym had the country on his side. He certainly had the City on his side, and mobs could probably have been got to shout for his acquittal as they had shouted for Strafford's blood. It is at least possible that Pym and his friends fled because a trial would have involved some most inconvenient revelations. It is even conceivable that they were guilty of High Treason, knew themselves guilty, and feared that the King might have sufficient evidence to prove their guilt before the House of Lords. They certainly fled.

Charles strode into the House. He told his followers to wait outside, but one of them held the door open so that the members could see the cocked pistols and naked swords. "By your leave, Mr. Speaker," said Charles to Lenthall, "I must borrow your chair a little." A glance had already told him that Pym was gone, and he could do nothing but carry off a defeat with some show of dignity. He apologized to the House for the necessity of intruding : he was careful of their privileges, but no privilege covered Treason : while there was Treason abroad, the House could never be "in the right way, that I do heartily wish it." He called the five names, but there was no answer. "I see all the birds are flown," he said. He asked for help in securing them, repeated that he contemplated nothing but a fair trial, and rose to go. Some cried "Privilege !" to his back. Some looked at the little army outside the door and expected a massacre. Charles led his followers quietly back to Whitehall, but one member ran home to make his will.

The City refused to surrender the members, and invited Skippon, a veteran from the Dutch wars, to take its trained bands in hand. Charles and Henrietta retired to Hampton Court. She said afterwards that his love had never shown so perfectly, though she confessed that it was through her and Lady Carlisle that the secret had leaked out. "Never did he treat me for a moment with less kindness than before it happened—though I had ruined him."

There was a weary road yet to tread before he knew himself ruined for ever. There were too many Englishmen, scattered over the country, who would not see the monarchy destroyed by manœuvres at Westminster : they would soon draw together into an army. Meanwhile the Commons struggled for control of the militia. Still Charles tried to placate them, accepted a Bill excluding Bishops from the Lords, even promised to put the militia under commanders approved by Parliament. Meanwhile he took Henrietta to Dover and sent her abroad, galloping along the cliffs until her ship faded from sight. Then he went to Newmarket to treat about the militia.

The Parliamentary list of commanders contained Harry Vane and one other commoner. The rest were the peers who had been supporters (as some said directors) of the opposition in the Commons. Essex was to control Yorkshire, the Hull arsenal, Montgomery, and Staffordshire ; Lord Pembroke, two Welsh counties, Wiltshire, Hampshire, and Portsmouth ; his son, three more counties in Wales ; Bedford, Saye, and Brooke, a county each ; Warwick, Salisbury, and Holland, two apiece. The great lords were demanding the keys of England. It was almost as if the Middle Ages had returned.

Charles met them with anger and gave the lie to their accusations. " Have I violated your Laws ? " he asked, " Have I denied to pass one Bill for the ease and security of my subjects ? " Pembroke begged him to grant them the militia temporarily. " By God ! " said Charles, " not for an hour."

Pembroke himself had no brain for politics, or for anything but horseflesh—James and Charles had used him mainly as a hunting companion ; but his defection was serious, for he was the richest man in England. Handsome, worthless, Holland was also very wealthy : he had been Henrietta's favourite, reaped every possible profit from a position at Court, but was now following Warwick, his brother and fellow-shareholder in the Providence Company. He was to change sides three more times until Parliament grew tired of him and had his head off.

A still more damaging defection was that of Northumberland, a politician and an honest one. His estates had suffered from forest enlargement, but he grumblingly followed the King until the last moment. He was Admiral, and with Warwick's help brought the navy over to Parliament. The men were inclined to Puritanism, and had been vilely paid and fed : they said Parliament could not treat them worse and might treat them better. Many repented the decision and rejoined the King,—when it was too late.

Charles began to roam round England, collecting money, pleading the justice of his cause, fighting slanders. Both sides began to raise troops. In Manchester the Parliamentary agents were recruiting, when in rode Lord Strange. He saw a crowd joining the Roundheads, he told his followers to charge and disperse them. Some of the citizens were wounded, one died of his injuries a day or two later. The Civil War had begun.

While his kingdom split asunder, brother taking leave of brother to fight on different sides, Charles visited for an hour or two one little oasis of peace, where politics dwindled to a distant and evil noise.

In the year of Charles's accession, a widowed lady had bought the ruined manor of Little Gidding, in Huntingdonshire. The former owners had turned the fields to grass ; the country people had vanished, but for one family in a shepherd's hut ; the church was a barn. Her son, Nicholas Ferrar, who had helped in Middlesex's impeachment, came to join her and escape from a turbid and unsatisfying world. Round them formed a little community, living very austerely, devoted to prayer, contemplation, and good works. They took no vows ; if any member wished to marry, Little Gidding gave its blessing —but it said good-bye. They taught children from the neighbouring town, practised and wrote music, printed, illustrated, and bound books : King Charles had been sent specimens of their work.

Naturally, they were called Papists by those who did not know them. A pamphlet begged Parliament to suppress the " Arminian Nunnery " ; its cover bore a crude woodcut of Mrs. Ferrar (strongly resembling Mrs. Noah in outline) leering out of a nun's hood and dangling a Popish rosary. Such is propaganda.

Charles had visited Little Gidding before in happier times. Now he brought with him little Prince Charles and Elizabeth's son, Rupert Palatine. The Ferrars came out to meet them, kissed the King's hands, and escorted him into their church. He asked where were the Popish images he had heard so much about, where even a single cross. Ferrar had kept the place absolutely bare, to avoid gossip. " What will not malice invent ? " said the King. They went to see the books, and Rupert was shown the engraved illustrations : years after he was to be the inventor of mezzotints, and one wonders if he remembered Little Gidding in his workshop. Then the young princes were given apple-pies and cheesecakes in the buttery, and they made Charles eat his share. He gave the community some money which he had won at cards. " Little Gidding is a happy place," he said, " I am glad to have seen it." The horses were brought round and the visitors mounted in the evening light. " Pray," said Charles, " pray for my speedy and safe return." Then he rode away. Next time he saw Little Gidding it was at dead of night, and he was a hunted fugitive.

On August 22, 1642, the King raised his standard in a field by Nottingham Castle. Eighty peers were to rally round it, a hundred and seventy-five of the Commons. The remainder—thirty of the Upper, three hundred of the Lower House—still sat at Westminster, still styled themselves the Parliament of England. Elections being out of the question, they co-opted new members, proclaimed the

absentees as traitors, and began to confiscate their estates.
They published a manifesto, accusing Charles of prolonged
misgovernment, and defending the recourse to arms as a
defence against plots for the violent subversion of Parliament. The manifesto denied that Parliament could be
an arbitrary power, or a breaker of law, for it represented
the nobility and gentry of England, and it was " most
improbable that the nobility and gentry of England should
conspire to take away the law, by which they enjoy their
estates, are protected from any act of violence and power,
and differenced from the meaner sort of people, with
whom otherwise they would be but fellow-servants."
Any one who imagines that Charles was fighting democracy would do well to study these words. His offence
was that he had tried to make rich and poor fellow-servants
of the Crown ; and he had done something to make them
fellow-servants of the community.

Meanwhile, at Wellington, the King took public oath
before his army that, whatever the outcome of the war, he
would make no attempt to destroy the authority of Parliament or even revoke the recent legislation : he was fighting
to defend monarchy from further aggression.[1] Both sides
were recruiting the poor and calling on the gentry to bring
their swords and followers to defend Liberty, Law, and
Religion. Some remained neutral, or tried to. Many
changed from one side to the other. Some families split
for conscience' sake, some (it was whispered) in order to
have a friend in both camps and save the property from
confiscation. Young Evelyn came to tell the King that
he was loyal but, as his estate was so near London, he could
not take up arms for fear of confiscation ; then he departed

---

[1] " . . . if it please God, by His blessing upon this army, raised for
my necessary defence, to preserve me from this rebellion, I do solemnly
and faithfully promise, in the sight of God, to maintain the just privileges
and freedom of Parliament, and to govern by the known laws of the land,
particularly to observe inviolably the laws consented to by me in this
Parliament. When I willingly fail in these particulars I will expect no
aid or relief from any man or protection from Heaven."

for foreign climes. Behind him nobler minds were making their choice.

We all know the kind of history-book which makes that choice an easy one : the frivolous and romantic, the obscurantist and the dupe became Cavaliers ; Parliament secured the serious-minded, the public-spirited, all who were alive to the real issue. The truth is, as usual, a little more complicated. A choice that sundered Milton from Juxon, Montrose from Cromwell, is not made without searchings of the soul.

The religious issue was the clearest. A Royalist victory meant the triumph of the ideas embodied in an old man who lay, almost forgotten, in the Tower. It would mean a Church governed by bishops, enforcing order, beauty, and some ceremony in her worship, enjoining charity towards Catholics. The victory of Parliament seemed to mean Presbyterianism (no one foresaw that the Parliamentary army would revolt against it), bitter cruelty to the Papists, a barer, or, as some thought, a nobler form of worship. It might mean more room for spiritual strugglings, more reaching out into the unknown, perhaps a more abundant life.

Politically, all was in confusion. The ancient machinery of co-operation, of sovereignty shared by King and Parliament, had broken down. No one had a real plan for the future, each side was busy blaming the other for the breakdown. Some accused Charles, believing that he had always despised Parliament in his heart, that he had tricked and thwarted its honest intentions, filched from it its ancient powers. Others held Eliot and Hampden and Pym responsible, saw only what was self-seeking in their aims, only the slander and injustice they had used to gain them : they believed the King had tried to satisfy all their reasonable demands and found them insatiable.[1]

---

[1] Margaret Eure to Sir R. Verney, 20/6/42 : " I am in such a great rage with the Parliament as nothing will pacify me, for they promised as all should be well if my Lord Strafford's head were off, and since then there is nothing better." [G. x. 213.]

Between the two views every man must judge for himself, and so long as men are men, they will differ in their judgment.

It is often assumed that the Cavaliers chose their side more by instinct, less by intelligence. It is an odd assumption to make of a party that commanded the allegiance of the Universities, and, on the whole, the majority of the best educated. It is perhaps true that a mere instinct of loyalty to the Crown was very potent, though a poor plea in disputation. When an institution is as old as monarchy and has sheltered millions through many centuries, the arguments in its favour are forgotten, the evil it does is apparent and easy to advertise. In our own day two institutions of immemorial antiquity— Marriage and Property—are in jeopardy : their power to do good has been unquestioned by the ordinary man for many centuries ; yet their defenders are curiously un- satisfying. Pick up a conservative newspaper, listen to the parson or the colonel in debate : most of their argu- ments are futile, they are constantly overwhelmed by the citing of one " hard case "—a poor man at the mercy of employers and landlords, a woman tied for life to a drunkard or a lunatic. Yet there are still good grounds for believing (with the majority of the best brains among our ancestors) that Marriage and Property are bare necessities to the continuance of human happiness ; for human salvation one must not mention nowadays, for fear of ridicule.

Instinctive or reasoned, warring convictions were soon to fill England with ruined homes, dead bodies, and weeping eyes. Some were riding to war with a sinking heart, some proud of their youth and unfleshed swords. Some dreamt of a new and better England, others only hankered for the swift decision that would send them home that winter to the petty round of dear and familiar things. Some hoped to free the King for ever from the rogues and tricksters who thwarted him in the dusty lobbies of Westminster. Some saw a mighty nation glad to be ruled by an assembly of its best and wisest, glad to be raised in dedication to a greater God than it had known before.

If anything survived from those bright August days, it was not to be the dreams. In eighteen years the Restoration would establish most of the evil in both parties—intolerance, intrigue, the greed of self-seeking courtiers, the opportunity for Parliament-men to dip hands into the public funds. And for two centuries the rich would make laws to extend their lands, their money, and their pride over the misery of the poor. Other lusts would have a swifter satisfaction : the avarice or personal spite to which war and confiscation gave an air of legality, the madness that destroyed beauty for no reason except that it was beautiful, the blind rage against fellow-Christians who looked to Rome for salvation, the murderous hatred for the Irish race.

CHAPTER SEVENTEEN

TRIAL BY BATTLE

1642–45

THEY will tell you in the Highlands that there is a curse upon the house of Stewart, most active in time of war. Consider the battles : Lostwithiel, Kilsyth, Killiecrankie, Prestonpans ; the victories are few and curiously fruitless. Sauchieburn, Flodden, Naseby, the Boyne, Culloden ; the defeats are utterly crushing. There are reasons for everything, if we can find them. Some see a hereditary strain of indecision, entering perhaps with Darnley, perhaps earlier, not expelled until the last and best loved Stewart, Bonnie Prince Charlie, drew sword in a hopeless cause. Even so, it is better to examine the particular circumstances of each failure. The Great Rebellion is the most decisive in the history of this unhappy race.

Many things contribute to success in war—enthusiasm, numbers, military experience, money, geographical position. Enthusiasm is almost impossible for a historian to weigh. The numbers in the Civil War seemed to have started about equal, or slightly to the King's advantage. The Scottish intervention upset the balance, and from that moment the Royalists diminished, the Roundheads multiplied. The same seems to have been true of the experienced soldiers : the King began by having more veterans from Dutch and German wars, but lost the advantage when the Scots joined his enemies. It is to our national credit that these experts did not manage to introduce into England the ghastly methods of the Thirty Years' War—though this was partly due to the desire of both parties to win the support of the neutrals. Rupert's sack of Bolton was

accompanied by atrocities, Montrose's Highlanders behaved
very badly in Aberdeen, and there was one horrible incident
on the evening of Naseby. Far the worst thing was done
after Philiphaugh by the Covenanters, when they butchered
300 women and children and, several days later, killed
50 prisoners to whom quarter had been granted, at the
order of the Lords and Clergy of the Kirk. Otherwise the
war was fought with unusually clean hands, until Cromwell's
army disembarked in Ireland.

Money the King lacked, especially towards the end.
He had many rich men on his side, particularly the Earl of
Newcastle. Lord Herbert (a very interesting person who
later anticipated James Watt by inventing a steam-engine)
poured half a million into his war-chest in two months.
Others melted their plate, diverted their rents, and mort-
gaged their estates for the King. Contributions were levied
on occupied territory. But, with a few important excep-
tions, Parliament had the support of the City merchants,
and, while the Navy kept the seas, London and most of
the ports produced a steady revenue to support the Roundhead armies. Towards the end, when both sides could
recruit as many men as they could pay and feed, Parliament's
greater and more lasting income was the decisive factor.

Finally, though the strategical positions were otherwise
equal, Parliament had in London an almost impregnable
base. There were Royalists or at least pacifists among its
poor, but the City as an organization, the City controlled
by merchants, shopkeepers, and apprentices, was Puritan
and Parliamentarian. Its offensive power was not negligible ; its trained bands fought well and were once induced
to march as far as Gloucester. Its defensive strength was
tremendous ; it was too big to be besieged, the fleet prevented its being starved out ; and it would be a bold army
that ventured into its labyrinth of populous streets.

Strategy was at a discount in the opening months.
If London, the ports, and a few inland towns, such as
Birmingham, were undoubtedly Puritan, nothing else was

certain, and the war was an affair of local feuds. The
gentry skirmished with each other and tried to capture the
arsenals. Trades and industries fought each other or
united against agricultural districts. Town and gown
struggled in Oxford and Cambridge, until Lord Saye
occupied the former, Cromwell the latter, disarming the
Universities and preventing them melting their plate for
the King. Cromwell's occupation was permanent, and
there is still a witness to it in the Elizabethan and Jacobean
silver (very rare in modern Oxford) which the Cambridge
Colleges kept hidden throughout the war. Meanwhile
active gentlemen secured the south-eastern counties for
Parliament ; Devon and the West, divided at first, were
won for the King by Sir Ralph Hopton's energy. Two
great recruiting-grounds, Wales and the North, fell to the
Royalists. Both had been under Prerogative government,
both were anti-Puritan ; the North followed the Earl of
Newcastle. The debatable ground was to be the Midlands
and the Thames valley.

Lord Essex began a larger game by a march into
Worcestershire. Charles advanced into the South Midlands, between him and London. He occupied the Cots-
wolds, hostile country where Brooke and Saye were the
principal landowners and their tenants refused food and
shelter to the Royalists. Puritanism was strong ; Banbury
was the traditional home of the Puritan who hanged his
cat for catching mice on Sunday. While the King's army
lay straddled across the three roads that lead into Banbury
from the north, news came that Essex was returning
from Worcestershire and lay to the westward, this side of
Stratford-on-Avon.

It was a Sunday morning in October. The county
people were beginning their weekly rest from the immemorial war against weed and weather. Very early in
the morning, the Royalists were awakened from their
scattered quarters and hurried over ridge and valley
towards Edge Hill.

They must have made a curious spectacle, hardly a pleasing one to the military eye. Some regiments were properly equipped with pike and musket. Some were mere crowds of men with bows, axes, and even sticks. Beside them rode gentlemen excellently mounted, some well armed, some bearing ancestral weapons unused since the Wars of the Roses or designed to slay deer and pheasants rather than men. One local squire had been found hunting in sight of the army on Saturday afternoon, and the King sent to ask whether he could not find something better to do when the kingdom was in jeopardy. He answered the call, and on Sunday night he lay dead below Edge Hill.

The place is well named. Here the broken hill country round Banbury ends in a sharp ridge whose western side is almost a cliff. Below lies the Vale of the Red Horse and the broad flat valley of Avon. It was noon before the army reached the top and looked across at Warwickshire. Its commander, Lindsey, was so tempted by the sight of that steep slope that he wanted to hold the crest as his position. If the war had been a professional one between well-supplied armies, the plan would have been excellent ; Essex had been a fool not to seize the ridge before the Royalists arrived, and he could never hope to storm such a position. But the amateurs knew better than Lindsey ; they wanted a battle : one battle would decide everything : the King must descend and fight Essex in the plain. They were supported by Rupert, who knew something of war. He, too, was tempted, not by the hill, but by the smooth fields below, so well adapted for his horsemen. He had trained them to charge home, not halt and fire pistols at the enemy in the old-fashioned style. Besides, to wait was to starve. There were no supplies, and some of the men had been thirty-six hours without food. Essex would gain strength ; Hampden was bringing up the cannon and the reserves from Stratford. The Council of War agreed with Rupert, Lindsey threw up his command in disgust, and the

17

army began to scramble down the slope.   The battle which
would decide everything was to be fought that afternoon.

The King had a late breakfast in a cottage on the hill.
With him sat Sir Edmund Verney, grizzled now, very
different from the youth who had struck a priest in Madrid.
He had grumbled at the war from the start ; it was all
about bishops, he said, and he detested bishops.   But he
had eaten the King's bread too long to desert him now.
The King gave him the royal standard to guard.   Then
he called for Dr. Harvey and gave him the young princes
to take care of.   Harvey took them behind a hedge and
lay there the whole afternoon, reading a book : he was
missing a great opportunity to study the Circulation of the
Blood.   Charles descended the slope and rode along the
ranks telling his men that at last the time was come for
" swords, not words."   Sir Jacob Astley was putting up
the famous prayer, " Lord, Thou knowest how busie I
must be this day ; if I forget Thee, do not Thou forget
mee."

Before them lay the many-coloured array of Parliament, better equipped with the proceeds of Hull arsenal,
somewhat inferior in numbers.   Essex's men were in
orange (among them Stapledon's troop with Captain Cromwell), and the whole army had adopted orange scarves as a
battle-sign.   Brooke's men were in purple, Holles's in red,
Mandeville's in blue : also in blue were the men Lord
Saye had sent under his son Nat Fiennes.   It was an odd
mixture of new and old.   Barons were revolting against
the King, Puritans were fighting for a new kind of Church,
City shareholders demanding a fresh system of finance.
Pym and St. John, fellow-shareholders, were organizing
war from London.   Hampden was bringing up his own
regiment of greencoats from Stratford.   Behind him, under
the tall spire, lay the remains of England's greatest man.
It was twenty-six years since Shakespeare had died, and
the England he had known was about to be blown to
pieces on a Sunday afternoon between Kineton and Edge

Hill. He had spoken often for rebel barons, more often for the glory and sanctity of kingship. On all men of lesser birth who interfered in government, he had poured an almost venomous scorn. But perhaps there was no motion in his grave when the cannon began to thunder twelve miles away.

A puff of smoke from a gun beside Brooke's regiment, and the battle had begun. Rupert was charging with the King's right wing : one troop of Parliamentarians deserted to him, throwing off their orange scarves ; the rest broke in hopeless rout. Rupert's men raced off in pursuit, killing the fugitives right into Kineton streets. Wilmot on the left made a similar charge, less successful. If he broke some regiments of Roundhead cavalry he left others unshaken, to take a decisive part in the battle. They wheeled in to help their infantry in the centre. The foot-soldiers were at it already, first with bullets and arrows, then spitting each other on pikes, clubbing away with musket-butts and cudgels. Parliament was having the best of it. Back and back the Royalists were driven, Rupert away and Roundhead horsemen circling round their flanks. The fight was hot round the royal standard. Verney's sword snapped in his hand, and he began to use the flagpole as a pike, until its spike buckled and broke. The hosts of the Lord compassed him about, and he disappeared. They carried away the standard : round its staff was clenched his severed hand. Soon the King himself was in danger : anxious courtiers wondered which way it would be safe for him to fly. He had no intention of flying. There was something of a rally as the autumn twilight began to fall. Rupert, after exchanging blows with Hampden in Kineton streets, had collected his men and returned. Charles was eager to order a last advance. He was told it was too late. Two tired and hungry armies lay down to sleep within sight of each other. Frost and damp came to add to the tortures of the wounded. The day was ended, one crowd of amateurs had run into

another and fought their battle. Five thousand Englishmen lay dead or dying on the field, and nothing whatever
had been decided.

Essex got home to London, the King captured Banbury
and then Oxford. Saye's men had gone, the town was
deprived of its arms, the Colleges became barracks and
arsenals. The King pressed on to London ; at Turnham
Green he found Essex protecting the capital with an army
twice the size of his own. There was talk of peace, but
the King would grant no armistice meanwhile, and ordered
Rupert to surprise Kingston. Parliament held this to be
treachery, and the negotiations came to nothing. The
King returned to Oxford.

Meanwhile Henrietta had returned, landing at Bridlington under the fire of Parliament's ships and risking the
cannon-balls to run back and rescue a pet dog from the
beach. After calling herself She Generalissimo, and leading
troops around the Midlands, she met Charles in July 1643,
near the battlefield of Edge Hill ; she had just come from
Stratford, where Shakespeare's daughter gave her welcome.

Her attempts to get help and money from abroad
never ceased for an instant. One of her messengers was
Sir Nicholas Crispe, who used to go through London disguised as a market woman ; his heart lies in the church a
few yards from Hammersmith Broadway. Better known
is her agent abroad, Sir Kenelm Digby, who had one of
the most picturesque careers of the century as a writer,
duellist, privateer, scientist, and romantic lover ; he was
one of England's strangest products, with an outlook on
life that sometimes recalls G. K. Chesterton's, sometimes
Admiral Beatty's. He was famous for his collection of
marbles and for a very gallant fight he had fought with
some Venetian galleys in the Levant. He was now at
Rome, and nearly hectored the Pope into sending Henrietta
money with no conditions attached.

Henrietta was established at Merton College, Charles
in Christchurch. The university still gave lectures and

conferred degrees, but war impinged everywhere. New College cloisters and tower became a powder-magazine, the Privy Council sat at Oriel, Magdalen Grove was a parking-place for guns. The King called the Law Courts to Oxford and made New Inn Hall into a Mint. He summoned what he called his " mongrel Parliament," and his followers who had left St. Stephen's Chapel assembled in Christchurch Hall. They were always busy with petitions for overtures of peace, never with proposals for winning the war. Charles must have smiled when the Westminster Parliament replied with demands that included the punishment of the King's followers.

He was happier when he left Oxford to accompany or lead his armies on the march. The temperate habits of a lifetime made simple food and poor lodging no hardship to him ; there was nothing unpleasant in having his frugal dinner in a Welsh cottage interrupted by his hostess coming to ask if the King had " finished with the cheese." Hidden in some remote corner of his complex nature was a strange interest in military things, first wakened by his brother Henry, which had made him, long ago, spend hours with manuals of war and problems of fortification. Like most men, he enjoyed the sight of well-mounted, well-equipped soldiers. Defeat found him ready to admire the bearing, if not the principles, of his enemies.

To return to Oxford was to plunge again into an atmosphere of jealousy, place-hunting, and divided counsels. The Cavaliers never forgot that they were independent gentlemen who had offered their swords and purses to the King, and unless they took a fancy to their commanders, commands were disputed and disobeyed. An amateur himself, the King could not secure unity among the professionals who were prodigal of conflicting advice. Rupert was proving the ablest soldier, both in strategy and in the training of new troops ; but Rupert, active, temperate, and fearless, was not at his best in a Council of War, and

a deal too fond of " seeming with a Pish ! to neglect all
another said and he approved not." [1]   The consequent
troubles did not seriously affect matters until defeat and
impoverishment began to work on nerves already frayed.
The Royalist strategy remained for a long time a model
of intelligence compared with the aimlessness of the
Roundheads.   For it required a Cromwell to save London's
counsels from all and more of the evils that afflicted
Oxford.

The armies became very different from the armed
crowds of Edge Hill.   Parliament, controlling the old
arsenals and the Kentish factory, had the better artillery.
But no one took much account of guns until it came to
siegework ; they decided no battles ; gunners were a
despised adjunct to an army, enjoying a particularly bad
name for foul language—due, said some, to their commerce with infernal substances.   Cavalry was very important ; its function was not yet, as the Victorian officer
said, " to add distinction to what would otherwise be a
vulgar brawl " : it was often the decisive arm.   Here the
King had, at first, a great advantage : his troopers were
better mounted, better trained, and better led.   Their only
rivals came from East Anglia, where Cromwell had grasped
the importance of training and was using a lighter breed of
horse, the product, largely, of King James's experiments
with Arab and Mediterranean strains.   They proved a
match for the old English " great horse," [2] which the
Cavaliers still favoured.   It is harder to make any comparison between the infantry on the two sides.   The very
complicated drill survives in military handbooks : since
there were no bayonets a regiment was half pikemen, half
musketeers with unwieldy matchlocks, needing an iron
rest to aim them, almost useless on rainy days.   The
handling of either weapon was an art, and one that England

---

[1] Warwick's memoirs.

[2] Contrariwise, the descendants of the " great horse " are now best
known in East Anglia, particularly the " Suffolk punch."

had long neglected.   It is not apparent that either side was quicker or better in relearning the lesson.

We have heard a great deal of the Puritan soldier, with his sturdy democratic tendencies, his occasional brutalities, his sober conduct, and the Bible in his knapsack ; enough, too, of the Cavalier gentleman ruining his fortune to supply the King, glad to forget privation and the growing threat of poverty and exile in songs and ribbons and fashionable oaths.   But few have had a word to say for the Royalist rank and file.   They suffered as much and more as their brothers in Parliament's ranks, starved and went naked more often, whistled more often for their pay.   They faced greater odds.   They, too, did cruel things, and they, too, worshipped God, perhaps a God more intelligible than the Puritan Jehovah.   They sweated and died unnoticed.   Few rose to command, none to ease or affluence.   Some returned, embittered or philosophical, to penniless homes ; many were drafted into the Parliamentary armies ; a few were sold as slaves in Barbadoes.   History knows little of their fate.   They were defeated.

There was little prospect of that defeat after the first year of war.   The King's cause was in the ascendant ; a strategic plan was emerging, sprung, probably, from Rupert's excellent if erratic brain.   There was to be a Triple Advance on London.   Sir Ralph Hopton was to push up from the west through Hampshire ; Rupert himself would march along the Thames valley ; Newcastle would come down the Great North Road.

The scheme was held up by the Puritan ports : there was insufficient artillery to bombard them, and " masking " them kept whole armies in idleness.   Hopton left Plymouth in his rear, but had to wheel north to help in the attacks on Bristol and Gloucester.   Bristol fell, but the central advance was still held up by the resistance of Gloucester.   Essex decided to relieve the hard-pressed town and marched the London trained bands across the

breadth of England. He raised the siege, but his way
home was blocked by the King, just south of Newbury,
and a long day's battle could not clear the road. Next
day, as the 'prentices prepared to renew the fight, they
found the King had drawn off, his ammunition all ex-
hausted. They got home to London with great tales to
tell. Rupert, still waiting for the Advance to get under
weigh, was raiding the Thames valley. Returning from
one foray, he heard that Hampden was in his wake, and
turned back, leapt his men over a hedge and charged across
Chalgrove Field. Hampden rode from the fight with a
pistol bullet in him, and reached Thame a dying man.
Charles sent the parson of Chinnor to ask how he fared ;
there were few of his enemies for whom he would have
done so much. But Hampden fared ill ; after many hours
of agony, he was dead. Meanwhile Cromwell was winning
laurels in the east : he had met Newcastle with the left
wing of the Advance, and hurled him back in Lincolnshire.
    Nevertheless, London was thoroughly alarmed. The
Triple Advance was stayed ; it might be resumed at any
moment : of defeating the King there seemed to be no
prospect.
    There was more talk of making peace. Even London
jibbed at Pym's war-taxes : long ago a lawyer had refused
to pay, gone to prison, and appealed in vain to the Petition
of Right. Now Pym was finding another Parliamentary
weapon to be double-edged. A deputation of Londoners,
bearing a petition against any treaty that meant surrender
to King Charles, was followed a day or two later by a mob
shouting for peace at any price. They were mostly women.
" Give us that dog, Pym ! " they yelled, and they would
not disperse until one had been shot down. Meanwhile
Pym, said a Royalist letter, was " crawling to his grave " ;
an internal abscess was eating away his life. In December
1643 King Pym was buried in Westminster Abbey and
lay there until the Restoration, when Charles II had his
body raked out and cast into a pit.

But Pym had left behind him one legacy, the Scottish
alliance, soon to be fatal to the King. The Scots had
offered their army to Charles. They had no quarrel with
him now ; he had conceded them everything, and upon
his concessions Argyle had built political power, the Presbyterians their Kirk. The price of their assistance was that
Presbyterianism should be forced on England too. Charles
refused, and the Scots addressed the same demand to
Parliament. Pym sent young Vane north to make better
terms. But bad news from the west induced Parliament
to give way : the Scottish conditions were accepted, the
Scots were to be paid £150,000 a month, and England was
to be made a Presbyterian country.

At Oxford, Montrose was begging for leave to go and
raise the Scottish Royalists before Argyle was ready with
his army. It seemed a hopeless venture, for no one knew
that Montrose could work miracles. Charles had begun
to rely again on Hamilton, who had repented of his double-
dealing and was soon to die for the King. Hamilton had
always disliked Montrose, and could point out that Montrose
had once been in arms for the Covenant. Charles had
little eye for men, never knew whom he could trust, and
certainly could not recognize the presence of a genius.
The fatal decision to do nothing was taken, Argyle went to
work unimpeded, and in the bitter January of 1643 a
" little old crooked man," now the Earl of Leven, crossed
the Tweed a second time, with 20,000 Covenanters at his
heels.

Rupert had just taken Newark in the Midlands. He
hastened north to meet the Scots, making a detour through
divided Lancashire. Cromwell had joined Leven, and
they were besieging Newcastle's army in the city of York.
Rupert released Newcastle from the besiegers, and the
united armies fell upon each other on the lonely moor
outside Long Marston. For the first and last time Rupert's
charge was broken, though Cromwell was wounded in the
fight. As the long day closed, the Royalist cavalry had

been driven from the field, and Newcastle's whitecoats, surrounded and past all hope, died grimly fighting in the twilight.   The North was lost for ever.

Events in Cornwall temporarily restored the balance upset on Marston Moor.   Essex was blundering westward with the best Parliamentary army.   Before him fled Henrietta, separated from her husband for the last time : at Exeter she gave birth to little Minette, who would never see her father.   Then, in great pain, she arrived at Falmouth, and escaped to Brest, fired on by a Parliamentary ship.   Meanwhile Essex was walking straight into a trap laid for him at Lostwithiel, some said by King Charles himself, some by a deaf old Scot of the Ruthven family, knighted by King Gustavus, made Earl of Brentford by King Charles.   It was his last fight, for Charles dismissed him ; no one knows quite what had happened, but the dismissal caused new quarrels among the Cavaliers.

Parliament's remedy for its similar evils was a committee of generals, with two civilian members in whose absence no decision might be taken.   The result was the second battle of Newbury : Charles raised the siege of Donnington Castle outside the town and escaped, with little loss, from an army that hemmed him round with nearly double his numbers : Cromwell's successful attack on his rear was rendered useless by the sloth or treachery of Manchester.

Meanwhile Essex, escaping by sea from Lostwithiel, had come to London to find a pretty kettle of fish.   Parliament was renewing its offers to the King, but demanding Presbyterianism, control of the army and navy, and punishment of the Royalist leaders.   Charles replied they would have " much ado " before he gave up his Church, his Crown, and his friends.   Manchester was for reducing the terms and making peace.   He and Essex talked of impeaching Cromwell, who determined to make no terms with King Charles.   Cromwell carried Parliament against the Lords, and there was no treaty.

The only impeachment was an ancient one, now carried to its horrible close against Archbishop Laud. Laud had stood aside at Prynne's trial, though it was only a matter of form. But it was no matter of form that Prynne was given the task of collecting evidence against his old enemy, ransacking his rooms, and producing his private diary—with certain inconvenient passages burnt away. Prynne found a Missal among Laud's books, and used it to substantiate a charge of Popery. Laud replied that he had spent much time refuting Popery and actually converting Papists, and had used the Missal for that purpose ; he asked whether a Koran he had always kept was evidence of Mohammedanism. Laud complained that his judges stayed in Court to hear the prosecution's evidence and strolled out when he began his defence. Even so, the Peers jibbed at the business, led by Essex. The Commons dropped impeachment and substituted Attainder. They were backed by petitions from the City. It was a cruel parody of Strafford's case.

Parliament had had good grounds for representing Strafford as a danger. Laud was a harmless old man who had been in prison for four years, occupied largely with charitable schemes ;[1] he was powerless to help the King, except with his prayers, it had always been his principle that life must not be taken for conscience' sake. But Parliament had passed the Attainder, and he was led to the scaffold, Clotworthy harassing him with foolish questions, until he turned to the executioner for relief. He knelt to pray for peace in England, for " brotherly love and charity." " Lord," he said, " I am coming as fast as I can." His head was struck off. He had been long in coming, for he was over seventy years of age.

One is glad to know that there were great crowds of Londoners to see him buried, and some brave enough to defy Parliament by reading the forbidden Prayer Book

[1] Reading still administers money that he left for apprenticing young men and providing dowries for poor girls.

service at the grave. It is also interesting to hear that one Abbot in Rome was glad to learn of Laud's death, because " the greatest enemy of the Church of Rome in England was cut off."

The murder of an old man could hardly help Parliament to defeat the King. The present methods were doing little to accomplish that object, and London felt that all its successes were being put into " a bag with holes." Cromwell had shown what new methods could accomplish : there was plenty of money to raise and train proper and permanent forces : in the winter of 1644–45 Parliament voted the formation of the New Model Army. To stop jealousies, the " Self-Denying Ordinance " excluded all Parliament men from military command. It was soon relaxed in Cromwell's favour, while it excluded Manchester ; but Cromwell had no hand in the training of the New Model. Fairfax and Skippon adopted his ideas and copied the East Anglian troops. The men were splendidly clad and equipped : for the first time an English army appeared wholly in scarlet. The training ground was Windsor Park ; here, under the windows of Charles's castle, the redcoats wheeled and manœuvred, learnt to handle pike and musket. Among them, perhaps, were the units that Charles II would take over, and christen the Coldstream Guards. Parliament had achieved a standing army.

It was to prove the ultimate threat. Charles had neither men nor money to meet it. Oxford was still in love with traditions and personal loyalties, still hampered by intrigue and jealousy. It could not defend itself against the business men of London, now that they were learning to make war in a businesslike way.

And then, for one glorious moment, the sanguine Charles must have thought that the whole structure of rebellion was about to fall to pieces. Its foundation was the Scottish army that had beaten Rupert at Marston Moor. Northern England was only kept from returning to its loyalty by the concentrated power of the Scottish Lowlands.

But there are hills beyond Pentland and streams beyond
Forth. Scotland would not be Scotland if it were only the
Lowland plains and hills across which Saxon and Norman
have spread their blood and their civilization. Beyond
them rose the mountains, sheltering an older and a darker
race ; it peopled in great numbers the valleys that have
now become lonely playgrounds for the rich. The soil was
poor, the living hard ; the Highlanders could eke it out
by plundering Lowland neighbours, who spoke of them
as mere savages, though they had an older culture and
language, shared with their Irish kinsmen. The Middle
Ages had passed over their heads, leaving their tribal law
untainted by feudalism, turning gangs of robbers into well-
knit clans. Many had ignored the Reformation, and the
chieftains kept their own priests, even sent their sons to
Catholic schools on the Continent. All hated Clan Campbell,
and had old feuds with Archie Campbell, who called himself
Argyle and had thrown in his lot with Lowlanders and Kirk
Elders. They had refused the Covenant and suffered terribly
from Argyle's cruel raids. They cared nothing for Parliaments and legality, mere machinery for hanging their best
champions as thieves in the Edinburgh Grassmarket. Now
Montrose had at last obtained a royal commission ; he
was coming to raise the Highlanders for the cause of a
king who had defied Parliaments, favoured Catholics, and
was himself a Highland Stewart. If it was centuries since
his ancestors had turned their backs upon the mountains,
centuries were nothing to the men who remembered
Cuchulain and Deirdre in their songs. They made a
strange army, ill-clad, barefooted, without a commissariat.
But they moved at a pace which made the daily march
of trained troops a laughing-stock. And even trained troops
found it difficult to stand against their charge.

The thing started in the oddest way. A small band of
Irish royalists landed on the west coast and attacked the
Covenanting Campbells. They were soon head over heels
in a muddle of clan feuds, thoroughly unpopular with

every one ; they were chevied across to Blair Atholl, and
there Montrose promised to meet them. They expected
him to come with drum and trumpet, and a respectable
army ;   all that arrived was a travel-stained laird in a
blue bonnet, with one companion at his heels. But his
name was sufficient to rouse the Stewarts and Robertsons,
who brought a few claymores and pikes, many sticks and
knives ; the Irish had muskets and one round of ammunition apiece ;   there were two lean horses in the army.
Three thousand strong, it marched to Tippermuir one
Sunday morning and encountered six thousand Covenanting infantry, seven hundred horse, and any number of
Presbyterian preachers. In a few minutes the Highlanders
had them all on the run ; by the evening they had killed
two thousand, captured Perth, and begun to requisition
cloth to cover their half-naked limbs.

Another defeat and the cruel sack of Aberdeen brought
Argyle out from Edinburgh. He was no soldier, but his
intrigues detached from Montrose some of the Lowland
lairds that had begun to join him. Their place was supplied
by Macdonalds and Macleans, Farquarsons and Camerons.
Montrose struck westward at the almost impregnable
strongholds of Clan Campbell, descending from wintry
moorlands to plunder the shores of Loch Awe. Argyle,
hurrying across from the east, hurried away again in a
fishing-boat ; but he summoned an army of 3000 from
the south, 5000 from the east. Montrose had 1500 left ;
he avoided one enemy by a desperate mountain march,
destroyed the other at the great battle of Inverlochy.
A month later he had marched right round Scotland and
captured Dundee. Driven north, he beat an army nearly
twice the size of his own at Auldearn, another, more equally
matched, at Alford, another at Kilsyth. Edinburgh sent
submission, explaining its disloyalty as due to the machina-
tions of a few traitors. Glasgow opened its gates, and
Montrose held a Parliament, proclaiming religious tolerance
and the end of Presbyterian tyranny. Then he turned

south to help King Charles in England. The blue bonnets
were coming over the Border.

They never reached it. The thing ended as suddenly
as it had begun. After each battle, Montrose had found his
Highlanders disappear to store their booty in safety or
settle private feuds. Few would think of accompanying
him to England. The Lowlanders were alienated by his
alliance with thieves and Papists, and the few who came
with him were half-hearted; only the Irish remained
reliable. Some of Leven's men had come home from
England, not enough to loosen Parliament's grip on the
northern counties, enough to catch Montrose napping in
a Border mist near Philiphaugh and obliterate his army
with terrible cruelties. Scotland was lost at a blow.

The year's campaign remains as one of the greatest
feats of arms in human history. Montrose had tackled
every military problem from the pitched battle fought
with infantry, cavalry, and guns, to the superhuman task
of getting thousands of drunken pillagers out of a town
menaced by vastly superior numbers. No one can say
what might have happened if King Charles could have
employed him earlier, and in England.

During the next hundred years the clans were to
rise many times for the Stewart cause. Their last and
greatest effort would carry them to Derby and so frighten
the English gentry that an Act of Parliament proscribed
the Highland language, dress, and weapons. Such chiefs
as had not been blown to pieces at Culloden were persuaded
into becoming landlords in virtue of a law of property
that had never run in the Highlands. Eviction turned
populous glens into silent deer-forest, and drove the
descendants of Montrose's clansmen across the Atlantic to
the farms, the shops, and the criminal gangs of nineteenth-
century America.

Their first venture had done Charles little good. Before
Philiphaugh was fought and lost, another disaster had
crushed his rising hopes.

Fairfax and Skippon had marched the New Model away from Windsor. Orders from London, still hesitating and contradictory, sent them into Somerset, brought them back to lay fruitless siege to Oxford. Then they were told to raise the siege and pursue King Charles, marching northward to join Montrose. Charles had fallen upon Leicester, captured and plundered the town ; then he turned back to meet the New Model Army.

In the very centre of England, the gentle undulations of the Midlands suddenly decide to reach a respectable height. A few miles south of Market Harborough lies a small steep hill : the homestead on its summit is called, in English fashion, Low Farm. It looks, southward again, across two smaller ridges, Dust Hill and Mill Hill, to a rather larger mass reaching 600 feet above sea-level. The district was once controlled by the monastery of Sulby Abbey : now the only important building is a fine gentleman's residence called Sulby Hall. The countryside is typically Midland, mournful in winter, very pretty in summer. It was June when the English monarchy was destroyed between those two hills. In some early age Danish settlers had christened the village beside Low Farm with the name of Sibbertoft ; another, hidden behind the crest of the larger, more southern hill, they called Naseby.

It was early in the morning when Charles and Rupert left Market Harborough and began to climb up to Sibbertoft. News had come that some soldiers of the New Model had arrived in Naseby last night. Rupert had always spoken slightingly of the New Model ; the event did something to justify him ; but nothing could justify giving battle to it on disadvantageous ground with little more than half its numbers. Probably Rupert had no such intention. His scout reported that there was no large body of the enemy within striking distance. The man may have been a traitor ; more likely he had found Sibbertoft Hill, Dust Hill, and Mill Hill sufficient for his morning's journey, and had not troubled to climb the last slope and look down into Naseby village. Nor could Rupert know that two nights ago the New Model had cheered Oliver Cromwell into their camp with his East Anglian troopers.

Fairfax was also unprepared for a battle, and his army was still in disorder as it came over the rise from Naseby and spread itself along the slope of Mill Hill. Cromwell made a virtue of necessity, telling his men that the Lord delighted to protect his unprepared host against the premeditated assault of the wicked : he might have added that, other things being equal, the Lord generally protects fourteen thousand men against the attack of eight thousand.

Rupert had ridden ahead, clad in a red *montero*, or general's cloak. He suddenly saw a Parliamentary army spread out before him and hastened back to form his battle-line. He took the right wing. Opposite him the Parliamentary cavalry was led by Ireton, soon to be Cromwell's son-in-law, for whom Cromwell had begged the command. Colonel Okey had advanced his dragoons (mounted infantry we might call them) to man a hedge in front of and at right angles to the battle-line : he hoped to gall the flank of Rupert's charge.

The two wings trotted towards each other. Suddenly Rupert halted, and the puzzled Ireton halted too. Rupert resumed the charge, smashed Ireton's regiments to pieces, captured their commander and raced off to chase the fugitives. As he galloped, he could see that the infantry in the centre had come to blows and that the Royalists were thrusting back the red coats : the New Model was not quitting itself well. In a short time Rupert was up and over Mill Hill, up the stiffer slope to Naseby. The Parliament's baggage guard saw him coming and thought it was Fairfax in flight, for Fairfax also wore a red *montero*. But when they heard Rupert's voice summoning them to surrender, they answered with a volley. He turned to

18

collect his scattered men : it would take a long time to bring them back to the decisive point.[1]

Fairfax was not in flight : indeed, that very brave gentleman could never be persuaded to remain at his post as general when a post of danger offered. He was in among the infantry, hard pressed by the King's centre. Skippon was down with a wound. Fairfax had lost his steel-cap, and was fighting bareheaded among the pikes.

It was Cromwell who saved the battle. He commanded the cavalry on the right wing. The ground here was rough and pitted with rabbit-holes. (There are still rabbits on Naseby field, descendants perhaps of the seventeenth-century conies who told their children to lie still while foolish humans made " such dreadful pother " overhead.) Across the warren rode Cromwell, hurling back Langdale's horsemen to where Charles waited on Dust Hill. Instead of pursuing, Cromwell wheeled inward to help the hard-pressed infantry in the centre, and caught the Royalists on flank and rear. Fairfax's men took new heart, Ireton was recaptured. One by one the Royalist regiments were broken. When Rupert galloped back, only one still held its place, fighting, says a Puritan soldier, " with incredible resolution." Round behind them swept Rupert to find King Charles and urge him to fly. Charles was desperately trying to lead a last attack. They would not let him. " Will you go to your death ? " they said, seized his bridle, and led his horse away. The battle was over, the King's army fled.

Everything was captured—flags, guns, baggage, even the King's private letters. The Puritans reached Sibber-toft in no melting mood. They had heard stories of the plunder of Leicester, of a Welsh colonel called Thomas recruiting for the King by slashing at objectors' legs with his sword. Thomas lay dead on Naseby field, and a good

[1] By taking Edgehill and Naseby as typical battles, I have been unfair to Rupert. In both he seems to have made a similar and disastrous mistake. There is no other instance of it in his other battles.

riddance. But in the King's camp were a hundred women, some Irish and Papist harlots, some respectable soldiers' wives. Next morning the Irishwomen were all dead, the English horribly gashed about the face.

London was overjoyed at the victory. The king's letters were published, and great capital made of his attempts to get help from Ireland, France, and the Pope. Cromwell's dispatch, after describing the battle, demanded fair treatment for the men who had won it, especially (since all manner of sects flourished in the New Model) liberty of conscience and freedom from Presbyterian tyranny. But men in London were talking of religious toleration as the Devil's engine, and the Commons deleted this part of the dispatch before sending it to the printer. Their censorship was comically ineffectual, for the Lords were simultaneously ordering the dispatch to be published in full.

It was all over with the Royalist cause. Naseby was followed by Langport and the loss of Goring's army. Some hope was built on the resistance of Bristol : Rupert wrote that he could hold it for four months while new armies were organized. On the heels of his letter came the news that he had surrendered the city with hardly a fight. Charles believed that even Rupert was turning traitor, and dismissed him from command. Meanwhile Puritan armies were closing round Oxford, and Cromwell trundled great guns through Hampshire, smoking out the Royalist strongholds. His last task was Basing House, where the Catholic Marquis of Winchester had often entertained Henrietta and her friends in the happier times of peace. Basing had beaten off three fierce assaults of Waller, fought starvation and the small-pox, and endured later sieges, replying with bold sallies in the night. It bid defiance even to Cromwell's guns : *Aimez Loyauté* was Basing's motto. Three days the cannon thundered : on the fourth, in the cold October dawn, Cromwell's soldiers carried the breaches by assault. There was a terrible carnage, for the garrison had refused quarter. Six priests were found and killed, four reserved for a crueller death upon the scaffold. Among those saved was Wencelas Hollar the artist and an old man, carried out in a blanket, who had once been the great Inigo Jones. The Marquis himself survived—to be ill-rewarded at the Restoration. Now Peters the preacher harried him with foolish questions : Why had he maintained the defence in such a hopeless cause ? " Basing is called Loyalty," said the Marquis.

As their cause grew more desperate, the dissensions among the Cavaliers grew worse rather than better. Rupert returned to headquarters, was absolved from the charge of treachery, but remained a focus for intrigues and quarrels until he left the country in despair.

Parliament's armies closed in upon Oxford. Fairfax camped on Headington Hill : Skippon, recovered from his wound, joined him there : Rainsborough captured Woodstock. On May 11, 1646, the city surrendered to its besiegers.

A fortnight earlier the King had slipped across Magdalen Bridge before daybreak, disguised as a servant ; his " master " was John Ashburnham ; with them went a clergyman called Michael Hudson. They rode towards London, across twenty miles of plain and up the steep slope of the Chilterns. At Nettlebed a soldier of Ireton's army insisted on joining the party. Charles told him that his master was a member of Parliament, then (as the man grew suspicious at a large tip handed to an innkeeper) a member of the Lords. Through Bix and Henley they rode : at Slough they shook off their unwelcome companion. It is thought that they expected a message from supporters in London, and Parliament, having heard of the escape, was prodigal of orders to stop the King coming. But at Harrow the party struck north. Charles had long been in communication with the Scots, and they had promised him shelter, perhaps armed support against their allies. From Harrow he rode to Downham, then, at

dead of night, to Little Gidding, up a slope still called
"The King's Close." There was no shelter here, for it
was Puritan country and the Ferrars were watched by
many jealous eyes. John Ferrar led the King to Copping-
fold in the night. Three days later Charles rode into
Southwell, dismounted at the "King's Arms" and ordered
a meal. It was his last in freedom. The Commissioners
came to escort him to the Scottish camp.

Far away, at Stow-on-the-Wold, his last army had
surrendered to Parliament. Its commander was Astley,
who had prayed so well at Edge Hill. "Gentlemen," he
said to his captors, "you have done your work and may
now go to play—unless you prefer to fall out among
yourselves."

CHAPTER EIGHTEEN

THE PRISONER

1645–48

IT needed no hint from Astley to make it clear that England was only at the beginning of her troubles. Since the war had grown out of mutual suspicions rather than a definite clash of principle, the victors had no agreed plan for a settlement. Still suspecting the King, they had begun to suspect one another. Mutual differences had been sunk for purposes of war : victory merely served to show that they were irreconcilable.

The Scots had lent a hand in return for two things— a promise of money and a promise that England should be made a Presbyterian country. Parliament had not paid them more than a fraction of their money, and was dilatory in its attempts to force Presbyterianism on a reluctant England. Cheated of their bargain, the Scots were beginning to suffer from a guilty conscience ; they were even asking themselves why they were in arms against a King who, reluctantly or no, had granted Scotland everything it had demanded of him. Short of money, they were making themselves unpopular by living at free quarters on the northern shires. Meanwhile they watched with apprehension the growth of England's military power and wondered how soon it would be directed to the conquest or plunder of Scotland.

Parliament, the ostensible victor in the war, was quite incompetent to use its victory. The best of the Parliamentarians were dead ; Essex had followed Pym and Hampden into the grave. The remainder were distracted in counsel and unpopular with the country. They had been raising great sums of money by the ordinary taxation and by the newly invented Excise : they were ruining great numbers of the Cavaliers by confiscating their estates altogether ; those who asked to buy them back by " compounding " with a proportion of their value were told they must first sign the hated Covenant ; and while many of the old clergy were expelled from their parishes and left to beggary or a tiny pension, Parliament had control of the great revenues of the bishoprics. As Parliament had ceased to keep any accounts, no one knew what was happening to the money. But it was common knowledge that members were growing rich on the bribery connected with the system of compounding, and that they had long been voting each other money as compensation for " sufferings " in the Parliamentary cause and for private money spent on the war. Meanwhile it was not only the Scots that remained unpaid ; the wages of Parliament's own army were months in arrears. Unpopular because of high taxation, suspected of very serious corruption, Parliament was proposing to force upon England a Presbyterian Church for which there was little enthusiasm and a great deal of violent opposition throughout the country.

That opposition was strongest in Parliament's own army, where there was an effective demand for religious toleration. It is only reasonable to assume that the majority of the soldiers would have been glad to disband and go home. But it was folly to expect they would do so while their pay was still denied them and their masters in Parliament were passing laws to bind their consciences, and even their daily habits, in bonds far narrower than any that Laud had forged. Parliament had only itself to blame when the troops refused to disperse unpaid, or be shipped to Ireland for further campaigns. The soldiers began to elect committees and " agitators " (agents, we should call them) to enforce their political demands. Each regiment turned itself into a debating society and discussed the most exalted interpretations of Christianity side by side with the wildest religious fads. They attacked Parliament's claim to represent England, and evolved democratic and even socialistic principles very interesting to a later age, very repugnant to the mind of seventeenth-century England.

Finally, there was the undoubted fact that the bulk of Englishmen, so far as they thought of politics at all, could only think in terms of hereditary monarchy. The clergy and Cavaliers, defeated and despoiled, were still unrepentant Royalists ; the majority of the Roundheads thought that the only problem was to frame restrictions on the King's powers, and were continually irritated by their leaders' failure to find a solution.

At first sight it might seem that Charles might be able to fish in such troubled waters with a fair hope of success. An adroit and unscrupulous man might soon have found himself in a stronger position than he was before the war. Charles was not very adroit ; he had some scruples, few, but quite unconquerable. He had, besides, two very serious disadvantages. He was more or less a prisoner, relying on such reports as his captors allowed to reach him, or on messages smuggled to him by secret agents. Rightly believing that most of England wanted a monarchy, he greatly overestimated the numbers and energy of those who would work actively for its preservation. Cut off from reliable information, he remained as sanguine as ever. In his whole life he had hardly known what it was to have the luck upon his side, to reap the full reward of a good move or avoid the bitterest consequences of an error. But he remained obstinately certain that the luck must one day turn. Only when the imminence of death convinced him that all was over, did he show the true courage founded, not on false hopes, but on despair of everything this world can offer.

There is also a darker side to the picture. He had always been a bad judge of men, not knowing whom to trust and whom to suspect. In the discreditable years that followed civil war, he came to the conclusion that he could trust no one, certainly no one who had once been in arms against him. He thought merely of playing off one man against another, using only their baser instincts, utterly ignoring their ideals. He would not actually break his word to them, or set his name to conditions he could not fulfil : short of that anything was justifiable to hoodwink a set of rebels whose schemes for a peaceful settlement of the country they had disturbed seemed to him the merest moonshine. The fact that he was invariably patient and courteous towards them, conquered them again and again by his personal charm, merely served to convince them, when the spell was shaken off, that they were dealing with a slippery rascal.

It must be allowed that his adversaries were not overscrupulous towards him or towards each other. Charles's first move, the flight to the Scottish camp, had plunged him into the midst of a very dubious game.

Richelieu was dead ; his successor, Mazarin, had dispatched an envoy, Montreuil, nominally to mediate between the contending parties, but with secret instructions to make sure that the result of his mediation was neither a strong monarchy nor a strong republic in England. At Montreuil's suggestion, the Scots had invited Charles to join them, behind the back of their allies in London. They promised to secure him " in conscience and honour " and restore him to " his rights and prerogatives," but they refused to put their pledge in writing. Charles promised to content them as far as possible in religion, and was willing to " receive instruction " about Presbyterianism. He had no intention of being converted, but not unnaturally the Scots took this as an indication that he intended to change his faith in order to regain his Crown. The game of deception had begun.

As soon as the Scots had possession of his person, they marched off to Newcastle and attempted to persuade him of the truth and necessity of Presbyterianism. Alexander

Henderson, original champion of the Covenant, was
brought from Scotland to argue with His Majesty. Charles
was at his best in theological controversy, and Henderson
went home to Edinburgh to die without having made the
least impression. Persistent rumours represented Henderson
as not only converted, but repentant for all that he had
done ; a death-bed confession was published, in which
Henderson lauds Charles to the skies and wishes Scotland
had been guided by his wisdom from the first. It is, in
all probability, a Royalist forgery.

But others seem to have feared the power of the King's
persuasive tongue. Parliament refused his offer to come
to London and discuss the terms of settlement. They
sent a deputation to Newcastle with a set of conditions
which the King must accept or reject as a whole. Charles
asked why so many dignitaries were sent to present the
terms when " an honest trumpeter could have done
the business." The demands included Presbyterianism,
Parliamentary control of army and navy, the punishment
of prominent Royalists. Charles could not possibly accept
them as they stood. The most he would do for the Presbyterians was to let them have their way for three years and
then call a general conference to re-settle religion. In
three years' time he did not doubt that he would be able
to re-establish Episcopacy. Henrietta wrote to him from
France suggesting that he should accept Presbyterianism,
and bargain for military control in return : she could see
no difference between one Protestant heresy and another,
but an army was an army. The poet Davenant arrived in
Newcastle to back her arguments, and talked as though
forms of religion did not matter. Charles dismissed him in
anger ; he had lost his kingdom, but he would not regain
it at the price of the Church. He believed that his Coronation oath bound him to uphold bishops ; he was sure that
to sanction Presbyterianism was to hand over the spiritual
guidance of England to everything that he considered evil.
He was living in a different world from Davenant's, and

one in which material advantages cannot be purchased by spiritual surrender. Later ages blessed Charles for his unshakable resolve, preserved through two years of tempting offers, preserved finally under the threat of death ; the Church of England made him its martyr. It is difficult to feel enthusiastic about the diplomatic methods whereby the resolve was defended, but, if the history of succeeding centuries is any guide, Charles was certainly defending the settled purpose of England against a minority of doctrinaires.

The Scots, finding that he was no use as an instrument for attaining their religious ends, began to think about the other side of their bargain. Parliament was ready to grant them a good proportion of their money, and after some haggling, they agreed to give up the King and return home. It was unfortunate for their reputation that the money arrived in Newcastle on the very day that Charles was handed over to the Parliamentary commissioners ; their already uneasy consciences were not quieted by the taunts that they had sold their King. Some of the townsmen of Newcastle flung stones and shouted " Judas ! " at the retreating columns, as they wound out of the town towards the Border.

Charles was brought southward to Holmby House, in Northamptonshire, for Parliament still feared his presence and influence in London. The journey served to fortify his conviction that England was Royalist at heart. People crowded to welcome him on the road, the gentry escorted him on his way, everywhere there were shouts of " God bless Your Majesty ! "

His new masters denied his chaplains access, and sent him Presbyterian divines ; Charles shut himself up in his bedroom and read over the Prayer Book service in solitude. They even passed a resolution that his Communion plate should be melted down and made into a dinner service for him. In other respects he was not badly treated, and much deference was shown him. He was always patient

and considerate, winning the regard, and in some cases the
loyalty, of the servants whom Parliament sent to attend
him.   He read much—theology, poetry, and Shakespeare's
plays.[1]   He played cards and chess, and, since there was
no bowling-green at Holmby, was allowed to ride over to
Althorpe for a game.

He was willing to entertain any proposal submitted
to him, but he still evaded the definite answer, delaying,
arguing, raising false hopes.   It was an exasperating game
for his opponents.   He simply disbelieved in the sincerity
of the men who came to bargain with him, and was perfectly
sure that they could not lay the foundations for a lasting
peace.   The only thing that mattered was to gain time,
for time would make England speak with a clear voice
and demand to be ruled by her King, not by a corrupt
clique of Parliamentary politicians.   Perhaps the most
exasperating thing of all was that the King was probably
right.   He was waiting for the Restoration, and, by any
ordinary calculation, the Restoration might have come
any time within the next few years.   What upset ordinary
calculation and delayed the thing for fifteen, was a phenomenon that King Charles could hardly appreciate.   It was
the genius of Cromwell.

It is hardly possible to be just to this very remarkable
man within the limits of a biography of King Charles.
His greatness, outside the military sphere, is not yet
apparent ; the most questionable part of his life is under
review.   Anathema to the Royalists, he would soon be
detested by the majority of his Roundhead colleagues.
For more than a century after his death, he was generally
regarded as an unscrupulous and hypocritical adventurer,
and the evidence for this view was collected mainly from

---

[1] " The constant companion of these his solitudes," says *Eikono-
klastes*.   The source is suspect, as the book accuses him, in earlier days,
of indecent behaviour with women in the theatre, and hints at parricide
and sodomy.   Such are the methods of seventeenth-century controversy, yet one is sorry to see them under the name of John Milton.

the years that led up to King Charles's death. More
recently he has become a popular hero ; the new legend,
probably far nearer the truth, is based principally on later
achievements.

The case against him is easily stated. He joined the
party which denounced King Charles for ruling without
Parliament, levying taxes of doubtful legality, punishing
the opposition of individuals in arbitrary courts of law,
and dictating a certain form of religion to England. He
used his party's triumph to make himself a king in all but
name. He then destroyed Parliament and put nothing in
its place to check his own despotism. He raised taxes of
unheard-of proportions without the consent of the taxed ;
he arrested and imprisoned men by arbitrary power ; he
proscribed the religion that had been, and was again to be,
that of the majority of Englishmen. He altered laws and
interfered with the life and liberty of the ordinary Englishman as no Stewart ever dared to do. His power was based
on the force of armies, which overawed England, conquered
the Scots, and behaved in Ireland as no body of Christians
can behave without defying every precept of religion and
common decency. Military strength and a large revenue
enabled him to win a prestige for England which, to some
Englishmen, justifies all Cromwell's career. It was used to
enforce a barren and unintelligent foreign policy ; for my
Lord Protector retained much of the ignorance and prejudice
of a petty Huntingdon squire.

So much must be granted of his political career. The
man himself can be represented in an almost more unfavour-
able light. When the tide of opinion began to turn in his
favour, nearly a century ago, Carlyle lent it strength by
republishing, with comments, the surviving letters and
speeches. We are out of tune with Carlyle to-day, for we
resent being shouted at. Sandwiched between slices of
Victorian rhetoric, Cromwell's own words strike rather chill.
There are bursts of real eloquence, and a great deal of
sound sense. But the level of intelligence is not a very

high one : there is little consistent thinking or grasp of principle ; a few speeches read like the wanderings of a disordered mind.   Behind all is the assumption, far more irritating than the Divine Right of Kings, that God is always on Cromwell's side, and on the side of whatever party Cromwell happens to be supporting.   Victory is a proof of it, whether over Royalist or Dutchman or Spaniard ; a nasty little defeat in the West Indies is no disproof. There is no arguing with such a mind, except by steel and lead ; and when steel and lead are in play, this man had a trick of winning the argument.   The secret of his greatness is not yet apparent.

It will always remain hidden from those who think too precisely.   It does not lie in intellect :   intellectually Cromwell is below Strafford and even Buckingham.   It lies in instinct and energy, and in that English quality for which we have coined the untranslatable phrase of Common Sense.   His brain could not follow the arguments of trained lawyers, and, from mere impatience, he said that English law was a " godless jumble " ; but he was obviously right.   And when instinct prompted him to say that it was wicked to hang a man for stealing six-and-eightpence, it is useless for a lawyer to put in a demurrer or cite a precedent.

A man cannot be the first soldier of his day without some great qualities.   If he applies them to politics, he may be unscrupulous and do much incidental harm, but something of enduring importance is likely to result. Cromwell made two contributions to the Puritan cause, beside making all the difference between its success and failure in the field of battle.   He could not make it tolerant, but he checked and modified its intolerance.   He saved England from the rigid Presbyterians, and gave freedom to everything except the Mass and the Book of Common Prayer.   Secondly, he had something of Strafford's hatred of " particular interests " and Strafford's love of good government.   He rescued his party from the

domination of rich aristocrats, pushing Essex and Manchester aside, driving Saye into obscurity. His task was
easier than Strafford's in that he had an army to support
him, and a vastly greater revenue (for he had no hesitation
in raising heavy taxation and, even then, in leaving huge
debts behind him). But he insisted on a strong central
power, and he used it to govern efficiently in what he took
to be the interests of the whole nation.

It might be imagined that, politically if not personally,
Cromwell had a good deal in common with King Charles.
An alliance between the two may not appear unthinkable,
and, for a moment, it looked as though that alliance would
come about. Two things made it unreal and ephemeral :
Charles represented legitimacy and continuity. If Cromwell's capacity to rule justified his seizure of power, then
England would be for ever at the mercy of adventurers
who imagined themselves to have a similar genius. Rebellion would follow rebellion, and of ultimate stability
there was no hope. The legitimist argument was indeed
justified by the collapse and anarchy that followed
Cromwell's death. Secondly, the personal factor was all
important : Charles and Cromwell were impossible allies.
There was a certain lack of continuity in Cromwell's nature
as in his politics—a constant friction between the temperament of an English country gentleman and the alien,
excitable religion that alternately comforted and tor-
mented him.[1] By middle age he had partially conquered
his difficulties. But he was given to the kind of horse-
play that suggests nervous repressions : he did many of
his most famous actions in fits of irritable temper. The

---

[1] He was Welsh by extraction, his real name being Williams. His
great-grandfather adopted the grander name of Cromwell from a brother-
in-law, the famous Thomas Cromwell, plunderer of the monasteries.
Oliver's mother, Elizabeth Steward, came of another family enriched
with monastic lands. But the theory which attributes his religion
and politics primarily to such origins breaks down at a vital point.
Oliver was a cadet of the family ; the chief monastic spoils went to his
uncle and namesake, Sir Oliver of Hinchinbrook, who remained a Churchman and Royalist to his death.

story that, as he signed the King's death-warrant, he playfully smeared ink on his colleague's face is not evidence of levity; it may be indication of a fevered mind, at war with itself.

Such a temperament, dynamic, fraught with good and evil in undigested confusion, was entirely outside the range of King Charles's sympathies, which demanded self-possession and good taste as mere preliminaries to co-operation. The two complex personalities were about to come into unprofitable contact.

One day, as Charles was playing bowls at Althorpe, his guardians suddenly interrupted him with the news that a large troop of horses was in the neighbourhood. The game was stopped, the party hurried back to Holmby. Late that night the King was awakened by the sound of angry voices in the passage and a heavy knocking on the door. It opened to reveal a young subaltern with a stupid face,[1] holding a loaded pistol. Joyce was his name; he would not say who had sent him, but he had come to fetch His Majesty away from the hands of Parliament's commissioners. The King told him to wait till morning. He rose early and summoned Joyce, asking by what authority he was acting and where was his commission. Joyce pointed out of window to a troop of cavalry drawn up before the house. "It is as fair a commission," said Charles, "and as well written as I have seen a commission written in my life," and he proceeded to compliment Joyce on the appearance of his men. At his own suggestion, Joyce took him to Newmarket, and it soon became clear who was Joyce's master. When Fairfax and Cromwell met the King, both denied that they had sent the troops to Holmby. Charles told them he would believe that when they hanged Joyce and not before. He was doing Fairfax an injustice, for Fairfax was a good soldier but no politician. It was Cromwell who was lying.

[1] There is a contemporary portrait of him, pistol and all, attributed to Vandyke's pupil, Dobson.

It was hardly possible for Cromwell to tell the truth, for he had to keep a foot in both camp and Parliament, and the Commons were outraged at the King's abduction. They ordered Charles's return to Holmby, but they were powerless to coerce the Army, and Charles refused to return. He was about to see whether he could not make Cromwell and the Army serve his turn.

The unnatural alliance depended mainly upon Charles's power to deceive Cromwell. He was curiously successful for a time. While the Army threatened Parliament, expelled its obnoxious members and occupied London with · troops, Charles moved about with the officers from New-market to Hatfield, to Windsor, Caversham, and Hampton Court. Cromwell complained indeed that the King might be " more frank " and wished he was not tied " so strictly to narrow maxims." But he assured a friend that Charles " was the uprightest and most conscientious man of his three kingdoms."

Charles was better treated than by Scots or Parliamentary guardians, he was allowed to see his friends and even his chaplains. From Caversham, Cromwell rode with him to Maidenhead where Charles saw his younger children again (Prince Charles was in France with his mother). There was no deception in the King's love for them, and Cromwell actually wept at the scene of reunion.

The upshot was that the Army, silencing Parliament by military force, offered Charles far better terms than any he had yet seen. The scheme, drawn up by Cromwell's son-in-law, Ireton, was called the *Heads of the Proposals*. It was exceedingly generous, startling in its originality, perhaps ahead of its age. It allowed Episcopacy, though without political rights or power to coerce : it insisted on a new and more democratic franchise that would have made Parliament more representative of the nation. It is easy to see why Charles rejected the scheme, it is impossible not to blame him for refusing to discuss it in a more sympathetic spirit.

19

No doubt he distrusted the sincerity of Cromwell and Ireton ; certainly, when they had fuller powers, they did not put their democratic ideas into practice. But the settlement was worth an honest trial. Charles hardly thought of it as a settlement at all, but only as a sign that the Army was begging his favour : he hoped that he would soon be able to dictate terms to them. " You cannot do without me," he told the officers ; " you will fall to ruin if I do not sustain you." One of his servants was astonished at the King's confidence. " Sir," he said, " Your Majesty speaks as if you had some secret power that I do not know of."

Such a secret power Charles believed himself to possess. He was sure of regaining his throne, and preferred to do so with the help of Royalists rather than of a pack of rebels. Argyle had offered him an army in return for a promise to make England Presbyterian. He had returned an uncompromising refusal. Now Argyle was losing ground in Edinburgh, Hamilton was gaining. Hamilton was persuading the Scots to accept the King's suggestion of three years' Presbyterianism, and then a new settlement. He was in touch with the discontented Royalists in England. The northern gentlemen were ready to rise, the home counties, hitherto loyal to the Roundheads, were growing tired of Parliamentary tyranny and military dictation. Lady Carlisle, a Royalist again, was spinning webs of intrigue in London. Henrietta was as prodigal as ever with hopes of continental assistance.

It is said that Cromwell discovered what was going on in a curious way. He was still waiting for the King's support. Rumour had it he was to be made Earl of Essex and gain great place in a restored monarchy : one Roundhead was saying that if Cromwell stepped into Buckingham's shoes, he himself would be a second Felton. Then a message came to Cromwell at Windsor, to warn him that he was building on shifting sands ; the proof of it was a letter hidden, unknown to its bearer, in the saddle-cloth of a messenger who was due to leave for the Continent that day. Cromwell and Ireton disguised themselves as troopers and hurried off to the Blue Boar Inn : they got a man to watch the inn yard and " sat drinking cans of beer till ten of the clock." When the messenger rode up, they ran out with drawn swords, carried off his saddle and, ripping it up, discovered a letter from the King to Henrietta. The saddle was returned, the messenger proceeded to Dover ; Cromwell and Ireton sat in the tap-room of the Blue Boar and read how the King was deciding to trust the Scots rather than the Army.

The picturesque details may or may not be true : the fact is beyond doubt : Cromwell suddenly ceased to trust Charles. Cromwell may have aimed solely at the welfare of England, he may have been moved by personal ambition : probably both motives were at work in his mind. In any case the King had become an obstacle to his schemes. Cromwell sent Charles a letter warning him of danger : the soldiers, he said, were so angry at the King's refusal to accept their terms on the spot, that they were planning to seize and murder him at Hampton Court. Charles was already thinking that he had better play his dangerous game from some place farther from London ; Cromwell's warning letter may have hastened his departure. Escape from Hampton Court was easy ; the guard was under the command of Colonel Whalley, a first cousin of Cromwell's, and there is little doubt that Cromwell was glad to see the King get away. One night Charles retired early to his bedroom, ostensibly to write letters before going to sleep ; next morning they found that he had disappeared.

He had reached Titchfield, in Hampshire, seeking some safe refuge. Ashburnham, who rode with him, suggested the Isle of Wight : Hammond, Governor of Carisbrooke Castle, was a cousin of the King's chaplain. Charles objected that he was also Cromwell's cousin. He refused to go until Ashburnham had sounded Hammond and obtained from him an oath that he would not prove another gaoler. Hammond was in Parliament's service, and could give no such oath : with incredible folly (treacherously, as some said) Ashburnham nevertheless told Hammond where the King was, and brought him across to Titchfield. Charles was appalled at this disobedience and folly. " Oh, Jack," he said, " thou hast undone me ! " But when Ashburnham offered to retrieve his mistake by going downstairs and killing Hammond, Charles refused to let murder be done.

There was nothing for it but to trust Hammond and hope for the best ; that night the party left for Carisbrooke. The King had escaped from one prison to another.[1]

Meanwhile the war clouds were scudding up. The Northern gentry rose, seizing Berwick and Carlisle. The Welsh Royalists were on the move. The troops occupying London had to shoot at a mob that occupied Westminster, crying, " For God and King Charles ! " Kent and Essex were up in arms. Part of the Fleet mutinied and helped the Royalists to seize Deal and Sandown. Hamilton, bitterly opposed by the Scottish clergy and the veterans of Marston Moor, was nevertheless gathering a large army to invade England. King Charles's friends were laying plans to help him escape from Carisbrooke.

---

[1] The curious combination of suspicious circumstances gave rise to the story that Cromwell had engineered the whole business. It is enshrined in the Ode addressed to him by his friend and admirer, Marvell :

> " Twining subtle fears with hope,
> He wove a net of such a scope
> That Charles himself might chase
> To Carisbrooke's narrow case ;
> That thence the royal actor borne
> The tragic scaffold might adorn."

The story is only acceptable on the supposition that Ashburnham was in Cromwell's pay. Ashburnham's enemies point out that he was given curiously easy terms when he came to " compound " for his estate with the Commonwealth. Charles was positive that he was a fool, but no traitor.

The second Civil War lasted barely four months. The
alliance between Presbyterian Scots and English Cavaliers
was hardly a happy one, and their mutual endeavours
were hopelessly mistimed. Before Hamilton crossed the
Border, Cromwell had already broken the back of insurrec-
tion in Wales, while Fairfax cleared the Royalists of Kent
and Essex into Colchester and shut them up in a siege.
Cromwell marched north to find Hamilton's troops strag-
gling along many miles of Lancashire roads, cut them in
two at the battle of Preston, and destroyed them piecemeal.

Charles's attempts to escape from Carisbrooke were as
fruitless as Hamilton's generalship. The first was balked
by an iron bar across his window : Harry Firebrace, who
was managing the business, wished to saw it through ;
Charles thought that to do so was to give the plot away at
the start, and having tried with his head, he was confident he
could squeeze his whole body through, in spite of the bar.
Night came ; Firebrace arranged for horses outside the
walls, and waited below the King's window to conduct him
to them. He heard the King scuffling and groaning above
him while he waited on tenterhooks below. Then suddenly the sounds ceased : a lighted candle appeared in the
window : it was the signal that all had failed. Charles
had miscalculated the size of the window, just as he had
miscalculated the political forces that were bringing him
from throne to scaffold.

It was proclaimed High Treason to help the King
escape, and a man was put to death for attempting it.
Every scheme was betrayed to Hammond by some treacherous accomplice : one, it was said, was a mere trap concocted by Hammond's lieutenant, Rolph, who waited in
the dark to shoot Charles if he took advantage of the
arrangements.

Meanwhile Parliament had grown tired of Cromwell
and the army, and had even refused to declare itself against
the Scots whom he had hurried off to fight. While he was
away, it hoped to conclude an agreement with the King.

Still refusing to let him come to London, it arranged for a proper discussion of terms at Newport, a few miles from Carisbrooke. Charles was released on parole, and allowed his secretaries and advisers to assist him. Parliament's commissioners were surprised at his skill in argument, and Lord Salisbury remarked how much the King had improved. " No," answered a secretary, " he was always so, but your Lordship has too late discovered it."

The terms were high : Parliament demanded an acknowledgment that Charles alone had been the aggressor in the first Civil War, while they had acted in self-defence ; bishops and Prayer Book must give way to a rigid Presbyterianism ; every one, from the King downwards, must sign the Covenant. Charles would go no further than his original offer of a provisional Presbyterianism for three years ; he refused to authorize the selling up of the bishops' lands. He doubted whether he was not betraying his trust by conceding large restrictions upon the political power of the Crown. But while the discussions proceeded, Fairfax captured Colchester ; Cromwell occupied Edinburgh and made a bargain with Argyle to keep the Scots quiet. The Army turned southward from the war.

Colonel Cooke, one of the King's attendants, at Newport, noticed that new troops were landing on the island. Late one night he begged leave to go out and see what was afoot. Everywhere he stumbled on soldiers. Cooke soon learnt that the Army had resolved to seize the King once more : they did not wish to treat with him or to let Parliament do so ; they had come back from the war determined to do him to death. Returning to the King's lodging, Cooke begged him to fly : a guard had been set in the meantime, but Cooke had the password. Charles did not believe that Cooke could get him free : he was sure the attempt would anger all parties : he was under parole to Parliament. Cooke argued that Parliament was now helpless and the parole of no force. But the King refused to move. Cooke urged once more the greatness of the danger. "Never let that trouble you," said the King; "I would not break my word to prevent it." [1]

Of the danger there was no doubt. Charles was roused at daybreak, hustled into a coach, and driven to the western end of the island. Beside him rode Rolph, abusing the King as they went. Hammond, too scrupulous for the Army's purpose, had been summoned to Headquarters and put under military arrest. When the coach reached the seashore a boat was waiting to convey the King across to Hurst Castle, a desolate little fortress built on a rock among the waves. Here stood a new gaoler, Captain Eyre, a melodramatic figure, bushily bearded, armed with halberd and basket-hilted sword. One of the officers told him to stop swaggering and treat the King with respect. Eyre collapsed into obsequiousness, but it was a poor lodging he had to offer: it was December, and the rooms so dark that candles were needed at midday: the air was dark and unhealthy; the King's only diversion was to walk out to the litter of sharp stones, that served for paths, and watch the ships passing up and down the Solent. Two faithful servants remained with him, Herbert and Harrington, but when the latter began to speak approvingly of the King's arguments at Newport, he was dismissed by the officers. It was a dangerous matter to discuss at all, for Parliament had just voted the King's concessions an adequate basis for a settlement, and the Army had resolved that there must be no settlement which left King Charles alive.

There had long been talk of killing him, especially among the wilder spirits in the military committees. The Second Civil War had given an edge to their words, and they were beginning to affect responsible men. There seemed no other way to prevent the King and Parliament

[1] The King had been entertaining the idea of escape during the negotiations, perhaps of an immediate escape and breach of parole. If the evidence was more conclusive, and not contradicted by the conversation here described (Col. Cooke's *Narrative*), the charge of duplicity against Charles would be proven.

coming to an agreement which would leave the Army in the cold. The Army chaplain, Peters, anticipating his enemies' blasphemies that were later to make comparison between Charles's sufferings and our Lord's, compared the King to Barabbas, the red-coats to Christ, and demanded, since one must be destroyed, that it should not be the latter. He marched with Colonel Pride to the House of Commons and helped to point out the members who were certain to favour an agreement with King Charles : two hundred were refused admission to the House, forty more were arrested for protesting and hindering the " Purge." Still the House fought against the King's trial, trying to strike a last bargain : even the officers were divided in Council, Fairfax refusing to entertain the proposal, Ireton slowly convinced, Cromwell (though the Royalists represented his reluctance as hypocrisy) probably the last of all. A month after Pride's Purge the last pressure was applied to Parliament : a bare forty-six members assembled to vote on a proposal for erecting the Court to try Charles : it was passed by a majority of six, but even the shadow of legality was destroyed when the remnant of the Peers threw out the Bill.

Meanwhile the soldiers had brought Charles from Hurst to Winchester, from Winchester to Windsor. He was still greeted with acclamations on the road and prayers for his preservation. A last plot to rescue him at a lonely spot near Bagshot was foiled by the lameness of a horse. He was still patient and cheerful, rallied Herbert for not waking him early in the morning, and sent out to the Windsor shops to buy him an " alarm-watch." But he had barely a month to live.

At Windsor he had a momentary view of Hamilton, a prisoner, and marked to die within a few days of the King. It was his last glimpse of the old world in which he had once lived in ease and happiness. It had passed away beyond hope of revival.

Buckingham had been twenty years in the grave, and

with him some part of Charles's heart. Of the men who had ridden with them to Madrid, Dick Graeme and Cottington were in exile, Endymion Porter was busy saving his estate by proving to Parliament that, though he held the King's commission, he had never actually been in arms against the Roundheads. The bride they had ridden to seek had died, after fifteen years of marriage to her Austrian cousin, the Emperor—too soon to see her husband's dominions find peace, after the long agony of the Thirty Years' War. It was four years since war had parted Charles from Henrietta ; she was growing a narrower Papist, would one day disregard his last instructions for his children's religion, and even turn her son from the door because he refused to abandon his Protestantism. Lucy Carlisle, once queen of the world of elegance, was a fast prisoner in the Tower, shuddering at the rack that was shown her in hope of frightening from her the secrets of her tortuous intrigues. Vandyke was dead : his and the other pictures that Charles had so lovingly gathered were soon to be sold and dispersed, Parliament at first ordering that all representations of Christ and the Virgin must be burnt : King Philip and Mazarin sent agents to the sale. Laud was dead ; the clergy that had held fast to his principles were driven from their livings, some to penury, a few to death : the most horrible fate had overtaken Dr. Hudson, who had ridden with Charles from Oxford. Surrendering with the garrison of Woodcroft House, he had been attacked by the victorious Roundheads ; as he attempted to climb down the walls, they had cut off his hands and then clubbed him to death in the moat below. Everywhere the churches were being battered and defaced ; the royal chapel at Windsor was a plundered wilderness. Little Gidding was deserted ; Basing House had been razed. The whole kingdom was a grave for loyal gentlemen ; the last and most gallant was Lisle, executed under Colchester walls, calling out to the firing - party to come nearer or they would miss him as they had so often missed him in battle.

Such deaths were not on his conscience ; there was no ghost to haunt him, except Strafford's ; but for that one sin, he had done his duty as he saw it, however narrow and imperfect his vision. There was one more task before him. Two years ago he had written to Digby : " I desire you to assure all my friends that if I cannot live as a king, I shall die like a gentleman, without doing anything which may make honest men blush for me." He had often been charged with breaking his promises ; this one he was going to keep.

CHAPTER NINETEEN

THE SCAFFOLD

January 1649

IT is difficult to overthrow a monarchy by revolution without ending, sooner or later, with the killing of a king. Sometimes it is done in mere defiance, sometimes to prevent reaction. The revolutionaries may take their victim to a cellar and shoot him without formality, and that is perhaps the honestest way. They may erect a tribunal to try him, and invent some new law against which he is supposed to have offended. For it is generally the misfortune of revolutionaries to find that their king has done nothing that can be cited in a law court as a capital offence. Two charges were brought against Charles. The first, that he had deliberately engineered the first Civil War in order to win for himself an " unlimited and tyrannical power," will not bear a moment's inspection. The second, that he had corrupted Parliament's allies and servants into renewing the war, has a little more force. Yet it is difficult to blame a king for attempting to recover by force what force has taken away. No one can doubt that he believed that a Royalist victory in the second Civil War was the only chance of a just and lasting settlement. And by killing him, his enemies were provoking yet a third war, even more destructive.

These considerations would bear less weight if the Regicides could have made good their boast that they were acting in the name of the people. If there is anything certain about England in these dark days, it is that the vast majority of the people were appalled at what the Army was doing. Even Parliament, to whose authority

287

the Regicides hypocritically appealed, refused its sanction, though Parliament might be imagined to contain
the King's bitterest enemies.   His partisans had left the
Commons seven years ago, and their seats were bestowed
on Roundheads.   This packed House had to be reduced
from 500 to 46 by military pressure before it would consent to the trial of the King, and then it passed the Bill
by a majority of six ; and when the remnant of Roundhead
Lords threw it out, their action had to be ignored.   The
ordinary judges naturally refused to touch the business.
Of the 135 Commissioners specially appointed to form the
tribunal, barely half could be got to take their seats, and
only 59 to sign the death-warrant.   The execution is
difficult to justify on any system of morality.   It certainly
had no sanction of law or popular consent.   It left its
perpetrators with no alternative but ten years of military
despotism, and discredited every political and religious
principle that they had once fought for.

It has been defended on grounds of political necessity.
The defence is valid to those who think it necessary for
the Army to impose its will on England and for Cromwell
to rise to supreme power.   It has some force with those
who believe Charles to have been an utterly faithless man,
incapable of abiding by any settlement to which he gave
assent and quick to find conscientious reasons for breaking
his word.   It is not possible to accept such a view of the
King.   His methods of treating for a settlement had been
exasperating and deceitful ; but they had been those of
a desperate man fighting against attempts to make him
sign some agreement he could not in honour observe.   If
he had been the slippery politician that he is sometimes
represented, he could have taken any one of the dozen
chances that had lately offered and signed an agreement (as,
for instance, Henrietta had urged him to do) only to repudiate it by force or fraud.   There are signs that, by
refusing to do so, by delay and argument and prevarication,
he had arrived in sight of a settlement with Parliament

that he could honourably accept. But it was one that left Cromwell and the Army unsatisfied, and it was hardly remarkable that men accused Cromwell of killing the King in order to prevent it.

Pride's Purge and the military occupation of London had reduced Parliament to a handful of partisans willing to vote what the Army required. But the officers still hesitated to order what England abhorred as a crime. They laid a last temptation before Charles, offering to ensure his acquittal if he would accept their terms; the most important were that he should authorize the sale of the bishops' lands and resign the royal power of vetoing what the Commons voted. The first, as Charles saw it, was to legalize robbery and cripple the only form of Church that had any authority or chance of permanence in England. The second was to destroy the monarchy he had been born to preserve and to destroy it in favour of a small group of evil men acting under the dictation of the sword. It is just possible that another man might have saved his life by accepting such a humiliation, in order to reverse it as soon as circumstances permitted. It is inconceivable that Charles should have done so.

He had never been afraid of death, and it was coming to him in a form more welcome than any. The issues were clear at last: he was dying to save the Church from Puritanism, the monarchy from rebels; and his death, whether he knew it or not, was to be the best blow he had ever struck for his Cause. There was no chance now for miscalculations and hesitations, for twistings and turnings and delay. Men noticed at the trial that even his lifelong stammer left him, so that he spoke firmly and clearly. Strongest of all was the feeling that everything his enemies did was a further justification of his life's work. He had always foreseen that, whatever reverence for law they had pretended, the end of their politics (and his forced concessions to them) was injustice and anarchy. There was only one thing on his conscience, and he acknowledged that if it increased his accusers' guilt, it justified his own punishment. He was dying because he had consented to Strafford's death.

His old enemies were refusing to countenance this last result of rebellion.   Fairfax, still nominal commander of the army, would have no hand in what Cromwell was determined to do.   Manchester and Northumberland opposed the ordinance for the King's trial: Prynne had been excluded by Pride's Purge before it could be passed.   The Army had driven Holles and Clotworthy into exile.   Vane, the avowed Republican, was still in the House but voted against the business.   St. John would have nothing to do with it.   Saye was doing a characteristic thing : looking round for a safe refuge, he jockeyed the owner out of the Isle of Lundy and retired there to await the Restoration ; then he returned to accept high office under Charles II and carve up at Broughton, where he had once plotted with Pym and Hampden, the bland motto, " It is pleasanter not to remember the past."

There is hardly one of the old names to stand beside Cromwell's on the list of judges.   There were a few officers who had won distinction in the war, Ireton and Ludlow, Okey and Fleetwood.   There was the old reprobate, Henry Marten (Charles had once refused to attend a race-meeting if "that whoremonger" was to be present), and Mauleverer, whom Parliament had arraigned for horse-stealing.   Of the other names, hardly one had achieved either fame or notoriety ; some were gentlemen, some tradesmen, a few workmen.

They must be granted great courage, and probably conviction.   They were braving the terrible death that overtook fifteen of them at the Restoration, while the rest went into prison or exile.   If the King's trial disgusted the moderate men, it also weeded out cowards from among the extremists.   One has for his memorial an imperishable phrase which he flung at the Restoration judges ; when custom prescribed the summoning of a long string of unnecessary witnesses to prove the guilt of the Regicides, he protested against the arid formality. " This thing," he said, " was not done in a corner."

The King was brought from Windsor to St. James's ; orders were given that he should not be treated as a king, but as a prisoner. Meanwhile they were clearing Westminster Hall of the booths and stalls that had sprung up in it, bundling out old Mrs. Breach the pamphlet-seller and Samuel Pecke the scrivener. The hall was divided across the centre by two wooden fences ; the narrow lane between was partitioned off into three boxes, and in the centre one was placed a chair for the King. It faced a table on which lay the mace and sword of state ; beyond, a dais was erected across the end of the hall to accommodate the sixty or seventy judges who had consented to sit. In the back half of the hall stood the soldiers, and, later in the trial, a number of spectators. Other spectators thronged the galleries that ran down the side walls. The scene was set.

At two o'clock on Saturday, January 20, the judges were meeting for a last consultation in the Painted Chamber, while Charles was brought in sedan chair from St. James's to Whitehall, and thence by barge to Westminster. Cromwell, standing at the window, saw him land in the gardens of Cotton House ; he turned to ask his colleagues what was to be the crucial question of the trial. How should they answer the King if he demanded by what authority they were trying him ? Marten suggested that they must claim the authority of Parliament and of " all the good people of England." With that resolution they marched across to Westminster Hall and took their seats on the dais.

An obscure lawyer called Bradshawe had been found to preside, and he discharged his difficult task with considerable ability. The first formality was the reading of the Commons' ordinance for setting up the Court. The next to hold a roll-call of the judges. Half the names remained unanswered, and when Fairfax's was read out a woman's voice from the gallery cried, " He has too much wit to be here ! " Then a party of soldiers was sent to fetch the prisoner from Cotton House. He appeared, dressed in black, wearing his George and Garter. He sat down in the little box, carefully avoiding any sign of deference to the judges. Bradshawe addressed him, accusing him, in the name of the Commons, of all the innocent blood that had lately been spilt in England. He ordered the indictment to be read ; it had been composed by a Dutchman called Isaac Dorislaus who was soon to return, unwisely, to his native land and be murdered by Royalist exiles at The Hague. It was drawn up in the name of the English people, and it fixed the charge at High Treason. Charles, after attempting to speak once, sat laughing to himself. Then Bradshawe required him to answer to the charge.

There was only one answer he could make. He could not plead at all until he knew by what authority he was on trial—" I mean," he said, " lawful authority—for there are many unlawful authorities in the world, robbers by the highway." He had been in negotiation with the Houses of Parliament ; they were " upon the conclusion of a treaty." He had suddenly been carried away and " brought from place to place, like I know not what, until I came hither." He demanded to know under what law this had come about, before he spoke further. " Remember, I am your King, your lawful King, and what sin you bring upon your heads—besides those other judgments you bring upon the land. . . . I have a trust committed to me by God, by old and lawful descent. I will not betray that trust to a new, unlawful authority, for all the world. Therefore, let me know by what lawful authority I am come hither and you shall hear more of me. Resolve me in that and I will answer."

The deadlock was complete. Bradshawe did not help matters by suggesting that Charles was being tried by " the People of England, by which people you were elected King." Charles scored a debating point by replying

that the English monarchy had not been elective for
" near this thousand years," and Bradshawe could not
begin to justify his claim that the judges represented the
people. " I do stand more for the liberties of my people,"
said Charles, " than any one that is here as a judge." He
had taken the only possible ground, and it proved a very
strong one, stronger than any that Pym or Eliot had
pleaded against him. The only justification for his death was
that the leaders of the Army thought it expedient in order to
preserve peace under their supremacy. They were arrogating to themselves that emergency power which Charles had
been blamed for exercising, and arrogating it without the
sanction of law, custom, and heredity which had placed it
in the King. The formality of trying him could have no
aim except to show that they were acting according to
law, and Charles was beating them at their own game.
And it was not very pleasant to hear his speeches greeted
with cries of " God save Your Majesty ! " from the galleries.

The Court was adjourned over the week-end, and
Charles was taken back to St. James's. Two soldiers were
stationed in his bedroom, and he refused to go to bed while
they remained. Next day Peters was sent to preach and
pray at him, and on Monday the Court reassembled in
Westminster Hall.

Neither that day nor the next was any progress made.
Charles indeed waived his kingship and the illegality of
trying a king. " It is not my case alone," he said, " it is
the freedom and liberty of the people of England. And—
do you pretend what you will—I must justly stand for
their liberties. For if power without law may make law,
may alter the fundamental laws of the kingdom, I do not
know what subject he is in England can be assured of his
life or anything that he can call his own." He was stealing
his opponents' thunder with a vengeance, and Bradshawe
had to interrupt him and, refusing to hear any argument
against the jurisdiction of the Court, to order the King's
removal.

20

Tuesday's session was shorter, Charles still demanding his right to give reasons for denying his judges' authority, Bradshawe refusing to permit it.

On Wednesday and Thursday a private committee of the judges sat to hear " evidence " in the Painted Chamber : a row of witnesses from different parts of the country gave unnecessary testimony that they had seen the King in arms against the Parliamentary forces. It is probable that the delay was welcomed as a means of fortifying the wavering resolution of the judges. There was much to make them waver. They were not popular in London : the Presbyterians were against them and the pulpits thundered denunciation. Bradshawe was given new lodgings in Dean's Yard, where he could be guarded ; even so he wore a bullet-proof hat, lined with steel. It was feared that Fairfax might put himself at the head of the discontent, and even make trouble among the soldiers. The Scottish commissioners sent to London by Argyle were protesting violently against the King's trial. A more pathetic appeal came from Prince Charles in Holland— his signature on a blank sheet of paper ; the judges were invited to write what terms they liked, so long as they spared his father's life.

Whatever qualms they felt, the judges were induced to close their ranks and carry through what they had begun. On Friday, sixty-three of them met together, agreed on their sentence and resolved to meet next day and summon the King to hear it read.

As soon as he appeared he endeavoured to speak, but Bradshawe, arrayed now in a scarlet robe, silenced him for the moment. But as Bradshawe began to speak and had pronounced the words " in the name of the people of England," the same woman's voice that had cavilled at Fairfax's name on the first day was heard from the gallery. It was Lady Fairfax. " It is a lie ! " she cried, " where are the people or their consents ! " Another woman called out " Not half or a quarter of them. Cromwell is

a traitor ! " Colonel Axtell commanded the soldiers in
the body of the hall to present their muskets and to shoot
if the drabs tried to speak again. When Bradshawe
resumed it was to say that the prisoner would be allowed
to speak before sentence was pronounced, but that the
Court could not entertain any more objections against its
authority or against the right of the House of Commons
to establish it.

Charles used his opportunity to make a last request ;
he asked to be confronted with Parliament itself, Lords
and Commons together. At this one of the judges, Downes,
rose in his place, trying to speak in favour of the King's
request. His neighbours told him to sit down again and
be quiet, but he demanded an adjournment. It was
granted, but to no purpose : he could find no colleague to
support him in urging that Parliament must at least be
informed of the King's request.

The judges returned, and Bradshawe pronounced
against the King's plea, quoting Magna Charta, with
hypocritical irony, to the effect that justice must not be
delayed to any man. Delay would be very dangerous to
the judges ; to reopen discussion in Parliament was
impossible, for the army had virtually destroyed Parliament before it could get its way. Charles may not have
known about Pride's Purge, but he must have guessed
from Bradshawe's prevarications that the Lords had
refused to vote for his trial. The Court could not grant
his appeal without destroying its own existence.

" Sir," he replied to Bradshawe, " I know it is vain for
me to dispute. I am no sceptic to deny the power that
you have. I know that you have power enough. Sir, I
confess I think it would be for the kingdom's peace if you
would have taken pains to have shown the lawfulness of
your power." He made a last appeal to Parliament. " I
do require you, as you will answer it at the dreadful day
of judgment, that you consider it once again." Beyond
that he had no more to say, only asking that his words

be recorded. He could only await what was inevitable, "an ugly sentence which I believe will pass upon me."

Bradshawe prefaced it with a long lecture on the lawfulness of calling kings to account, and the evils of Charles's reign. He was full of pedantries, he contrived to obscure the fact that it was not Parliament which was condemning the King, and he relied overmuch upon vague denunciations of him as a "traitor and murtherer." Nevertheless the speech is an able and sincere performance, far more so than the statement (prepared but never delivered) of the prosecuting counsel, who had raked up venomous old scandals—the poisoning of King James, a deliberate plot to betray La Rochelle to the Papists, the incitement to murder Protestants in Ireland. Bradshawe deserves better consideration than Lawyer Cooke, who had waited in vain for Charles to plead and give him an opportunity of prosecuting. Bradshawe's speech, his references to the King's "breach of trust," his "miscarriages," the sad state of his country, aiming against Charles's mistakes rather than his sins, would be an easy one to answer in a court of law. But it proclaims the man's conviction that, if the thing he was doing was unjust, it was also necessary.

Charles attempted to interrupt once, asking leave to reply to Bradshawe's "imputations" before sentence was pronounced. Bradshawe quashed him, drove straight ahead to his peroration, and commanded the clerk to read the formal sentence of death. Again Charles asked leave to reply. Bradshawe refused it, and ordered the guards to remove the prisoner. As they did so, Charles repeated his appeal, a little feverishly now. "Guard, withdraw your prisoner!" thundered Bradshawe. "I am not suffered to speak," said the King, as he was led away. "Expect what justice other people will have."

Axtell was scoffing aloud as he went, the soldiers laughing and blowing smoke in his face. One had spat in his face on the second day of the trial. Now several were calling out "Justice! Execution!" "Poor creatures," said the King, " for sixpence they would say as much of their commanders." One indeed cried, " God bless you, sir ! " so that his officer hit him with a cane, and the King told him that the punishment exceeded the offence. He was hurried into a sedan chair, and the porters took off their hats to him until Axtell beat them into covering their heads again. At the door of St. James's he met his personal servants whom the soldiers were sending away ; seeing them weep, the King told his captors that they might forbid their attendance but not their tears. He sent away his dogs, asking that they might be taken over to Henrietta.

Of his children, only two were at hand. Mary was with her husband in Holland ; James had escaped, disguised as a woman, to join Prince Charles abroad. Elizabeth, thirteen years of age, and the little Duke of Gloucester, three years younger, were brought to St. James's on the Monday night. She was to die in prison before the next year was out, he had another ten years to live. Both were weeping now, though Charles told them that they must not sorrow overmuch, because he was dying gloriously for law, liberty, and true Protestantism. He charged the girl with a last message to Henrietta, quaintly but characteristically recommended her to read certain books of theology, and told her to forgive his murderers but not to trust their word. He warned the little Prince that they might try to make him King for their own ends, but that he must not consent while his elder brothers lived. " I will sooner be torn in pieces ! " said the boy. Charles divided some jewels between them, kissed them, and said good-bye. He spent the evening with Bishop Juxon. It was a happy chance, for Juxon had been one of the only two to bid him refuse consent to Strafford's death. That he had done so and yet retained the respect and even affection of the Puritans is the best of testimonies to his saintly character. With Juxon's blessing and absolution Charles slept his last sleep on earth.

Meanwhile it had been no easy matter to get sufficient

signatures to the death-warrant. The first document was wrongly dated and addressed to two officers who refused to take a hand in the business; those who had signed it might draw back and refuse to put their hand to an amended order. It was safer to change the two names and the date by erasure and substitution. Not for the first time King Charles's enemies resorted to forgers' methods.

Even so, the list of signatures was a meagre one, and great efforts were made to increase it. When the Restoration came, the captured Regicides were prodigal of stories about the pressure and intimidation under which they acted, especially about Cromwell's brutal insistence. There is little doubt that part of their tale is true. By one means or another, fifty-nine judges, not quite half the original number, were induced to sign the death-warrant.

Tuesday, the 30th of January, dawned raw and bitter. The Thames was frozen, and a light snow was sprinkling down; next day it would fall in earnest, enough to make a pall upon the White King's coffin as the little band of devoted Royalists carried him to rest in the plundered chapel at Windsor.

Charles rose early. He had asked Herbert to bring in his pallet-bed and sleep beside him. Herbert told the King he had a strange dream of Laud knocking for admission and conferring with his master. Charles asked Herbert to give him two shirts to wear, lest men should see him shiver with cold and imagine he was afraid. Then Herbert gave place to Juxon, who was alone with the King for an hour. Finally the three of them said the Prayer Book service together. A little before ten Colonel Hacker knocked at the door. The King stepped out into the air. " March apace ! " he called out to the soldiers, for it was very cold. Rogue, his spaniel, attempted to follow him on his last journey, but was taken up by a bystander. As the party passed Spring Gardens, Charles pointed out one of the trees and told Juxon that his brother

Henry had planted it thirty years ago. The wheel of his life had come full circle.

At Whitehall, the King received the Sacrament. Even to the last the Puritan preachers tried to force their attentions on him, but he made Juxon tell them to pray for him as they had often prayed against him, but he would have them do it elsewhere. He refused dinner, but took a piece of bread and a glass of claret. He had many long hours to wait ; no one knows the reason for delay, perhaps there was a difficulty in finding an executioner, perhaps the remnant of Parliament had to meet and pass an order forbidding any one to proclaim King Charles's successor after the ancient custom. The winter afternoon was half spent before the summons came.

The scene that followed is worth trying to envisage : even its details were not without their effect upon our history.

A man, let us suppose, has come out from London to see the end. He walks along the Strand, passing the fronts of the great men's houses, whose gardens run down to the river behind. As he is about to swing left towards Whitehall, he sees the ruined stump of Charing Cross, demolished two years since because Parliament had voted it a monument of superstition. Beyond it are a few houses, then Spring Gardens, and the open country. The landmarks are Goring House (where now stands Buckingham Palace), the villages of Knight's Bridge and Paddington. Nearer in is the isolated mass of St. James's where the King slept last night. To the right, probably visible over the roofs of the nearer homes, is Windmill Hill and Pickadilly Hall where, a few years ago, " was a fair House for Entertainment and Gaming, with Handsome walks with Shade, and where were an upper and lower Bowling Green, whither very many of the Nobility and Gentry of the best Quality resorted, both for exercise and Pleasure." [1] Now the City is beset with a Puritan Army,

[1] *Clarendon Rebellion*, i. 241.

there is little gaming for the Nobility and Gentry. The spectator leaves the ruins of Charing Cross and turns down to Whitehall.

He is at the head of a kind of square, enclosed on three sides. To his right, where now the Horse Guards stand, is the Palace Tilting Yard. Ahead of him, instead of the straight broad street of Whitehall, the view is blocked by buildings of Henry VIII's time, straddled across the way ; only Holbein's turreted gate gives a glimpse into the Privy Garden and the right-of-way that leads through it to Westminster. To his left, the third side of the square is formed by the Banqueting Hall, the only part of Inigo's rebuilding scheme which there had been money to complete. From its north end, nearest the spectator, a little red-brick wing or addition has grown out. The scaffold has been built in an L-shape, its long arm running down the left side of the square under the main windows of the Banqueting Hall ; its shorter arm turns the corner and connects up to the red-brick wing, whose first-story window has had its sill broken down until it is a door whereby King Charles can step on to the scaffold.

The whole square is crowded with people, grown stiff and cold with waiting. They fill every window, and swarm on roofs and chimneys. Soldiers stand in line to keep them well back from the scaffold. A troop of cavalry is drawn up under Holbein's gate, another blocks the opposite end of the square, near the stub of Charing Cross. The snow has ceased, and the sun struggles through.

There is a stir at the broken window, and a small party appears on the scaffold—two or three officers, two executioners, masked and disguised, the King, and Bishop Juxon. They advance, turn the corner of the Banqueting Hall, and halt beneath its fourth great window. They are only visible to the waist, for the railing of the scaffold has been hung with black cloth ; the low block, the plain deal coffin, are completely hidden from the crowd below. Charles has a small paper in his hand, notes of a speech he

had intended to make to the people ; but the soldiers have
kept them so far back that his voice will hardly reach them ;
he was never a good speaker. He turns to the group on
the scaffold, to the few soldiers within earshot. Some
one tried to take down his words in shorthand, but " it is
done so defectively it deserveth not to be accounted his
speech, by the testimony of those that heard it." [1] He
spoke of the illegality of his execution, of the destruction
of Parliament, and the pressure put upon its remnant ;
his judges were " out of the way which he would gladly
put them into ; out of the way, because the Kingdom
consisted of three Estates, King, Lords, and Commons,
and they were devolved into one, and that but a piece of
one, and that under a power." He suggested three remedies.
The national synod he had proposed at Newcastle and
Newport to settle religion. " For the King, that a lawful
succession may be, by authority of Parliament ; for the
People, that a free election of members be, to represent
them in Parliament." Urged by Juxon, he declared that
he died a firm Protestant. Nothing, he said, " lay so
heavy on his conscience as his consenting to the death of
the Earle of Strafford." Then he gave his stick and cloak,
his jewels and watch to the Bishop, directing him to send
them to his family and friends. Seeing a man stand
near the Axe, he said, half-humorously, " Do not hurt
the Axe, though it may me." They had driven staples

[1] Fuller's *Church History*, 1655. All the details of the scene (especially the position of window and scaffold) are hotly debated. Far more
important are Charles's last speeches. Two accounts appeared within a
day or two of the execution. I have followed Dillingham's in the *London
Intelligencer*, except for the words about an " incorruptible crown,"
which come from the second pamphlet, by Peter Cole. Parliamentarians will prefer the latter : though it agrees in making the King speak
of Strafford and of the National Synod, it omits the passages about
Parliament acting under pressure and about " free election," and makes
the King die an unrepentant absolutist, saying that government
is " nothing pertaining " to the People, " a subject and a soveraign
are clean different things." The pamphlet is " published by special
authority."

into the flooring of the scaffold and brought cords to pull
him down if he resisted. They had misjudged their man.
He assured the Bishop that he was light of heart. " I go
from a corruptible to an incorruptible crown," he said,
" where no disturbance can be, no disturbance in the
world." He told the executioner he wished to pray for a
moment, and would then give him a sign to strike. He
knelt down.

He was invisible to the waiting crowd. There was a
pause and a silence. Then they saw the headsman move,
the axe rise and fall. " The blow I saw given," says an
onlooker, " and can truly say, with a sad heart. At the
instant whereof, I remember well, there was such a groan
by the thousands there present as I never heard before,
and desire I may never hear again."

Then the two troops of cavalry set spur to their horses
and rode forward to clear the square, jostling aside the
people of England in whose name murder had been committed in Whitehall.

APPENDIX

A FEW days after the King's death, a small book called *Eikon Basilike* was published in London, purporting to be the meditations of King Charles upon the political events of his later years. The reasons for accepting it as genuine are practically flawless : the arguments for its spuriousness are equally convincing. No satisfactory solution has been found to this highly complicated problem. I believe a few passages to be the King's writing, or an uncannily accurate reproduction of his thought : the passage on Strafford's death (with its repetition, from his genuine letter, April 23, 1641, of the rather odd word "conjuncture") seems to me most likely to be genuine. Otherwise I have ignored the book.

A good selection of his letters will be found in Halliwell's *Letters of the Kings of England*. The originals shown in the British Museum give a very interesting demonstration of how handwriting can change. For his speeches, proclamations, etc., I have used May's *Parliamentary History* and *Bibliotheca Regia*, published in 1658. His religious controversy with Henderson is reprinted in Aiton's *Life and Times of Alexander Henderson*.

Other original authorities are far too numerous to quote, and quotation without a full discussion of their reliability (which would run to several hundred pages) is quite useless. The only unimpeachable source is the *Calendar of State Papers*. Clarendon gives the most interesting account, from the point of view of an Opposition member converted after Strafford's death to a moderate Royalism. The best written ultra-Royalist history is Echard's, 1707, quite unreliable in detail. The most powerful mind that has tackled the period is Hume's ; he is too disgruntled and disillusioned to be a Royalist, but he is a furious anti-Parliamentarian.

Far the most complete and capable study of the period is Gardiner's great history : its footnotes are an excellent guide to authorities. I believe the view taken of Charles's character to be radically mistaken, but there is no question of Gardiner's attempt to be fair. It breaks down in curious ways : I suggest reference to his account of Felton's remorse (vi. 359), the words "hardly mattered " on p. 456, vol. viii. (compare what Charles said of the business in *Cal. S.P.* Dom. cccxxiii. 14.6.39), the curious account of Pym's motives in vol. ix. chap. xcviii. (*e.g.* p. 351, line 15), and finally, the extraordinary conclusions drawn from the second Army Plot (x. 399–400). Consciously or unconsciously, such things colour the whole narrative and affect the reader's mind.

New facts and new points of view have greatly modified our view of the period since Gardiner wrote. The most important will be found in the following books :—Wade, *John Pym*. R. R. Reid, *The King's Council for the North*. Hugh O'Grady, *Strafford*. Penn, *The Navy under the Early Stuarts*. G. Callender, *Naval Side of British History*. G. N. Clark, *The Seventeenth Century*. Muddiman, *Trial of Charles I*. C. S. Terry, *History of Scotland*. M. James, *Social Policy during the Puritan Revolution*. G. R. S. Taylor, *Oliver Cromwell*. E. M. Leonard, *Early History of English Poor Relief*. Chesterton, *Short History of England* (worth a great many more learned books). H. G. R. Reade, *Sidelights on the Thirty Years' War*. H. Belloc, *Richelieu, Cromwell* and *Warfare in England*. H. F. Russell Smith, *Harrington and his Oceana*.

Two works of reference must be mentioned. I have taken about half of my facts from the *Dictionary of National Biography*. And my work has been enlivened by the excellent map of Seventeenth Century England, published with an interesting introduction by the Ordnance Survey Office.

INDEX

Abbot, Archbp., 6 n., 9, 87, 140, 158, 182, 185.
Aberdeen, 198, 243, 258–9.
Absolutism, 56–7, 60, 203, 231, 273, 301 n.
Agincourt, 71, 123.
Alford, 258.
Althorpe, 272, 276.
Alum, 163–5.
Amboyna, 43–4, 123.
America, 14, 24, 34, 36, 187–8, 193, 231.
  modern, 2, 10, 259.
Amsterdam, 43, 114, 117.
Andalusia, 97.
Anne of Austria, 30, 48–9, 125.
  Boleyn, 146.
  of Denmark, 1, 6, 26.
  Queen, 122.
Arabic, 179.
Archie, 32, 47, 195.
Argyle, Archie Campbell, Marquis of, 40, 198–9, 208, 227–8, 253, 257–8, 278, 282, 294.
Armada, 16, 33, 35, 95, 102.
Arminians, Arminianism, 13, 133, 142–3, 237.
Army, 94–5, 101, 199–200, 270.
  Plot, 216–7, 231.
  New Model, 256, 260–4, 267–8, 277–8, 280–4, 288–9.
Arundel, Thos. Howard, Earl of, 151–3, 200, 211.
Ashburnham, Jn., 264, 279–80 n.
Assembly, Kirk, 183, 197–8, 201.
Astley, Sir Jacob, 246, 265–6.
Attainder, 213.
  of Strafford, 213–24.
  of Laud, 255.
Auldearn, 258.
Austen, Jane, 72.
Austria, 3, 21, 25–6, 39. *See* Emperor, Hapsburg.
Axtell, Col., 295–7.

Bacon, Francis, 27–8.

Bagg, Sir Jas., 111.
Bagshot, 284.
Balliol, 181.
Baltic, the, 25, 118.
Banbury, 244–5, 248.
Barbadoes, 251.
Barham, 50.
Basing House, 263–4, 285.
Bassompierre, 106.
Bastwick, Dr., 188.
Baxter, Richard, 187, 193.
Beatty, Admiral, 248.
Bedford, Francis Russell, Earl of, 190, 207, 210, 216, 227, 235.
Benevolences, 59.
Berkshire, 65.
  Francis Norris, Earl of, 6 n.
Bingley, 35.
Birmingham, 243.
Bishops, Episcopacy, 14, 89, 169, 188–90, 220, 222, 225, 270, 289.
  Scottish, 183, 189, 194, 229–30, 235, 277, 282.
Bix, 264.
Blackfriars, 151.
Black Rod, 92, 117, 143, 210.
Blair Atholl, 258.
Blake, Robert, 162.
Bohemia, 25–6, 118.
Bolton, 242.
Bordeaux, 122.
Boulogne, 30.
Bourchier, Sir John, 165.
Boyle, *see* Cork.
Bradshawe, John, 291–6.
Breache, Mrs., 291.
Breda, 44.
Brest, 254.
Bridgewater, 162.
Bridlington, 248.
Bristol, 251, 263.
  John Digby, Earl of, 29–30, 32, 34, 37, 115, 119, 136, 140, 210, 214, 217, 219.

305

21

314   INDEX